D0122430

Affairs at State

By the Author
Libya: The New Arab Kingdom of North Africa
Affairs at State

Henry Serrano Villard

Affairs at State

Thomas Y. Crowell Company

Established 1834   New York

Designed by Judith Woracek Barry

Manufactured in the United States of America
by the Vail-Ballou Press, Inc., Binghamton, New York

Library of Congress Catalog Card No. 65-21413

First Printing

For two children of the Foreign Service,
Dimitri and Alexandra

Introduction

by James Reston

Associate Editor, *New York Times*

This book is about the professional diplomatic service of the United States and was written by Henry Serrano Villard, who is one of that remarkable generation of diplomats that served the United States from the days of its isolation in the late 1920's until the period of world leadership in the 1960's.

Ever since the time of Benjamin Franklin, the Adamses, and Thomas Jefferson, American diplomats have been recording their observations on the style and problems of American diplomacy, but there is a great difference now.

For the first time in 2,000 years, the world is having to adjust to the fact that the most powerful and influential nations now lie outside the Continent of Europe in the United States and the Soviet Union. It is not an easy thing to do, for these two nations are not only the most powerful on earth but the least experienced in the conduct of foreign affairs—each with an untraditional style of diplomatic procedure.

Almost the first announcement out of Moscow after the Soviet Revolution, for example, was that the Bolshevik regime was withdrawing from the Western diplomatic community. Trotsky in November of 1917 denounced what he called the "intrigues, codes and lies" of the Old Diplomacy, and promised to substitute something new and "open." At least he produced something "new."

President Woodrow Wilson likewise brought the United States

vii

shortly thereafter into the forefront of world diplomacy by denouncing the Old Diplomacy and promising "open covenants openly arrived at." He was himself immediately denounced and repudiated by the Senate of the United States.

Ever since then, almost every major move by these two countries has affected the interests of many other countries, but after forty years of experience with Washington and Moscow, the diplomats of other countries are still complaining that they do not understand either the sudden "closed" diplomacy of the USSR or the open democratic diplomacy of the United States.

This book does not attempt to explain the foreign policy of the United States over the last thirty years, but it does tell a great deal about the conflict between the professional Foreign Service of the United States and the professional politicians of the United States who have to work together on the foreign policy of the country.

Mr. Villard served six Presidents—Coolidge, Hoover, Roosevelt, Truman, Eisenhower, and Kennedy. Throughout this long period, he held responsible positions both in the Department of State and overseas. He served in Teheran, Caracas, Rio de Janeiro, Oslo, and Geneva among other places. He was assistant chief of the Division of Near Eastern Affairs and deputy director of the Office of Near Eastern, South Asian, and African Affairs in the Department of State. He pioneered United States relations with Africa and became the first chief of the Division of African Affairs. He was also a member of the Department's Policy Planning Staff and a representative of his country at numerous special conferences, including the San Francisco conference that established the United Nations. Mr. Villard finished his career as head of mission to the Kingdom of Libya and finally as Ambassador to the Republic of Senegal and the Islamic Republic of Mauretania.

In the process, he had the opportunity to live through the extraordinary years of transition in the State Department and the Foreign Service. When he was born in 1900, there were less than 100 men on the staff of the State Department. When he entered the Foreign Service, the correct attitude of a Foreign Service officer was not so different from John Quincy Adams' definition of an American diplomat in 1794: "It is our duty," Mr. Adams wrote, "to remain the peaceful and silent though sorrowful spectators of the European scene." But by the time Ambassador Villard retired, the State Department had over 24,000 members, and American foreign service officers were no longer "sorrowful spectators" but influential leaders of every diplomatic corps in every capital of the world.

Mr. Villard makes clear in this book the real problem: the United States has changed its role in the world before it has had time to change its habits of mind. The Congress and the public still regard the Foreign Service the way they did back in the days when foreign affairs were thought to be a nuisance. If things go wrong with other countries, as they inevitably do and will, somebody must be at fault, and the popular view is that the blame must be allocated to the State Department and its principal professional servants.

This troubles the Ambassador. He is proud of the Foreign Service and with good reason. He regrets that it has been diluted with a vast army of public servants whose responsibility is propaganda rather than diplomacy. He feels that the more the United States assumes responsibility in an increasingly complex world, the more it must depend on the professional Foreign Service.

In another generation, this view will probably be more widely accepted, but meanwhile it is useful that the story of Villard's generation of Foreign Service officers should be told, as George F. Kennan and Robert Murphy, among others, have tried to tell it. The United States has been kinder to its soldiers of this period than to its diplomats.

Villard's generation of Foreign Service officers was roughly the age of the century. They were trained in their twenties and thirties to be observers of the world scene, and then had to change, in their forties and fifties, as America's role changed, to be leaders in the accommodation of world problems.

❀ ❀

The surprising thing is not that they made mistakes but that they did so well under the circumstances. Mr. Villard's book is an affectionate lament for his profession. "The ambassadors of peace shall weep," the prophet Isaiah warned in 700 B.C., and most ambassadors have been confirming this ever since.

♔ ♔

Preface

On July 1, 1964, a thousand invited guests gathered in the Diplomatic Lobby of the State Department to observe a notable date, the fortieth anniversary of an Act of Congress which combined the old Diplomatic and Consular Services into a single "Foreign Service of the United States" and laid the cornerstone of the career as it exists today. When this forward-looking piece of legislation was passed, under the sponsorship of the late John Jacob Rogers of Massachusetts, there were but 54 diplomatic posts—now there are more than 100; there were only 633 Foreign Service officers and about the same number of American clerks—today there are nearly 4,000 officers; and, in addition, some 1,300 members of what is known as the Reserve; there are more than 4,000 in the clerical or Staff Corps, where there were only 600-odd before. In this span of time the United States has assumed, reluctantly, the burdens of an altogether different world; it has changed completely its outlook on the international scene; and its Foreign Service has become of truly vital importance to the national security and to world peace.

Public appreciation of the role played by American Foreign Service officers has not increased proportionately. Although the work of the Service, more than ever before, should be a concern of the American people, a great gap remains between its accomplishments and an understanding of its problems and difficulties. There is also much misapprehension of the role which the State Department plays in our foreign affairs—of what it can and cannot do to realize some of America's ideals, of the limits placed upon its actions by the White House, by Congress, and by public opinion.

Looking back over forty years, we may take pride in what the career established by the Rogers Act succeeded in doing. The principle of entrance into the Service after examination and promotion on merit produced outstanding officers who worked their way up from the bottom and gave unstintingly of their talents to advance the interests of the country. Robert Murphy, whose book *Diplomat Among Warriors* has contributed much to the history of our times, was one of them. Three who became ambassadors to the Soviet Union—Charles E. Bohlen, George F. Kennan, and Llewellyn E. Thompson, Jr.—developed into top specialists in Russian affairs, whose professional skills any nation must envy. Despite its loose-tongued critics, the Foreign Service has nothing for which it need apologize. American diplomats who were trained through the ranks have held their own everywhere —reporting, negotiating, protecting American interests, and meeting successfully the adept officers of other governments on their own grounds.

In devotion to duty and conscientious performance, the Service's return to the taxpayer is second to none in the diplomatic world. At the same time, we must feel dismay at some present-day tendencies which threaten not only the original concept of the career but the efficiency and expertise of its operations. Appropriations for the State Department are paltry in comparison to other government expenditures. Bureaucracy is rampant; tightening control by an administrative machine is gradually effacing the individual and downgrading the human factor in foreign affairs. Adulteration of high standards and political influence in key places are lessening the appeal of an inspiring type of lifework. A prime victim of McCarthyism and of other irresponsible forces, Foreign Service morale is far below the point where it should be today.

The fact that the Service, despite the heavy going to which it has been subjected, has steadily developed into a first-class professional organization is a tribute to the individuals who compose it and to the strength and wisdom of Congressman Rogers' founding legislation. The public image, however, is uncertain and unclear. Never before have we needed so much ability to deal with so many aspects of our relations with so many countries, old and new. Unless the American people give the Foreign Service its due, the Foreign Service cannot render the best service to the people. The time has come to take a new look at what constitutes our establishment for foreign affairs.

Contents

The Unhappy Image

Of the thousand flowers that bloom in the lush gardens of Washington bureaucracy, none is so exotic as the Department of State. The mere fact that its roots derive nourishment in strangely named distant places sets it apart from such homely varieties as Interior, Agriculture, or Commerce; its mushroom growth since World War II, its wealth of administrative flora, its far-wandering offshoot—the Foreign Service—and the jungle of committees that surround it, all give it a special cachet in the Capital family. Even the Pentagon, which State is beginning to rival in size and complexity, looks commonplace and dull compared with the cosmopolitan specimen that flourishes in the fertile soil of Foggy Bottom.

A rose by any other name may smell as sweet. But to those who dislike what they do not altogether understand, who distrust the foreign on general principles, or who, perhaps, are secretly jealous of an institution for which they themselves possess no qualifications, the State Department is far from fragrant.

In a country that proclaims it has never lost a war or won a peace, the vision conjured up by our foreign affairs establishment is cloudy at best, tinged with treason at worst. To some, as Churchill said of Russia, it is a riddle wrapped in a mystery inside an enigma. It satisfies no one, least of all itself. If it does not produce a quick answer to a current crisis, it is derelict in its duty. If it is not victorious in a brush with our adversaries, it is weak-kneed or softheaded. If it does not call the turn on a palace revolution, it has ignored the portents or fallen asleep. Diplomat is synonymous with wearer of striped pants; and associated with that badge of his trade are nefarious deals which threaten to undermine the republic, willful acts of appeasement, and a propensity—unless checked by a vigilant citizenry—for selling out the nation in favor of world government. Public praise of the diplomat is rare; yet blame falls unerringly on him if things go wrong.

When Cuba was captured by Castro, a book titled *The Fourth Floor* was written, which laid the blame on the desk officers in the State Department who were concerned with Cuba. When a proposal was made to put the Agency for International Development under the State Department, a prominent senator said he could think of nothing which would foul up the program quicker. When another senator aired his complaints in the *Reader's Digest,* the article's subtitle asserted that the State Department was "a study in indecision, timidity and inefficiency." When a bomb exploded at the door of the American embassy in Cyprus, a "sick and tired" correspondent wrote to the *Washington Star:* "We should neither have been surprised, shocked, or even faintly chagrined at what occurred. . . . The State Department should have known exactly what was happening, and what the end result would be. Why, oh why, when we spend so much for diplomacy and intelligence, do we get none?"

Whether it is the unhappy image that arouses the scorn, or whether it is the scorn in which it is held that creates the unhappy image, Congressional niggardliness in the annual appropriations for the Foreign Service is notorious. Despite the most painstaking estimates of the minimum amounts it considers necessary, the State Department is regularly denied what it asks for. Its supporters and defenders, wherever one looks, seem always absent.

The fact is that no other branch of officialdom is so often berated in public, so frequently accused of pursuing the wrong policy, so roundly scolded by the demagogues from the grass roots, so thoroughly misunderstood by the masses in whose behalf it labors. Badgered by Congress, kicked around by the ill-informed, tackled by the politicians like a dummy at football practice, the department which bears the chief burden for our safety in a predatory and tricky world is everybody's whipping boy.

Exasperation and frustration sometimes lead to extreme proposals. In the spring of 1964, a bill, H.R. 11070, was introduced in the House of Representatives by Republican Congressman Samuel L. Devine of Ohio to abolish the State Department and to start all over again with a "Department of Foreign Affairs."

The origins of the Foreign Service, like many another chapter in American history, can be found in the Continental Congress, which existed from 1774 to 1789. In the latter part of 1775, the congress sent secret agents to Europe to present the cause of the colonies in their conflict with Great Britain and to sound out the possibility of help in the event of a final break with the mother country. They did their work well in France, where arrangements were made for military aid even before the Declaration of Independence.

Control of foreign relations was first exercised by a secret committee, created to find arms and ammunition: the Committee of Secret Correspondence entered into communication with persons in England to ascertain sentiment toward the colonies and to obtain other information. After 1776, secrecy was no longer necessary and a Committee for Foreign Affairs took form—the progenitor of the vast State Department of today. That early body of patriots was served by one secretary at $70 a month; the committees today are legion, and the clerical personnel in Washington numbers in the thousands.

What was put together as the diplomatic service of the Revolution shed luster on a young America; its work abroad during the fighting years, during the negotiation of a satisfactory peace, and in the immediate postindependence days was distinguished. The story of the Foreign Service as it developed over the next 150 years is a record of hesitancy, inadequacies, and vicissitudes; but it is also an account of extraordinary devotion and self-sacrifice.

During the last couple of generations, its coming of age has been hastened by cataclysmic events and phenomenal changes in foreign affairs. The map of the world has been redrawn, and the destiny of the world depends to a great extent on the foreign policy of the United States.

In the present atmosphere of concern for world peace and our national security, the role of the State Department is of transcendental importance and the role of its Foreign Service no less so. Appointed by the President, by and with the advice and consent of the Senate, the Foreign Service Officer today is the link that connects international events with Washington; his responsibilities in carrying out the foreign policies of the President, in helping to formulate some of those policies, in protecting American interests, in reporting in depth to his government, and in promoting relations with other peoples are scarcely known to his fellow citizens. The Foreign Service Officer represents the eyes and ears, and sometimes part of the brain, of the United States. He is both perceptive and receptive. He is trained to observe events in every corner of the earth, to furnish the raw strands from which foreign policies are spun, and to recommend how best to implement them. He is as patriotic and dedicated an American as the next man— and he may be pardoned if he is sick and tired of the unhappy image associated with his name.

Most Americans who have heard of the Foreign Service Officer— and there are probably millions who have not—seem to think of him as a lightheaded fellow addicted to a costume seldom seen nowadays save at funerals or weddings, who occasionally does a stint of work for his countrymen but is principally engaged in living it up abroad at the taxpayer's expense. The myth persists that he prefers duty in the banquet hall and the ballroom to the more onerous tasks of what we call the American way of life; that he is somehow unmanly, unorthodox, or unequal to the demands at home; that his existence is one long round of fun and games in the heady atmosphere of London, Paris, Rome, or Madrid.

Before the advent of the Foreign Service as a professional career, there may have been grounds for the belief that diplomacy was a pastime of the idle rich. But in the jet age, the unflattering stereotype of the diplomatic fop in striped pants and top hat is as dated as Karl Marx, as obsolete as powdered wigs and knee breeches.

When our embassies were filled with men of means, because no one else could afford the posts, the diplomat was dismissed as a social dilettante. After World War I, it was the vogue to satirize him as "a messenger boy in white spats." While Prohibition held sway, he was derided as a drinker of tea, and when water turned into wine, he was berated for attending cocktail parties. There never was a time, in fact, save in the birth pangs of the nation, when the American who served abroad was not looked upon askance. Now, in addition to the stigma of striped pants, he squirms under the epithet of "cooky pusher."

It is much easier to trace the origin of that unpalatable phrase than to explain why cooky pusher lingers on as a symbol of the Foreign Service Officer. During the Congressional hearings held in 1924 to decide whether the diplomatic and consular services—then separate—should be combined into a single foreign service, Ambassador Hugh Gibson testified on the relation of private wealth to appointments in the diplomatic branch. Gibson tried to emphasize that a number of undesirables had gained positions which they never would have had if it had been possible to make the service more attractive and induce better-qualified men to enter. He argued persuasively; little did he realize that his words were to be pinned like the donkey's tail on a reborn American Foreign Service:

"You hear very frequently about the boys with the white spats, the tea drinkers, the cooky pushers," he remarked in what proved to be an unguarded moment, "and while they are a very small minority, they make a noise entirely disproportionate to their numbers. . . . Our great problem now is to attract enough men so that we will have a real choice of material and crowd out those incompetents and defectives."

As so often happens when a catch phrase is pulled out of context, the headlines of the day heralded the reference to the spats

✿ ✿

and the tea and the cooky pushers; the "very small minority" of incompetents and defectives described by Gibson—such as are found in any large organization—were obscured, while "cooky pushing" was ascribed to the whole Foreign Service, it seems forever.

Still another tag has been pinned on the man who makes his living in the esoteric realm of foreign affairs—that of "stuffed shirt." To some people he is pompous, close-lipped, overbearing, impressed with his own importance. It is not his fault if he gives this impression. From the moment a young Foreign Service Officer enters the confines of bureaucracy, he feels the disciplines of caution and conformity; his mind may be as devoid of the "little grooves" which the late Texas Senator Tom Connally ascribed to it as that of a babe in arms, but by the time he reaches his first post, he has become part of the system.

Even worse, the Foreign Service Officer became publicly identified with the "ugly American," thanks to the widely touted book by that name. There is certainly no pride of face on the part of the typically self-effacing officer in the Foreign Service; but he resents the libel on his craft by the widespread acceptance of the book title as an accurate description of himself. Actually, if one takes the trouble to unravel that particular piece of fiction, the "ugly American" was a shrewd, self-made engineer who turned the tables on government technicians and diplomats—but who by no stretch of the imagination could be regarded as a diplomat.

There may still be misfits and malingerers in the recesses of the State Department, as in every firm or business corporation, but the career of diplomacy today requires more than sartorial elegance, the balancing of teacups or cocktail glasses, or "cooky pushing." In Washington the diplomat is sometimes thought of as an ant in an anthill, engaged in unspecified or undisclosed bureaucratic chores until the round of evening parties begins. In foreign parts, he is supposed to lead the glamorous life that enthralled the readers of E. Phillips Oppenheim. Neither picture is correct. On assignment in the Department, dealing with the affairs of one or more countries, he must keep a schedule a good deal stiffer than that of the nine-to-five businessman who takes an afternoon off for golf; in the field he must be on his toes from dawn to dusk, and from dusk far into the night, playing his part as a personable and persuasive agent of the United States. If he were a woolly-brained social gadabout, he would not last long; he is much more likely to be as well informed and hardheaded as a city editor, as sharp-minded in negotiations as a horse trader.

Throughout their professional lives, officers of the Foreign Service are conscious of the cares and obligations resting upon them as representatives of the United States; they often feel—and look—as though they were Atlas, carrying the weight of the world on their shoulders, as indeed they are in a sense, for they deal with the most ponderous problems and can never divorce their private personalities from their official selves. They are fated to wage a perpetual inner battle to preserve their individuality; as anyone knows who stays in it too long, public service contains a built-in threat to creativeness and originality.

Appearances, on the other hand, can be deceiving. That bland and sometimes solemn bearing that irritates the uninitiated may conceal an active, analytical brain geared to moves and motives in the great game of politics, international style; that outer shell may be merely the product of environment. Certainly, a carefree, freewheeling attitude in the negotiation of deadly serious matters, while admittedly spectacular, would hardly be consistent with the task of maintaining world peace.

Harold Nicolson, dean of British diplomatists, had a word or two on the subject: "The manner of suspended judgment, of skeptical tolerance, of passionless detachment which denotes the trained diplomat is often taken by outside observers to suggest that he is conceited, lazy, stupid—or very, very ill." Aldous Huxley put it another way in his description of Simmons, the gentlemen's gentleman, who "had that statesmanlike dignity of demeanor which the necessity of holding the tongue and keeping the temper, of never speaking one's real mind and preserving appearances always tends to produce in diplomats, royal personages, high government officials and butlers."

Restraint in word or deed is not only traditional among diplomats, but a necessity when the fate of a nation may hang on the turn of a phrase, or even on a smile or a look. In the early days of the Foreign Service, there was no such word as "laugh" in the codebooks, as the unconventional onetime Undersecretary of State, Joseph P. Cotton, discovered to his discomfiture—and therefore no way to instruct a chief of mission to "laugh it off" when an embarrassing predicament arose. Laughing was unthinkable in this business, and to encode the colloquialism it was necessary to resort to an awkward and roundabout simile. If a diplomat can preserve his sense of humor when all those around him are losing theirs, he is sure to stand out among the herd—like the Department employee who wore white gloves to work in the hope of getting noticed (it proved the contrary, for the frowns of his superiors drowned out the smiles). That, perhaps, is why the Italian author Daniel Vare entered the diplomatic service and out of sheer perversity produced a novel called *The Laughing Diplomat* —a contradiction in terms.

It may be that the image of our Foreign Service is inherent in an age-old profession which has always been suspected of Machiavellian intrigue, duplicity, and outright lying for one's country. In ancient days, envoys bearing gifts were distrusted as a matter of course, and they in turn distrusted the courts to which they were sent—to such an extent that an ambassador would take along his own cook and food taster. The Byzantine emperors practically made prisoners of ambassadors to their capital, for fear they would learn too much; the Muscovite authorities used to jail ambassadors who showed too much curiosity; and in Venice, the death penalty hung over the head of any citizen who made contact with a foreign diplomat. No wonder it became second nature for a diplomat to watch his step.

Times have changed, yet a cool and deliberative outlook—often mistaken for timidity—is still the hallmark of the trade. Furthermore, exposure to the cross fire of international politics endows the man who stands on our first line of defense with a degree of worldly knowledge vouchsafed to few others; it is sure to stamp

him as something of a cynic, and this does not endear him either
to his fellow citizens or to their chosen representatives in Congress,
who are less subject to sophisticated influences.

Precisely because the questions he deals with are so complex and
so subtle that the average person cannot possess the full background, the Foreign Service Officer is widely criticized and misunderstood. I had firsthand experience with this fundamental fact
when, in the face of violent public opposition, we maintained relations with Vichy France, the collaborationist regime of Marshal
Pétain. Backed into a corner at gatherings of friends, I could
never fully explain to their satisfaction why we pursued the policy we did—for the reasons were not only complicated, but could
not be divulged until after the American landings in North
Africa. In a subsequent chapter the reader will hear more about
this episode.

Not knowing the entire background, then, the man in the
street is almost bound to disagree at one time or another with
what is said or done by the State Department. President Kennedy
once put his finger on this truth when he reminded an audience
that all those concerned with great affairs sooner or later face the
possibility of criticism. "Those who cannot stand the heat," he
added, "should get out of the kitchen"—as Truman once said.

It is worth noting that no Foreign Service Officer ever volun-
teered to get out of the kitchen because of the heat. No Foreign
Service Officer whose mind was closed or made up, whose outlook
was circumscribed by the cocktail circuit, who fancied himself
over the human beings he strives to serve, could stand today's
boiling kitchen. If the picture so often painted of him were accurate, he would have been on his way out of his competitive career almost before he had started.

On Capitol Hill there are exceptions that prove every rule, but
the majority of congressmen have little affinity for the "career
boys" of Foggy Bottom and the lands beyond. If there is not
something offbeat about those who, by choice, spend their lives on
problems remote from the domestic scene, they seem, at least, always to be trying to see the foreigner's viewpoint instead of stand-

ing up forthrightly for the United States. Congressmen may not say so aloud, but privately they are inclined to regard the striped pants brigade as made up of effete creatures, spineless and lacking in red corpuscles, contaminated by association with those who plot the overthrow of the existing order, and more inclined to sell the country down the river for the sake of peace than to strike a blow for American rights. Captious critics who shoot from the hip and a press more concerned with local politics than with world affairs frequently lend encouragement to this line.

Although one has to assume that in the sophisticated city of Washington a member of Congress constantly adds to his grasp of foreign affairs and of the functions of the Foreign Service, he must also, in the last analysis, be guided by the views and opinions of the voters back home. The trouble is that the voters back home have few, if any, views and opinions about the Foreign Service; those they may have are likely to be garbled. Interest in foreign affairs is generally lacking; in some sections of the country it is conspicuously low in relation to the price of beef, the new state highway, the PTA, the baseball scores, or the alternating problems of flood and drought. In the larger cities a Council on Foreign Relations here, a World Affairs Council or a Foreign Policy Association there, can focus a spotlight on current events and instill an awareness of what the State Department does and what it can or cannot do. But for the man in Main Street, the Foreign Service has no appeal; it has no catchy title like the Peace Corps—though it was the nation's original corps for the pursuit of peace. For some it is concerned with subjects too abstruse for ready comprehension; for others it has goals and activities too removed from the stock market or the comics; in the face of massive public apathy, it is not surprising that the politicians fail to become enthusiastic about the diplomats and their works, especially when the returns on this investment of the taxpayer's money are neither tangible nor immediately apparent.

To show how difficult it is for the public to get a true perspective of the Foreign Service, one need only consider the experience of a senior officer who addressed a town meeting on the subject of

China. How come, he was asked by an irate listener, that the Foreign Service lost China for the United States? The officer launched into the background of the Opium War of 1839–1842, the Boxer Rebellion of 1899–1900, which was sparked by resentment against Western interests in China, and various other sidelights of history, concluding with an observation to the effect that what China did was dictated by the Chinese and not by the United States. "If that, then, is the case," was the response, "the treachery in the Foreign Service goes back much farther than I thought!"

The State Department, of course, is not the only federal agency that lacks a rapport with the public. Perhaps some of the suspicion with which the typical American regards the functions of government, as well as some of the resignation with which government workers accept the little recognition accorded them, may be traced to the frequent changes made by party politics in the higher echelons. As an article in *Holiday* magazine put it: "The civil servant . . . watches the political appointees move into their paneled throne rooms with their freshly signed photographs of the new President and their radical innovations. During their tour of duty, which usually lasts about 18 months, they may succeed in making slight changes of emphasis or direction in a particular program; but long after they have returned to their board rooms and their faculty lounges, the career official will still be sitting at his desk, initialing inter-office memoranda."

It is the uncomplaining official from the career who needs to be understood; it is he who must keep the wheels turning while the politicians take turns in manipulating the controls at the top. The State Department is no exception to this rule.

For a long time the Department recoiled in horror—if one can imagine an impassive Department recoiling—at the mere thought that it should interpret policies or answer critics through the mass media of communications. If anyone was interested—well, he could study the formal speeches or mimeographed press handouts of the Division of Current Information; the diplomatic official himself was inscrutable. Spokesmen for the hierarchy left the public unenlightened even when explanations could readily be made; the time-honored attitude was one of aloofness and reserve. Although the heavy hand of caution is still evident, a Bureau of Public Affairs is now doing something to change the picture—to provide information, to prepare studies of public opinion, to distribute pamphlets or periodicals, and to answer queries on current policy. Much remains to be done, however, if the Foreign Service is to enlist active backers of its cause, if the gulf between civil servant and private citizen is to be bridged adequately with understanding. The subject of foreign affairs must be repeatedly explained to be understood.

In retrospect over the years since the word "cooky pusher" was coined, every imaginable roadblock seems to have been thrust into the path of the Foreign Service in its development as a career. Not only has its performance been hamstrung by lack of money, but its morale has been dealt staggering blows by irresponsible accusations of disloyalty and by betrayal of the principle that entrance and advancement should depend solely on merit. Its entrance standards have been lowered in the name of recruitment, its operations choked by the rank weed of bureaucracy, its top posts bartered away for political purposes, its career men ignored in ambassadorial appointments. And as we shall see in subsequent chapters, the advice of its experts has been disregarded by the White House, its best thought contradicted by politicians for the sake of domestic politics.

To its lasting credit, the much-condemned Foreign Service and its equally denounced parent body, the Department of State, have done a remarkable job of protecting and furthering American interests all over the globe. Together they have developed a versatility in the handling of our foreign affairs that would have been unthinkable a couple of decades ago. Gibes and jeers notwithstanding, the Service has evolved into a highly competent corps that more than holds its own on every sector of the international front.

Nevertheless, there is room for improvement in our foreign

affairs establishment. Even in a city built by bureaucracy, the State Department is an object of bureaucratic awe. Housed in a mammoth eight-floor edifice that covers four square blocks, whose exterior, according to James Reston of the *New York Times,* "has about as much character as a chewing gum factory in Los Angeles," the Department has some five miles of corridors—in the reaches of which it is so easy to lose the way that visitors are given floor maps to help them reach their destination. Like Pelion upon Ossa, administrative and management units are making the structure top-heavy; so many programs, projects, and plans for the personnel jostle the process of policy formulation that one wonders when—not whether—the machine will master the man. Home staffing has flourished and personnel have gone forth and multiplied at every embassy overseas. Although there may be reasons for such madness, including the obligation to perform chores for other agencies serving the public abroad, the bystander can be forgiven if he asks: Is such size really necessary for what the administrators refer to as our "foreign affairs complex"; and if not, why does it take so many to do a given job? The comparable bureaucracies of other countries, such as Britain or France, have changed scarcely at all since before World War II; they do not, of course, have comparable responsibilities, but their basic business of conducting relations with other countries does not seem to call for double or triple the former staffs.

Under the chairmanship of Senator Henry M. Jackson of Washington, a Senate Subcommittee on National Security Staffing and Operations delved exhaustively into questions affecting the image and the operation of the Foreign Service during hearings held in the summer and fall of 1963. It brought to light some of the extraordinary handicaps to which the State Department is subject in the policy-making process; it turned the beam of publicity on faults in the structure and gave a selected group of ambassadors the chance to unburden themselves of pent-up suggestions and recommendations. This constructive exercise pointed up one of the chief difficulties, which goes hand in hand with the proliferation of personnel: the stultifying practice of decision by committee. Endless committees and endless committee clearances are required before policy decisions can be carried out, although efforts are made periodically to discourage their growth. The Department —like a Hydra-headed monster—seems to sprout two committees every time one is knocked off. Committees naturally cannot thrive without untold man-hours of meetings; and nothing can stall a decision, inhibit the thought process, or take the teeth out of a foreign policy faster than to submit a problem to an inter-office conclave or a huddle of spokesmen from different branches of the government, each with an itchy finger in the policy-making pie. Secretary Dean Rusk himself was a witness at the hearings and testified on these internal obstructions to the free flow of thought.

Other impedimenta thwart the maker of policy and contribute to his reputation—wholly undeserved—as inept, inefficient, or incompetent. To an extent that may be unimaginable on the outside looking in, those on the inside looking out are subject to influences quite unrelated to what would be considered by the public a logical and normal course of action. An expert may recommend; but those who decide must take into account any number of considerations not readily visible on the surface; possible repercussions in Congress; the reaction of that amorphous specter, public opinion, to, say, the recognition of a Latin-American dictator; the pressure of a senator pressed for votes; the attitude of an ally, as in the Skybolt affair with the British, and the consequences to that ally of a unilateral move; whether one or more of our vocal minority groups will approve or object, as in the signing of a nuclear test ban with Russia; whether some hidden aspect will play into the hands of the political opposition. As we shall note in more detail later on, it is not always simple to set a policy in motion; if the Department sometimes swings like a weathervane in the prevailing breeze, it may be that its better judgment has been subordinated to factors which few know exist.

Considering the earth-shaking changes wrought by two great wars, which dropped the liabilities as well as the privileges of leadership into our unreceptive laps, and considering the small cost to the taxpayer, the Foreign Service functions today with astonishing efficiency. Like a picked battalion, it keeps a vigil around the clock. To prevent wars from brewing, to safeguard the American stake in foreign lands, to promote the American ideal, to gauge the climate of a Cold War, State Department officials never sleep. There is, however, urgent need to attract more people with superior—rather than average—qualifications; to encourage them to look forward, at the peak of their careers, to becoming ambassadors instead of seeing the ultimate prizes carried off by politicians. There is need to rescue the morale of the career from the parlous state into which, for a variety of causes, it has drifted. There is urgent need to reduce the red tape and to use a scythe on the paper underbrush that retards the policy makers in their work. There is need to strike a responsive chord in Congress, in the press, and in the mind of the public—in short, to replace the tarnished image with a shiny modern version.

The Foreign Service Officer is, in brief, a prophet without honor in his own country; judging by foreign comment, more sympathetic understanding exists abroad. To see ourselves as others see us, let the London *Economist* hold up a candid mirror:

The American Foreign Service has always worked under extreme difficulties and looked forward to few rewards. Its members always knew that both the important diplomatic positions and the desirable, but less important, ones would go to the politically faithful—and that their role would too often be the thankless one of trying, from subordinate positions, to prevent international illiterates from making major blunders. In their declining years they might find themselves, if they were lucky, as Minister in some capital with an unpleasant climate. Under the circumstances, the United States got more devoted service and more efficient work from its diplomats than it deserved.

The Service could do with a little encouragement. Instead of carping, instead of censuring out of hand a professional corps that devotes all its energies to their welfare, the American people might try to study the working of the State Department and to make allowances for some of the intricacies of its problems.

🎖 🎖 🎖 🎖 🎖 🎖 🎖 🎖 TWO 🎖 🎖 🎖 🎖 🎖 🎖 🎖 🎖

Foggy Bottom

To understand the State Department and the complexity of its task, it is worth taking a look at what Congressman Samuel L. Devine would like to do away with at one stroke. Unsatisfactory as such an institution may appear to be to some people, the State Department does house indispensable machinery for maintaining relations with the diverse governments of the world. If it did not exist, we would have to invent it. And the manner in which our relations are conducted with different countries—comparable to playing a hundred games of chess at the same time—has become critical to the survival of the United States as a great nation.

In drawing up the Constitution, the founding fathers had the role of the Secretary of State very much in mind. Although our foreign interests were few, and our policy was to go it alone as far as the Old World was concerned, he was to be the senior confidant of the President and the right-hand dispenser of advice on many matters, internal as well as external. Sitting in a key spot in the official family circle, he would bring to the President a wide perspective. He would speak for the President before Congress, the nation, and the rest of the world, and serve as interpreter to the President of the desires and complaints of other countries, practically all of whose policies are now likely to affect our own in one way or another. The significance of this strategic position has increased proportionately with the speed of communications, for hardly anything can happen in any part of the world today that is not immediately known in another. A hundred years ago the news of Lincoln's assassination reached India three weeks after he had died; the murder of President Kennedy was known within minutes.

As a federal department, State ranks first—if not in the hearts of its fellow bureaucracies, then at least in the order of precedence among other government agencies. It is to State that the President turns, or should turn, first in the hierarchy; a sign of the times, however, is that the Secretary of Defense has more to say than ever, since the problems of national security are, in most cases, inextricably bound up with those of foreign affairs. The public is apt to forget, when it takes exception to a national policy, that it is the President, not the Secretary of State, who is responsible for the conduct of our foreign affairs—subject to certain powers of Congress. The Secretary of State is the instrument placed in his hands for that purpose. The Secretary's authority is derived directly from the President; an act of 1789 provided that he "shall perform and execute such duties as shall from time to time be enjoined on or entrusted to him by the President of the United States, agreeable to the Constitution." The Secretary, it was also specified, should conduct the business of the Department "in such manner as the President of the United States shall from time to time order or instruct." It is inconceivable that the State Department would embark upon a course of action that did not have at least the tacit approval of the White House. It is altogether possible, however, for the White House, depending on the type of President, to take action in some sphere of foreign affairs that the State Department does not learn about until much later.

If the Department resembles the hub of a wheel with spokes radiating to the ends of the earth, it is, in reverse, the focal point of lines bearing down upon it from the same distant places. Washington is the center of attention for more than a hundred sovereign and independent nations, with more on the way; not all have opened diplomatic missions, but that does not mean the capital of the United States is neglected in anyone's political, economic, or cultural calculations. Representatives of most foreign countries beat a constant tattoo on the doors of the State Department, seeking to advance their interests in the United States or hoping to get the United States lined up behind their particular points of view. Foreign relations are a two-way street—and the traffic is not only heavy but sometimes loaded with dynamite.

To handle its multitudinous affairs, the Department carves up the globe into five unequal politico-geographic parts. Europe, Latin America, the Far East, and the Near East were all discovered long ago, and their arbitrary boundaries spelled out so that no divisional chief would encroach on the territory of another. When the thunderheads of Nazi imperialism began to rise over Africa— Hitler's grand design was to take over the continent's resources for the New Order in Europe—the way was paved for recognition of another area. The European Division, which had jurisdiction over the European colonies on the African land mass, transferred them—for want of a better place—to the Division of Near Eastern Affairs; and in return it received the Balkans, no doubt the biggest and most one-sided real-estate deal in history. Africa came into its own as a separate Division at the height of the war in 1944, when it fell to my lot to be tapped as its first chief.

Today each geographic fifth is a bureau run by an assistant secretary, his deputy, and a myriad of office directors, country desk officers, special assistants, deputy special assistants, assorted advisers, and liaison men for AID, USIA, UN, politico-military and other specialized affairs, and an ever-growing host of that prolific species, the administrative officer. There are, of course, such high level incumbents from the Secretary down as the Undersecretary, the Deputy Undersecretary for Political Affairs, the Deputy Undersecretary for Administrative Affairs, a total of thirteen assistant secretaries or their equivalent, a counselor who is also the head of the Policy Planning Council, and the legal adviser. But when one examines the tortuous chart of the organization and tallies up the distribution of "slots" for the various fields and functions, it is difficult to see the wood for the trees in a forest of administrative timber; along with the supernumeraries who deal in specialized subjects, clusters of budgetary, personnel, and management drones form the crowded base of a pyramid, at the top of which is a small squad of overworked decision makers whose noses are still at the grindstone when the functionaries depart and who do not get home till long hours later. In short, it is the lengthy, unwieldy administrative tail which, to the detriment of efficient operations, threatens to wag the politico-geographic dog.

Like the insidious termite, the bug of bureaucracy got into the venerable structure on tree-lined Pennsylvania Avenue early in World War II, undermining the small, closely knit organization that ran the nation's foreign relations before the upheaval. Although State overflowed during the battle years into "temporary" quarters in remote parts of the city, its heart continued to beat in the same place for a year after V day. After the retirement of Secretary Cordell Hull came the zestful, silver-haired Edward J. Stettinius, Jr., of United States Steel, an old friend of mine from school days in New York. Together with a number of aides brought in from Lend-Lease, who earned for him the irreverent title of "Snow White and the Seven Dwarfs," Stettinius made a noble effort to bring business order out of wartime chaos. But the creeping evil had started its deadly work. More divisions were set up, more boxes appeared on the organization charts; office chiefs became political advisers, political advisers became directors, directors became assistant secretaries—and more hands were hired at lower levels to put more papers into more pigeonholes. Secretary James F. Byrnes, whose frequent absence in attending international gatherings led to the saying that "the Department fiddles while Byrnes roams" was persuaded to install a string of "executive assistants"—a fatal expedient that gave the green light to ever more expansion later on. Resistance was useless; the office that handled European affairs, for instance, protested to the last that it needed no administrative professional to run its business, but in the end it was forced to accept one. It was a portent of things to come.

By the time General George C. Marshall took command in 1947, functional cells had subdivided themselves so often that it

🎖 🎖

was no longer possible to house all the key bureaus under one roof. So, like an army on the move, the chieftains broke camp and transferred their quarters from the hallowed site adjoining the White House to the vastness of Foggy Bottom—where they took possession of an air-conditioned home, within sight of the Potomac, no longer needed by the Joint Chiefs of Staff. Old State, with its ghosts of great names and events, was left to second-string or odd-lot units; later it became an executive office of the President and was saved from the bulldozer only by historically minded citizens.

With the exodus and transfer of 1947 went something akin to the "soul" of policy making, when policy makers met informally over a pipe or cigar and conferred in a semicircle around the Secretary himself. Even after the outbreak of World War II, I was able to join half a dozen others in front of Cordell Hull's littered desk in Old State and mull over a course of action related, say, to the free wheeling General de Gaulle and the Free French. Discussions were unruffled, wide-ranging, and unhampered by squads of technicians and specialists. But in the dehydrated air of New State, jobs were further compartmentalized, policy papers were composed and "staffed" along military lines, and decisions were made by a yes or no on a line reserved for concurrence or not. One of the penalties of a modern bureaucracy is that it erects ever more barriers to the interchange of thought and that policies, instead of flowering in the friendly contacts of a qualified few, are almost as devoid of life as the air in which they are made.

King Canute himself would never have tried to stem the tide of government workers which the postwar years brought in. By 1948 State Department personnel had swollen to 5,652, or nine times what it was just ten years earlier; the overseas staff had also increased, from 3,749 in 1938 to 12,294 in 1948. The influx in Washington, of course, was not limited to State; but it takes on particular interest when one considers the range of subjects now within the purview of a department of foreign affairs. At the core of the expansion has been the appearance of new states. To establish, maintain, and foster our relations with "emerging" countries

has required more than twice as many political desks as when the
United Nations was born at San Francisco. But to create more
desks and divisions to handle the everyday business with scores of
countries—new or old—was not enough. Economic problems and
economic aid bulk large in our foreign operations today; so do
cultural and educational exchanges; so do the United Nations in
all its ramifications, the global enterprise of the United States Information Agency, and the Central Intelligence Agency. Now the
Peace Corps has joined the family. The State Department inherited many parts of the disbanded wartime agencies and felt
obliged to assert a policy interest in others; no one can quarrel, of
course, with the need to support our forward lines with adequate
facilities in the rear, but the simple matter of logistical backing
for the tasks of other government agencies has in itself produced a
growth in the State Department and Foreign Service that would
delight the most ardent disciples of Parkinson's law: "Work expands to fill the time available."

It did not take long to remedy our unfamiliarity with these
orphans of the storm. Liaison officers were appointed; since their
multiplication could not be stopped, the best that could be done
was to try to co-ordinate their activities. The New State of Secretaries Marshall, Acheson, Dulles, and Herter was soon bursting at
the seams, so that the present $60-million behemoth, New New
State, came into being. To Dean Rusk went also its thriving
cousins AID (Agency for International Development) and
ACDA (Arms Control and Disarmament Agency). Even this
fantastically outsize complex is inadequate. Spilling over into nine
rented buildings, using nearly 1.5 million square feet of space, the
State Department premises are already far too small; if AID,
ACDA, and USIA are added, the total is twenty buildings with
2,547,377 square feet. Offices are overcrowded; tenants must
double up, conference rooms must be lopped off, new outlets
sought; and high priority has been assigned to a spacious annex
for the immediate future. The preferred site for this latter project
is a nearby 21-acre tract which would provide 1.1 million additional square feet of space; the cost is estimated at $30 million.

Titles are as abundant in New New State as blossoms in May, and afford a fair cross section of what concerns the bureaucrat in the mid-1960's. To pick at random, there are the Deputy Assistant Secretary for Politico-Military Affairs, the Chief of the Administrative Management and Personnel Division in the Bureau of Educational and Cultural Affairs, and the Officer-in-Charge of Development Policy and Finances in the Office of International Economic and Social Affairs. Picture a committee composed of the Chief of the British Commonwealth, Northern and Central Europe Division of the Office of Research and Analysis for Western Europe in the Bureau of Intelligence and Research, the Chief of Regulations and Procedures Staff in the Office of the Deputy Executive Director for Administration, and the Officer-in-Charge of Financial Operations in the Office of International Finance and Economic Analysis in the Bureau of Economic Affairs. No wonder we need, to sort things out, a Deputy Assistant Secretary of State for "Evaluation."

Alice in Wonderland was never confronted with such a bewildering array of place names and titles. Undoubtedly she could have set up a functional unit of her own in this Washington dreamland, with the Mad Hatter and the Red Queen as special assistants, and never even have been noticed.

Twenty-five years ago one would, indeed, have been in wonderland if it had been necessary to consult a thick directory filled with cabalistic clues as to who handled what. No chart was then posted at the end of a corridor to tell you where you were and show you where you wanted to go. No floor plan, filled out at an information booth, was required to start you on your journey.

In today's labyrinthine Department, interminable interiors— fluorescent-lighted and soundproofed like a hospital—befuddle even the inmates; those on the inside of the gargantuan cage have no windows to tell them whether there is rain or shine outdoors. Personnel by the thousands ride in silent, automated elevators, slip into or out of cubicles behind a nightmare row of numbered doors, or mill around the cafeteria at lunchtime—bureaucracy uncontrolled and, one fears, uncontrollable.

🏵 🏵

The mechanics of carrying on the business of the Department have so many convolutions that the ultimate product is often distinguished by its lack of distinction. When 1,500 cablegrams pour into the mill every day, and at least as many flow out, the wheels must grind continuously at high speed; the number of messages on any one day may suddenly rise, sometimes to 4,000, and the telegraphic verbiage may total 400,000 words or more. It is an open question, however, whether the resulting grist is worth all the effort in coding and decoding; despite periodic pleas and exhortations to cut down on telegraphic verbosity and to use airmail instead, despite watchdogs at the source to censor superfluous phrases, the stream seems undammed and undammable.

An elaborate distribution schedule spreads the incoming message, classified as to secrecy and according to content, to all who may have a right to know; those who must run to meetings while they read are provided with summaries. But for the outgoing message, so many cooks are apt to haggle over the ingredients that the final broth may contain neither body nor nourishment. A draft instruction to an embassy remains a draft as long as anyone can be found to give it his attention; whatever the degree of urgency, it may take three days or it may take ten before the last initial appears in the clearance column. Inevitably, in a department as large as State, those who must be consulted are infinite in their jurisdictional duties. In the most complicated cases, where other government agencies must see, criticize, and make suggestions, it may be weeks before the final product is dispatched.

Mostly to blame for the delay is the committee system—what has been jocularly described as "the unwilling called by the unfit to do what was unnecessary." Although such a disparaging reflection is certainly not applicable to all State Department thought, it is as difficult to win concurrence from a committee as it is to pull the teeth of a reluctant dragon; each member, invoking to the full the much-abused principle of checks and balances, contributes his mite to slowing up a decision. Government by concurrence throttles decisions, for a paper filled with concurrences is not only a compromise on policy but a sacrifice to boldness of thought.

In the Washington world committees are spawned in direct ratio to the number of bureaucrats, and State is no exception to this Parkinson-like law. When a policy proposal passes through more than one committee, the evil is compounded: qualifications, reservations, and adulterations soon make a simulacrum of the original version. If discussions are prolonged, a quagmire of complications and amplifications is sure to stall quick action. Charles F. Kettering, the industrialist, once voiced this uncharitable view of committees in business: "If you . . . set up a committee of experts to handle the matter, then I can tell you that the surest way to kill the new ideas that are sprouting around your offices is to submit them to that committee. The best way to get the great, grand, epoch-making idea of yours reduced to the simplest, lowest, most commonplace form of mediocrity possible is to get that committee to pass on it." No more appropriate words could be applied to the committee in government—unless they are the words of Secretary Rusk in testifying before the Jackson subcommittee on "layering."

"Layering," admitted the Secretary in a model of understatement, "is an obstacle to the extent that it is burdensome." By "layering" Rusk meant the number of offices and officers that intervened between him and the handling of a given issue. An incoming telegram must follow its appointed course through the establishment and back to the particular bureau where it belongs. If it does not, said the Secretary, "somebody feels that he is being deprived of his participation in a matter of his responsibility." And no more heinous sin can be found in the wondrous world of bureaucracy than to deprive a bureaucrat of his participation in a matter for which he shares a modicum of responsibility.

Accompanying the committee system is the array of position papers which surround the taking of a decision, almost any decision. To sift the sea of documents which might, or might not, be relevant to a policy in the making can be a full-time occupation —as first became apparent to me during the battle of Washington in World War II. The sudden surge of papers into the "In" baskets, as a result of our stepped-up concern with world affairs, required Herculean efforts to control and steer into the "Out" baskets. I used to shudder to think what would become of all the papers after they left my room, what monumental files were building up; and I often wondered when someone would do something to stem the flood. But that was a war emergency, temporary in nature and not expected to continue; since then, the Department has grown fourfold and the files have become like Augean stables—no matter how fast they are swept out to be microfilmed and placed in the archives, more papers keep coming in ever greater profusion.

As a House Subcommittee on Census and Statistics discovered, the paper jungle is a "serious menace," but it did not need an official committee to point out that its very existence breeds overstaffing and empire-building. More people are progressively needed to collect, compile, arrange, and file more papers. Some years ago the Hoover Commission reported that government paper work alone costs the taxpayers $4 billion per annum. Although no breakdown for today is available, one way to bury us may be with the towering mountain of papers in the State Department a few years hence.

In the Vatican Museum stands a piece of marble sculpture familiar to every school child who studies the history of art— Laocoön and his sons caught in the coils of two serpents. Titian made a caricature of this group, in which he replaced the boys by monkeys—which perhaps gives us poetic license to compare the figures with State Department officers caught in bureaucracy's endless miles of red tape. According to the encyclopedias, Johann Joachim Winckelmann, father of modern archaeology, derived from the original statue the attributes of "noble simplicity and quiet grandeur." Winckelmann called attention to the fact that none of the figures is really crying aloud, but only "mildly sobbing." Nothing could more graphically symbolize the struggle, the noble simplicity, and the quiet grandeur of an officer in the Foreign Service assigned to a desk in Washington. He may not always feel like a monkey, and he may not be crying aloud, but he is certainly mildly sobbing as he strives to free himself from the strangling effect of committee meetings, conferences, position papers, and tedious clearances of his proposals.

If a man from Mars were to walk into State and say, "Take me to your leader, I have a project to discuss," he would first fill out a questionnaire, then find himself shunted through a succession of offices until his plan came to rest—not in front of the Secretary but before a subordinate officer far down the line dealing with Martian matters. In the interval, there would have been confusion as to which division had proper jurisdiction; indecision as to how the subject should be handled; suspensions of judgment by all those remotely interested; and interoffice memorandums by the score. Senator Paul H. Douglas, in his book *Economy in the National Government,* admirably described the situation which would have arisen because of the number of hands through which the proposal would have had to pass. Excessive numbers, he wrote:

. . . delay work and make it more difficult, for, in order to develop plans the subordinates have to clear matters with one another. Then they must start their projects upward through the administrative hierarchy. At each level there must be consultations, discussion, and modification. By this system of horizontal, vertical, and traverse clearance and discussion much time and effort are consumed. . . . The chief energies of the large staff are consumed in communicating with one another.

The job eventually does get done. But to the taxpayer it may partially explain why so many people are required to do what a smaller staff might accomplish in less time and at less expense. Aside from the natural tendency of government to grow, the chief reason may be our lack of experience in playing the lead in the huge arena of the modern world. Americans simply have not had the time to acquire the readiness, the skill, and the confidence to handle so many complex roles in so many sectors of the globe with surety, dispatch, and economy of operation. The principle is one which would have been familiar to Voltaire: We have not the time to be brief. We must do it the hard way—if not with an excess of zeal, then with an excess of personnel. Adding more actors, though not all are in the category of stars, seems to be the only way we know to cope with the diversity of plots in the theater of our foreign affairs; once under way, the proliferation is progressively more difficult to control. It is also hard to control the proliferation of automobiles in our city streets; but sooner or later a beginning must be made if all forward motion is not to be choked by the traffic.

The multiplicity of memorandums at home is matched only by the prolific reports—many of them to languish unread in the maze of bureaucracy—from fruitful embassies and consulates abroad. Although efforts have recently been made to cut down on their length and number, just as economy moves in the past have resulted in a temporary reduction of personnel, reports are so all-embracing and so demanding that their preparation takes precious hours, days, or even weeks; those of a routine or periodic variety clog the works with administrative minutiae. Or, on the spur of the moment, some Washington official requests a report to close his own information gap; sometimes this assumes the form of a circular telegram calling indiscriminately on all posts for a comprehensive survey. Essential requirements must be met, of course, to keep the wheels of government turning, but the test is "what is essential?" I once received, as vice consul in Teheran, a request for a study of the market for artificial golf greens. Although there might have been a sales outlet for such a product in a country as dry and barren as Persia, had there been any golf courses, no one had taken the trouble to find out first that Persians did not play golf.

We seem congenitally unable to stop the burgeoning, whether in papers or in staff. In our London embassy, as Secretary Rusk told the Jackson subcommittee, it was a matter of some concern that at least forty-four agencies of the government were represented—a matter "that would have to be looked into." Not only do other agencies feel free to establish branches in our diplomatic missions, but one attaché usually leads to another. With a foot in the door, he must have an assistant; the assistant, too, must be assisted, until there is a vested interest and an ever-growing staff in the office. To complete the vicious circle, the administrators in the home office must make room for more staff to serve the additional representatives overseas.

As an example of the size of an important embassy, our mission in New Delhi, at the time this was written, contained 109 persons high enough in rank to be named in the Foreign Service List, including the military attachés and those belonging to the United States Information Agency but excluding typists, code clerks, and administrative personnel. Attached to the embassy is the Agency for International Development—Mission and Technical Staff—which outnumbered the embassy proper with 111 persons likewise exclusive of clerical assistants. A few titles taken at random give an idea of the scope of the interests of the agency which have to be serviced: agricultural marketing and processing adviser, program documentation clerk, regional legal adviser, assistant director of physical resources, educational program assistant, malaria adviser, soils adviser, assistant supply adviser, nurse education adviser, entomologist. A new note, moreover, has crept into the embassy roster—six representatives, or associate representatives, of the Peace Corps who administer the program and direct the personnel of the corps in India.

Although the duplication was self-evident, I had on my staff in Libya a military attaché, a naval attaché, an air attaché, and an agent of Central Intelligence, all of whom vied with the trained members of my political section in gathering intelligence. Since the sources of information in that country were necessarily limited, those who furnished the intelligence were often taken aback at being asked the same questions by representatives of different agencies; those who did the asking stumbled over each other in their efforts to garner the available scraps.

Only an ambassador can say whether his executive, political, economic, consular, or administrative section is too large for his needs; but the fact remains that not even the Soviets have as much personnel as we have in some places. By comparison with the British and the French, we are top-heavy in nearly every post: the collective American representation in Rome is between 800 and 900, for example, while our allies make do with a tenth that

number. At international conferences the United States delegation, loaded with alternate positions, often outnumbers the others
two to one; its nearest rival is our Soviet adversary.

Still another reason for the size in our administrative structure
is that it seems easier to employ two persons of medium skill than
to pay for the services of one who is highly trained; after a
woman employee at a Central American post resigned a while ago,
with five years' experience, she was astonished to learn that she had
been replaced by two other girls. We start big, too. At our embassy in Usumbura, capital of the new African country of
Burundi, we opened with a regular staff of eighteen, or a total of
sixty Americans counting all grades of personnel and their families, more foreigners than the Belgians had when they ran the territory as a trusteeship. It was easy to foretell what would happen
at this far end of the line: the first question that came from the
duly impressed officials was "Now when do we get American
aid?"

Government salary tables have never been known to offer more
attraction than private business, and modest educational requirements do not necessarily translate into the highest standards of
efficiency when it comes to clerical or stenographic help. In addition to the regular civil service positions in Washington, the Foreign Service Staff Corps has some 4,000 employees who can be stationed either in the Department or abroad for technical and administrative duties. To recruit secretaries, communications clerks,
and teletype operators "willing to go anywhere in the world on
assignment," including Washington, positions were advertised in
the spring of 1964 at $4,215 to $4,715 plus allowances. For this
pay, the quality of performance is sometimes remarkable. But
padding of the rolls with Negroes under the impetus of civil
rights is another matter. No possible objection could exist, in a
department that deals daily with Africans, to employing Negroes
who have the necessary aptitudes, abilities, and temperaments—
already there are more Negro officers in higher paying positions in
State than in any other government agency. But when "equal
employment opportunity" means the appointment of those who,

admittedly, lack the "superior" qualifications normally required of others, the taxpayer is being asked to support a new kind of featherbedding. Even the Puerto Rican and Indian minorities now have their claimants for a place in the sun of foreign affairs, and if room must be made for them, somebody else must move over. For domestic political reasons the once-thought select occupation of toiler in the vineyard of diplomacy is being invaded by those whose capacity to learn must be cultivated before it can become effective.

The span of thirty years since I ran the consulate general at Teheran with two local clerks has brought an elaboration in the administrative machinery without which it seems impossible to operate. To keep the records, to compile the reports, to tally the accounts, to perform the many clerical duties now necessitated by our operating procedures, naturally require more personnel; as Parkinson might have noted, requirements expand as the establishment grows. When hearings were held by the House Subcommittee on Appropriations, on February 28, 1962, light was cast on the use of sixteen people to conduct the affairs of our embassy in Ouagadougou, a mud hut town of 65,000, which is the capital of the Upper Volta Republic in Central Africa. Ambassador Thomas Estes justified the need for four officers, four clerks, and eight local watchmen-laborer-gardeners by showing that he—an authorized deputy chief of mission—a third secretary, and an administrative officer composed the authorized executive staff; that with the deputy's position temporarily vacant, his secretary was employed full time as a records clerk and that the wife of the administrative officer, a trained secretary, was doing duty in the code room; that another American girl, an administrative assistant, was engaged full time on accounts in addition to her other duties, thereby saving an additional position for the accounting work; that the local staff was needed for a variety of chores in a country where "the standard of performance was extremely low"; and that since there were no local resources to fall back upon, these were called "do-it-yourself embassies."

❀ ❀

Chairman John Rooney may have made a point when he remarked, "Outside of the do-it-yourself business I have not heard of any work being done there." But there is always scope for work, even in a town of 65,000 Africans. It is the character of the work that counts: the bureaucratic apparatus which now seems to overshadow the real job of diplomacy not only keeps everyone busy full time, but it can no longer be curtailed without throwing the whole cumbersome system out of gear.

There are other reasons for all the bigness—advanced by those who attempt to explain, if not to excuse, the phenomenal growth. Other government agencies, rather than defer to State, would like nothing better than to set up their own foreign services, much like those represented in pre-World War II days by the trade commissioners and commercial attachés of the Department of Commerce and the agricultural attachés of the Department of Agriculture. Although those officers were assimilated into the regular Foreign Service in 1939, to the simplification of our overseas structure, an Agricultural foreign service was reborn after the war and others would doubtless arise if given the opportunity. Carried to their logical—or illogical—extremes, such separate activities could lead to separate courses of action and separate responsibilities; the United States would speak with different voices, in various keys, without the knowledge or consent of the department primarily concerned in the field of foreign affairs.

Not only Commerce and Agriculture, but many other federal agencies have a natural bent for branching out abroad. Army, Navy, and Air attachés are always with us. The Agency for International Development is an expanding career. Labor, Treasury, and Central Intelligence have well-developed units overseas. Justice, Interior, and Health, Education, and Welfare find foreign lands irresistible. Our international cultural and educational activities alone involve an interest on the part of a couple of dozen different agencies. In addition, semiofficial or private organizations —business, scientific, cultural, journalistic—many of them with political overtones, are engaged in operations around the globe;

mass movements, ubiquitous pressure groups, and philanthropic bodies spread their word and make their influence felt with or without benefit of government guidance.

The State Department and the Foreign Service spend a lot of time, and use a lot of personnel, compiling statistics on agriculture, prices, and crop conditions for the Department of Agriculture, notwithstanding the latter's own experts; on reporting financial or exchange conditions for the Treasury and Federal Reserve Board; on gathering data regarding prices, wages, and living costs for the Labor Department. Among its still other duties, State studies and reports on foreign harbor facilities, port rules, and hydrographic matters for the Navy; it performs countless chores for the Post Office and lesser agencies having a direct or indirect interest in foreign countries. Anything that may conceivably bear on a domestic problem is a legitimate demand on consular or diplomatic time; anything that any other agency can do, State can do too.

To keep tabs on the ever-spreading role of American enterprise throughout the world, to run interference for and to represent the interests of other government bureaus, say the apologists for a huge State Department, requires a huge administrative organ. If there were no one to ride herd on the mavericks, no one would know what they were up to. And without that supervision, of course, the State Department would be left with even less to say than it now has over the expanding programs and personnel policies of rival bureaucracies.

State would dearly like to give up the administering of others' affairs in exchange for stricter powers of control; but this is clearly a wishful thought and nothing more. Testifying before the Jackson subcommittee in November, 1963, Deputy Undersecretary William J. Crockett explained: "I have had other agencies say this to me: 'Our program abroad is our program, we have had it established by Congress and, therefore, it isn't any of your business trying to tell us whether or not we need more people and whether or not we should be doing certain things abroad; this is our program.' . . . For instance, there are about seventy people in the United States Government representing various agencies, who are interested in India. So our desk officer in charge of India has a real job of co-ordination."

There can be no doubt that the present administrative structure —the like of which has never been seen in the chancelleries of the world—is not likely to grow any smaller unless drastic steps are soon taken to bring that about. One way, say those who disagree with the thesis that bigness is inevitable, is to cut down on the number of specialists in the Department and rely more on the specialists in other agencies for specialized services. It is not essential, they hold, for State to know all about everything; it could use the output of the Labor Department or the International Labor Office on technical questions, of Commerce on international business problems, and so on, like the "general department" in the British Foreign Office, which calls up the specialists on given subjects as required. However, that prolific new breed, the liaison officer, seems here to stay as a member of the bureaucratic family. Every specialty must be cross-bred with every other specialty. Thus, in the office dealing with Far Eastern matters, there must be a liaison man for United Nations affairs, and in the office of United Nations affairs there must be a liaison officer for Far Eastern matters. And so, like guinea pigs in an incubator, the specialists multiply.

Like other administrative concepts that owe their origin to the changing times, the growth of the "specialist"—as opposed to the "generalist"—is fundamentally affecting the career. In the early days it was assumed that a Foreign Service Officer would develop the different skills which would fit him ultimately to take charge of, and to run with wide perspective, a diplomatic mission of his own. World War II, however, left the Service with a legacy of new and special subjects—labor, communications, science, petroleum, culture, international finance, civil aviation, and most particularly those in the budgetary-administrative category. As life grew more complicated, there was need for a specialist in every field and less time for a generalist to become familiar with each one of them. In the same way that specialists in different branches of medicine are elbowing out the old-fashioned family physician, the specialists in the Foreign Service are displacing the old-time generalists. Actually, as Deputy Undersecretary Crockett has explained, there is seldom a day "when we don't find the need for a new specialty or a new technique." The dawn of specialization has indeed come up like thunder in the land of Foggy Bottom; but the question remains whether the new age is producing statesmen or a solid phalanx of specialized organization men.

In the Wriston Report, to be discussed later, much stress was laid on the business theory of "developing an individual around his specialty, with generalism coming later." Like the often quoted creed of its president, Charles E. Wilson, "What's good for General Motors is good for the country," the successful businessman's idea of the specialist was applied to the profession of diplomacy. In other words, the specialty within the profession was to be more emphasized than the profession itself, in bland disregard of the fact that diplomacy is not business and that a properly qualified diplomat, skilled in political and economic analysis, negotiation, languages, and psychological insight, is himself a specialist of a rare order.

Specialists in certain subjects such as Soviet affairs, the Arab world and its language, in labor or commerce, will always be needed in the Foreign Service. At the same time, what is known as the "thrust" of the Career Management Plan acknowledges that officers should have some experience in fields other than their specialties and should be subject to interchange among the Department's various functional areas. After all, the generalists are the ones who count when the time comes to appoint the head of a diplomatic mission—for they must be grounded not only in a knowledge of how their embassy works, but in understanding of what it takes to meet either their associates or their adversaries on a wide topical front. The question may well be asked: Can a man who has spent most of his life engrossed in the details of his specialty step naturally into the role of ambassador without ever having served abroad or passed a language test? The answer is yes, according to the "new diplomacy" of the State Department. Generalists are fast disappearing from the scene; and with them are going the assets of perceptiveness, sound judgment, panoramic understanding, and intuition tempered in the fires of practical experience.

When Nicholas I, the "Iron Czar" of Russia, was at the height of his power, he is reported to have said: "I do not rule Russia. Ten thousand clerks do." One is tempted to apply this simile to the ever-burgeoning bureaucracy of the State Department, where the administrative maze has not yet reached the ten-thousand mark but is truly colossal by pre-World War II standards. What shocks the career officer in the Foreign Service, however, is not so much the battalions of employees who pour in and out of the Washington beehive, as the fact that the administrators in charge of the multitude have little on-the-spot knowledge of Service life or "feel" for Service problems.

It seems to be contrary to the modern view that the best results come from commanders who have served with the troops—that enlightened appreciation of Foreign Service aims rises from direct contact with operations in the field. The substitute for such old-fashioned thinking is the impersonal system of "career management," which trains the officer along a predetermined path, functionally specializing as he goes, while the higher qualities of the professional diplomat are downgraded or ignored. What this seems to lead to is an IBM technique—a computer-run organization, both at home and abroad. The groundwork was laid when thousands of employees were required to fill out questionnaires listing their "functional and area skills" for the Officer in Charge of Manpower Resources Planning in the Office of Personnel. The "new procedures for planning and deciding personnel assignment and career development actions," read a circular instruction, "will help the Department develop composite appraisals of the skills of officers and employees."

The Department's administrative circles are proud of the fact that their *Manpower Skills Handbook* has been taken as a model by foundations, universities, schools of management, libraries, and government agencies. It may be a model of its kind; but when foreign affairs are run like a "school of management," which decides how funds are to be expended or curtailed; when business machines decide which officer has the right qualifications for what post; when card catalogues are substituted for personal appraisal; when the composite diplomat takes over, we may tremble for the foundations of the Service itself.

Admiral Hyman G. Rickover, pioneer of the nuclear submarine, once made the salty observation: "Whoever has had anything to do with organizations will have observed the tendency of the administrators to gain control of the whole corporate body." In the State Department, the administrators are no longer the servants of the policy makers—they are rapidly becoming the masters. Rickover might have added that nothing can destroy the spark of genius quicker; if State Department administrators should ever gain control of policy decisions in the substantive sphere, they could not only kill the spirit of the organization, but in the next twenty years turn it into the depersonalized, machine-dominated institution portrayed by George Orwell in his book *1984*.

Empire building, as we have seen, is an old fault of government; administrative personnel begets more administrative personnel, and managerial staffs soon set up regulations which help to create both conformity and uniformity. It is unnecessary for our purposes to seek further for the origins of the present incubus than December 2, 1957, when a "Management Staff" was created in the Office of the Assistant Secretary for Administration to "advise on the broad management aspects of basic program and policy questions." This modest milestone in the bureaucrat's progress was to "develop comprehensive analysis programs covering the activities of the Department in Washington and abroad"; in carrying out its duties, it was directed to "work in collaboration with and through existing management aspects of the Department," such as the Foreign Service Inspection Corps, Office of Personnel, Office of Budget, and Regulations and Procedures Staff; it not only foreshadowed the ambitious managerial aspects of "career development" which threaten the extinction of individual initiative today, but suggested that the complexities of handling our foreign relations had reached a point where only more managerial blueprints superimposed on the administrative infrastructure could show what they were all about.

Trying to put foreign affairs on a big-business footing does not mean that business acumen is successfully employed, or that efficiency manual techniques are producing a streamlined establishment to house the new diplomat. The bigger the place becomes, the more does responsibility branch out; divided and subdivided, responsibilities become the charge of numberless petty despots who insist on having their separate say. Supposedly run on business lines, the elaborate machinery tends to become a manufacturing plant for international relations; the personal equation—so often the bridge between success and failure in diplomacy—becomes denigrated; and the machine, fed with functional formulas, turns out sterile policies in quintuplicate.

Costly experience has shown that business executives have little luck in managing the State Department. Many changes have occurred in the top administrative spot of the Department and the Foreign Service since the end of World War II—at one time the rate was one undersecretary every year and a half. Each administrator brought in from the outside had his own ideas how to apply managerial techniques to the peculiar combination of Departmental civil service and Foreign Service; of these one of the most conspicuously unsuccessful was Donald B. Lowrie, vice president of Quaker Oats, who became Undersecretary for Administration in the Republican year of 1953. Famed as a football player at Princeton, but green to the Washington wild woods, Lowrie rode head on into the McCarthy-McLeod nightmare. Even without the particular disruptiveness of that period, his short incumbency could have contributed nothing to the comprehension of the administrators as to what diplomacy was all about. Lowrie, no doubt, left a sadder but wiser man. Intelligent comprehension of the complicated factors involved in operative, as well as administrative decisions, together with astute judgment as to their possible repercussions both at home and abroad, are indispensable assets in the "management" of a foreign affairs establishment. In the late 1950's, an attempt was made to meet these requirements when

Career Ambassador Loy W. Henderson, under whom I once served as deputy for Near Eastern, South Asian, and African Affairs, was in charge for a five-year period. Whoever sits in the driver's seat should not only be well equipped to understand the "art and practice of diplomacy," but also be well versed in the ups and downs of Service life. The British publicly recognized this principle in the recommendations of a committee for the reform of the British diplomatic service, chaired by the former head of the British Atomic Energy Authority, Lord Plowden. Administrative affairs, said the Plowden Report, should be directed by an officer of the highest grade in the diplomatic service.

But the most important attribute of the post of Undersecretary for Administration should be its length of tenure. A single official, who would devote the better part of his career to running the Service, immune to partisan issues or change, might accomplish unsuspected miracles. But appointment on such a long-term basis is not the practice. Between 1961 and 1964, no less than three officials have successively tackled the job.

It remains to be seen whether the monster machine created by administrative Frankensteins over the last twenty years is the best suited, from a diplomatic standpoint, to meet the tremendous challenge of the times.

Evolution of a Career

"Let us strive for a foreign service which will be flexible and democratic; which will attract and retain the best men we have; which will offer reasonable pay; reasonable prospects for promotion, and reasonable provision against want when old age comes to a faithful servant who has served long and ably."

With these words the concept of a career was wedded to the existing haphazard system of appointing consuls and secretaries in the diplomatic service. Representative John Jacob Rogers of Massachusetts, speaking at the Institute of Politics in Williamstown on August 21, 1923, thus launched a drive in Congress which culminated the following year in the act which bears his name; it consolidated the consular and diplomatic branches into one Foreign Service, established a secure professional basis for its officers, and incorporated provisions of unprecedented liberality to induce men of high caliber and ability to enter. For this reason Congressman Rogers has been called the father of the modern Foreign Service. So has Wilbur J. Carr, Assistant Secretary of State from 1924 to 1937, who joined the Department in 1892 as a clerk after passing the civil service examinations and who tirelessly aided and encouraged the Congressional effort to create a unified Service on the basis of merit as opposed to political preferment.

So, too, has Benjamin Franklin, in whose memory stands a statue in the garden of the American embassy in Paris. Franklin's fame as the father of the Foreign Service stems from the fact

❧ ❧

that he was the first minister plenipotentiary of the United States of America, and that when he presented his credentials to Louis XVI, on March 23, 1779, he became the first American of that rank and title to be received by a foreign state. Whatever the effects of this mixed paternity, the Foreign Service has grown from an unwelcome foundling on the doorsteps of Congress to a virile, if ungainly, manhood. While its upbringing at the hands of a skeptical and indifferent public has been one of hard knocks, it has developed sinews of strength that allow it to take on all comers today; and if its progenitors could not now recognize their precocious offspring, they would have the satisfaction of noting that its powers of resistance have enabled it to survive with credit the onslaughts of detractors and reformers alike.

Much history is encompassed between the day our first envoy was sent to France and the present practice of appointing ambassadors to every geographical expression dignified by the name of nation.

In the beginning, the Foreign Service of the United States—which had its genesis in the Secret Committees of the Revolution—carried no sense whatever of a career mission. Diplomats of the earliest school regarded their appointments as temporary, while most consular officials considered the official duties they performed as a sideline to the commercial occupations which took them to a foreign port. During the pioneer period following American independence, diplomats were nonpolitical, tested as to talent and fitness for public service by the leadership they had displayed in the Revolution. President Washington set high standards, as did Thomas Jefferson, who became the first Secretary of State in 1790; their immediate followers, too, adhered to the principle of quality first in naming diplomatic envoys, until the introduction of the spoils system by President Andrew Jackson smudged the record. Famous names then studded the pages of our diplomatic history: in London we were represented by such outstanding men as Thomas Pinckney, negotiator of the 1795 treaty with Spain; Rufus King, distinguished Federalist senator; James Monroe, future Secretary of State and President-to-be;

John Quincy Adams, son of the first American representative to Great Britain and later President himself; Richard Rush, former Attorney General and successful negotiator of the treaty for joint occupation of Oregon; and Albert Gallatin, Swiss-born Secretary of the Treasury under Jefferson and Madison. In Paris the galaxy of star performers included Gouverneur Morris, Robert R. Livingston, Joel Barlow—forerunner of the literary figures that were to grace the list of nineteenth-century statesmen—and the versatile Monroe and Gallatin.

Nowhere could it have been harder for a new country to start relations with an old one than in the Great Britain of King George III. As minister plenipotentiary of the United States, John Adams had an impossible task to open relations with that less than friendly monarch and he could not have met with a more uncivil reception from the press. On his arrival in May, 1785, the *London Public Advertiser* extended this sarcastic greeting: "An Ambassador from America! Good heavens what a sound! The Gazette surely never announced anything so extraordinary before. . . . This will be such a phenomenon in the Corps Diplomatique that 'tis hard to say which can excite indignation most, the insolence of those who appoint the Character, or the meanness of those who receive it."

John Quincy Adams fared better than his father in a diplomatic career, serving successfully as minister to the Hague, to Prussia, to St. Petersburg, to London, as head of the American Commission at Ghent to make peace with Great Britain, as senator, Secretary of State, and President. His training and experience undoubtedly set an all-time record; beginning at the age of eleven, he had worked as secretary to Adams the elder during the latter's short tenure as American Commissioner in Paris; at fourteen he was private secretary to Francis Dana, American Minister to Russia; he studied international law in the Netherlands, and again acted as secretary to his father during the last stages of the peace negotiations with Britain. As a graduate of Harvard he had practiced law in Massachusetts, was fluent in French and German, highly intelligent and industrious, familiar at first hand with Eu-

🏵 🏵

ropean politics and America's foreign relations; he probably did more than any other individual to shape the foundations of the country's foreign policy.

Among the consuls, Lieutenant Colonel William Palfrey of Massachusetts, former Paymaster General of the Continental Army, had the double distinction of being the first to be appointed and the first officer of the Foreign Service to die under heroic or tragic circumstances. On December 9, 1780, Palfrey was commissioned "consul in France," with a salary of $1,500 a year, and shortly thereafter was lost at sea en route to his post. His name leads all the rest on the memorial plaque honoring those who have given their lives for their country. Thomas Barclay of Pennsylvania, commissioned "vice consul in France" on July 10, 1781, with the munificent salary of $1,000 a year, was the first consular officer actually to serve abroad. An American merchant residing in France, Barclay had previously been of service to Ambassadors Franklin and Adams; less than three months after his appointment he was promoted to consul in place of Palfrey.

Appropriations for "foreign intercourse" were as modest at the start as Congress could decree and as they have remained, relatively speaking, ever since. An act of July 1, 1790, authorized the President to draw from the Treasury a lump sum of $40,000 annually "for the support of such persons as he shall commission to serve the United States in foreign parts, and for the expense incident to the business in which they may be employed." The "Foreign Fund," as it was called, was augmented by provision for an "outfit," equal to a year's salary, paid to ministers and chargés d'affaires for the costs of getting to and installing themselves in their posts. No minister could receive a salary in excess of $9,000, while a secretary to a minister was limited to $1,350. As Secretary of State, Jefferson lost no time in opening the struggle with Congress for adequate funds, a struggle that continues to this day. Pointing out the difficulties of representing America on such low salaries—much lower than those of European diplomats of equal rank—he urged relief, "for the public good," and in small measure this was forthcoming. The costs of couriers, newspapers, translating, and printing were allowed as additional charges; and in 1796, the appropriation for regular expenses was increased to $60,000.

"Foreign intercourse," however, was elastically interpreted in the Act of March 20, 1794, and the Act of May 30, 1796, when spectacularly large sums were provided to purchase peace with the rulers of the Barbary States and to pay the ransoms demanded by the North African pirates for the release of American captives. The first act authorized the President to borrow one million dollars to defray such "additional expenses"; the second authorized an appropriation of $260,000 and a loan of $325,000 for the same purpose. This ignominious chapter in American foreign relations was brightened by the illustrious figure of Joel Barlow, who spent more than a year as the agent of our minister to Portugal, Colonel David Humphreys, negotiating the necessary deals with the dey of Algiers; and who, as American minister to Paris some fourteen years later, was to die of exposure in Poland while vainly pursuing Napoleon and an equally elusive treaty for the protection of American shipping against French depredations.

Barlow's death was a tragic and futile sacrifice. Put off time and again in his attempts to conclude a treaty, he was finally invited to continue the negotiations in Wilna, temporary headquarters of the French foreign office while Napoleon was conducting his invasion of Russia. But the arduous 1,500-mile carriage journey from Paris came too late. Shortly after his arrival at the Lithuanian capital, the American minister found that the invasion had turned into a rout. Barlow was forced to flee with the rest of the diplomatic corps. Joining the great retreat in the icy grip of winter, he soon contracted pneumonia; racked with chills and fever, he pushed on as long as he could, but in the little town of Zarnowice, on December 21, 1812, he reached the limit of his endurance. Lodged in the home of the town's mayor and postmaster, John Blaski, he died the day after Christmas.

Even more bizarre was an incident that occurred in 1801, when Yussef Karamanli, the pasha of Tripoli, repudiated his treaty with the United States and, to show his defiance, chopped down the

🏵 🏵

flagpole in front of the American consulate and expelled Consul General James Leander Cathcart. For the next four years the nascent United States Navy carried on a desultory war with the pasha. At length an enterprising and high-spirited Connecticut Yankee named William Eaton, agent of the Navy in North Africa and former consul in Tunis, resolved on an unparalleled land campaign to bring hostilities to a close. With the help of the pasha's elder brother, Hamet, who had been ousted from the throne, Eaton marched a miscellaneous collection of adventurers, including 38 Greek mercenaries, an English doctor and a handful of United States Marines across 600 miles of desert coastline from a base in Egypt. An Arab sheik provided the transport with a caravan of 190 camels; six weeks of travel across the shifting sands brought the Moslem crew close to starvation and on the verge of mutiny against the Christians in the party. In the nick of time, Eaton met with relief in the Gulf of Bomba from three American naval vessels, the *Argus,* the *Hornet,* and the *Nautilus.* Supported by gunfire from the ships, Eaton and his men succeeded in capturing the Cyrenaican city of Derna, part of the Tripolitanian domain. Entrenched in the fort overlooking the town, they withstood a month's siege until the forces of Yussef were driven off. However, before he could press on to Tripoli, still hundreds of miles distant, Commodore Samuel Barrow and Consul General Tobias Lear at Algiers took the wind out of Eaton's triumphant sails by signing an agreement with the pasha which terminated the war.

The battle for the port of Derna gave birth to the celebrated line in the marching song of the Marines, "From the halls of Montezuma to the shores of Tripoli." A century and a half after this improbable action, accompanied by my military attaché in the kingdom of Libya, I had the opportunity to place a wreath against the remains of the fort, where a commemorative tablet marks a shrine totally unknown to tourists and unfamiliar to most Americans.

The paucity of diplomats in the early days of nationhood was matched by the scarcity of diplomatic help. Since no provision existed for a career personnel, the quickest route to service abroad was by apprenticeship as secretary to a minister, arranged through personal ties of friendships. Without these apprentices, what work there was could not be done. There was no connection between service abroad and service at home; no relationship between diplomatic and consular service. Rudiments of a career appeared only in 1810, when legislation was adopted requiring Senate confirmation for any secretary of legation paid by government funds.

The stamp of the amateur likewise lay upon the first consular officers. Washington made seventeen consular appointments between February and August, 1790, none of which carried a salary; remuneration was to come from fees for consular services and from the private trade in which the officeholders were invariably engaged. Not until April 14, 1792, was any regulation of the consular service attempted; on that date an act was passed which remained its organic legislation for more than fifty years. Duties as defined therein were virtually limited to the protection of American citizens, but particularly American seamen who might become stranded in foreign ports. No restriction was placed on the nationality of those who were to represent the United States, no limits were imposed as to the trade they might pursue; and no salaries were authorized except in the case of consuls residing on the Barbary Coast, who were involved in semidiplomatic practices on behalf of the American ships, cargoes, and crews seized by the Barbary corsairs. In Tunis and Tripoli the annual salary was $2,000; in Algiers, center of this activity, it was augmented to $4,000.

America's expanding commerce and shipping were responsible for the relatively rapid growth of consular representation, compared with diplomatic. Seaports in Great Britain, France, Spain, Portugal, Italy, and the Low Countries, as well as in north Germany, Sweden, Denmark, Russia, and the Barbary States were logical places to fly the flag—as were several exotic ports of call in Latin America and in the British, French, Spanish, and Dutch islands of the Caribbean. Posts were even opened in faraway Capetown, Canton, Batavia, and Smyrna. By 1830, 141 consular offices had been established, compared with only 15 diplomatic missions. One of the latter, it is of passing interest to note, was in czarist St. Petersburg, where Minister John Randolph was instructed by the Secretary of State that "his official intercourse with the Russian Government was to have for its object the preservation of peace and good understanding and the consolidation of the most amicable relations with a long tried and faithful friend of the United States."

Consular fees belonged to consular officers—$2, for example, for the authentication of documents and 5 per cent of the estate of an American dying abroad; but since no uniform rules existed as to the manner of performing consular services or the fees to be collected, it became customary to charge all the traffic would bear. Supervision and guidance from Washington were scanty; the small staff in the Department of State was far too busy carrying on the current correspondence to flood the field with instructions such as pour forth today. For its freedom from administrative control, the consul's life must then have been a pleasant one.

A Department of Foreign Affairs had been established by Congress in 1789, whose business, as we have noted, was to be conducted by a Secretary "in such manner as the President of the United States shall from time to time order or instruct"; the name was changed, on second thought, to Department of State, when it was decided to add such domestic duties as keeping the great seal and the archives of the United States, publishing the acts of Congress, issuing patents, and recording the census. Since nearly all its "state" functions have passed to other agencies of the government, the Department is now, in effect, more than ever a "Department of Foreign Affairs." Its first home, as part of the federal government, then located in New York, was in a house on lower Broadway, and when Jefferson took charge—at a yearly salary of $3,500—his staff consisted of two principal and three subordinate clerks, one part-time French translator, and two custodians. Such a miniscule personnel would hardly be dignified by the name of "unit" in the Departmental complex of today.

Although the number of posts, both diplomatic and consular,

continued to grow steadily in the period preceding the Civil War, the foreign service, then as now suffered from public indifference; worse, the administration was happy-go-lucky, and the damaging spoils system reigned in our foreign representation. The eyes of the people were focused inward, not outward; in the absence of external threats, little interest was shown in affairs abroad, and Congress began to cast the mold of what has become its traditional attitude of tightfistedness toward appropriations for "foreign intercourse." In point of fact, there were certain members of Congress —as there no doubt are today—who would have been pleased to sweep the subject of foreign affairs under the rug and forget about the whole troublesome business, "to have with them," as Washington said of foreign nations in his Farewell Address, "as little to do as possible." According to the *Annals of Congress* for 1798, as quoted by Albert C. F. Westphall in *The House Committee on Foreign Affairs,* a Mr. Nichols is reported to have expressed the opinion that "the United States should have no ministers at all," and a Mr. Goodrich, that we ought to have no political foreign relations." Not only congressmen but many wishful members of the public today would like to see life thus reduced to the simplest of terms.

Worst of all was the pressure for patronage, an evil that still survives most notoriously at the ambassadorial level. The philosophy introduced by President Jackson in his first annual message to Congress, on December 8, 1829, makes strange reading in light of the professional character of current diplomacy. "The duties of all public officers are, or at least admit of being made so plain and simple," he proclaimed, "that men of intelligence may readily qualify themselves for their performance; and I cannot but believe that more is lost by the long continuance of men in office than is generally to be gained by their experience." The abuses of the system may be imagined. Partisan politicians claiming to be "men of intelligence" were appointed diplomats, but in most cases totally lacked competence compared with European professionals, while nonsalaried officers were made consuls, collecting exorbitant fees for their ill-defined services and giving rise to endless controversies and complaints. More posts were opened than were needed, for many American businessmen residing abroad pressed to serve in a consular capacity for the commercial advantage and local status this would bring. By 1860, on the eve of the Civil War, there were 8 consulates general, 226 consulates, 21 vice consulates, 24 commercial agencies, and 3 other posts; in addition, there were 198 consular agencies, which handled occasional routine duties usually connected with shipping—in all, many more than the number of foreign service posts today. Small wonder that America's consular service was in low repute or that Congress took a dim view of the size of our diplomatic representation. In 1832 the House Committee on Foreign Affairs first looked into "the expediency of reducing the number of our ministers resident abroad to three, viz.: to England, France and Russia"; in 1844 it recommended a drastic reduction in the number of diplomatic missions abroad "with a view to the diminution of public expenditures." Although no action was taken in either instance, the critical stance of Congress with respect to the diplomatic service was clearly evident. The framers of the laws permitted themselves only a grudging acknowledgment that an assistant to the minister was "absolutely necessary," the act of March 1, 1855, authorized the appointment of one secretary to each legation, but objections on constitutional grounds led to its repeal a year later. To meet the ever-present staffing problem, the Department of State had allowed its ministers, in accordance with European custom, to appoint unpaid "attachés"—generally young men of means who functioned as secretaries in return for the opportunity to study, travel, and reap the social advantages of life in a European capital; but the practice was terminated by the acts passed in 1855 and 1856, when charges of misconduct blemished the reputation of these gay blades.

Like the recurrent theme in a musical score, proposals for reform now began to run through the record. As early as 1833, inexperienced men and inadequate salaries had so scandalized the Secretary of State, Edward Livingston, that he presented to President Jackson a highly critical report of the whole consular system, with a recommendation that consuls be paid an adequate salary and prohibited from engaging in private business; at the same time he submitted suggestions for improvements in the diplomatic service. But neither Jackson nor his immediate successors were interested; nor was Congress, which remained unimpressed by all the inefficiency and inadequacies. Although improvement gradually did take place in the course of the century, the Livingston Report might have been written today in its description of how a diplomat's effectiveness could be destroyed by his having to live in a parsimonious manner: "A minister to a foreign power, whatever may be his grade, is the accredited agent of his country. If he is forced, from the inadequate compensation that is allowed him, to live in a manner that will not allow him to associate, on an equal footing, with others of the same grade, he is deprived of many of the advantages which social intercourse affords, to perform essential duties and to gain important information, which can only be obtained by mixing in the best circles."

Even more pertinent is the applicability today of Livingston's report on the lack of appreciation given to a diplomat's work. What was true then, is still unfortunately the case:

> Their exertions, their embarrassments, their laborious intercourse with the Governments to which they are sent, their anxious care to avoid anything that might, on the one hand, give just cause of offense, or to neglect or abandon the rights of their country or its citizens, on the other, are all unknown at home. Even the merit of their correspondence, from which, at least, the reward of honor might be derived, is hid in the archives of their department, and rarely sees the light. . . . A minister returns to his country, after years of the most laborious exertion of the highest talent, with an injured, if not a broken fortune, his countrymen ignorant of his exertions, and undervaluing them, perhaps, if known. On the whole, there is scarcely an office, of which the duties, properly performed, are more arduous, more responsible, and less fairly appreciated, than that of a minister to a country with which we have important commercial relations.

The earliest proposal for reform which turned into legislative action was that dated August 18, 1856—"To Remodel the Diplomatic and Consular Systems of the United States." This lonely landmark stood until the turn of the century, when exploratory steps were finally taken to apply the merit principle to consular appointments; it acknowledged existing deficiencies in administration and compensation and sought to remedy them by restricting the consular practice of engaging in trade and keeping the fees; by fixing salaries for the more important consuls; and by improving the pay and allowances for diplomats. A salary of $17,500 was authorized for the ministers to Great Britain and France; and for the next ninety years, despite the enormous decline in purchasing power brought about by the passage of time, that figure remained as the top pay of an American envoy. Not until the sweeping changes of two world wars had forced realization of its inadequacy was the maximum salary raised in 1946 to $25,000.

Helpful as the act of 1856 was, it did not go far enough; nothing was done to promote the career principle, to curtail political appointments, or to abolish once and for all the system of consular compensation through fees and private business. As might be expected, the low level at which consular salaries were set, particularly in posts where business on the side was curbed, brought loud protests from the incumbents. For example, the $7,500 salary at Liverpool carried with it a prohibition on trade and a requirement that the consul pay personally the sum of $4,000 for clerk hire. Nathaniel Hawthorne, most prominent of our literary lights to expand their horizons by service abroad, had been rewarded by President Pierce with the Liverpool post for a campaign biography in 1852, and had enjoyed a lucrative income of $15,000 in consular fees until he relinquished the consulship a few months before the limitations of the act became effective. The archives in Washington abound with tales of financial distress, as indeed they continue to do to this day; the only additional allowance was that given to consuls who were not engaged in trade, in an amount equal to 10 per cent of their salaries. This did not go far, as Consul Robert M. Hamilton at Montevideo complained in his letter of resignation, when one's salary was $1,000 a year and house rent alone was $800.

❀ ❀

Through the strains of the Civil War, when Union diplomats and consuls kept careful watch on Confederate activities abroad, through the era of Reconstruction, and through the early days of the Civil Service Act of 1883—which did not apply to the diplomatic or consular services and thereby redoubled the pressure on them for political appointments—the foreign representation of the United States expanded and the volume of business grew, but Congress was, if anything, more economy-minded than ever. For the fiscal year 1869, the number of clerks in the State Department was actually reduced from forty-eight to thirty-one, which, to make the most use of available resources, led to a basic administrative reorganization by Secretary Hamilton Fish. In 1870, the staff assigned to the conduct of diplomatic and consular correspondence totaled thirteen persons—an increase of only five from 1833. Far from acting to strengthen the foreign service, Congress allowed to lapse over the next thirty-nine years various proposals for reform, including a bill favorably reported in 1895 by Senator John T. Morgan of the Foreign Relations Committee, who strongly criticized Congressional neglect and indifference and, without much avail, supported his arguments by pointing out that American foreign trade—that is, exports and imports combined—had risen from $308 million in 1850 to $1,697 million in 1893.

Although several outstanding citizens were appointed to diplomatic positions in the second half of the nineteenth century, such as James Russell Lowell as minister to Spain and General Lew Wallace, author of *Ben-Hur*, as minister to Turkey, the quality of consular personnel deteriorated under the flagrant abuses of the spoils system. A call at the White House, a reminder of personal connections or of services rendered, was often sufficient to obtain a post. Under President Grant it was almost too easy; the applicant would present the President's card at the Department inscribed with this message: "I will be willing to give the bearer, Mr. ————, one of the best consulates now vacant. I have known Mr. ————'s family for many years, quite favorably." It was hardly surprising that the character of men attracted to the Service left much to be desired, and that cases of venality and vice came to light more and more often.

Toward the end of this era, a small concession was made by Congress in the name of modernity. Although the Department of State had subscribed to the rules of the Congress of Vienna that ambassadors were the personal representatives of their respective sovereigns and as such had precedence over ministers or any other type of diplomatic envoy, no American had ever been made an ambassador. In a democratic nation ministers were good enough; but they ranked lower in foreign courts than the ambassadors appointed by many smaller states. American prestige suffered accordingly. Finally, in 1893, Congress authorized the designation of United States representatives as ambassadors in countries which sent ambassadors to the United States. Today the practice of naming ambassadors has spread throughout the world, so that even the newest and smallest nation—whether it has anything else to boast of or not—has at least an ambassador to the United Nations and probably maintains several other embassies besides; only vestigial remnants of the species known as ministers can be found, and their legations are almost a forgotten relic of diplomacy.

On September 20, 1895, President Cleveland at long last took the ball away from Congress with an executive order which made a start on the reform of consular appointments. For the first time the selection of candidates was regulated, in part at any rate, by oral and written examination: vacant consular positions paying between $1,000 and $2,500 a year were henceforth to be filled either by a qualified officer of the Department or by a person designated by the President for examination and found qualified thereby for the position.

Whether Congress or the country liked it or not, the end of the Spanish-American War brought the United States to the threshold as a world power and compelled the acceptance of a much-overdue change in the method of selecting our foreign representatives. To President Theodore Roosevelt went the credit for the constructive initial move toward taking the consular service out of politics and introducing a higher standard of appointments.

Roosevelt's first message to Congress on December 3, 1901, urged "the just principle" that appointments should be made "only after a practical test of the applicant's fitness, that promotions should be governed by trustworthiness, adaptability and zeal in the performance of duty, and that tenure of office should be unaffected by partisan considerations." Annual messages in subsequent years reiterated these recommendations and added others: that the consular service be classified, that the Executive be given authority to transfer consuls from post to post, that the fee system be abolished in its entirety and salaries provided for all officers, that each consular office should have an adequate clerical staff, and that a satisfactory inspection system should be created. Senator Henry Cabot Lodge of Massachusetts introduced a bill embodying the Presidential views on December 6, 1905; it became law on April 5, 1906, and was supplemented by an executive order relating to examinations and promotions on June 27. Statutory confirmation of the merit principle took place in 1915.

Teddy Roosevelt also took the first tentative step toward application of the merit system to the diplomatic branch; his executive order of November 10, 1905, established the rule that vacancies for secretaries of legation or embassy should be filled by transfer, promotion, or appointment after examination. President Taft followed this up on November 26, 1909, with an executive order conferring civil service status on all diplomatic officers below the grade of minister, instituting a system of efficiency records, and specifying the scope of the examinations to be given candidates. At this point, after a careful reorganization by Secretary Philander C. Knox, the Department's personnel consisted of 35 ranking officers, 135 clerks, and 40 messengers, for a total of 210 persons. The establishment thus functioned peacefully and economically until World War I brought a rude awakening.

The financial handicaps under which consuls and diplomats labored abroad were ingloriously reflected from the start in the lack of official residences. No truer words were ever spoken than those of President Cleveland in his messages to Congress of 1895 and 1896, recommending the purchase of buildings in the capitals

ღ ღ

of the more important countries for the use of American ministers
and ambassadors: "The usefulness of a nation's diplomatic representative undeniably depends much upon the appropriateness of
his surroundings, and a country like ours, while avoiding unnecessary glitter and show, should be certain that it does not suffer in
its relations with foreign nations through parsimony and shabbiness in its diplomatic outfit." Parsimony and shabbiness in the diplomatic outfit were, however, of little concern to Congress and
more than a decade went by before serious attention was directed
to the subject. In 1909, public opinion pushed for action; the
American Embassy Association, a private organization, was
founded in New York and began a propaganda campaign for the
acquisition of permanent homes away from home for ambassadors.
Representative Frank O. Lowden, later governor of Illinois,
espoused the cause and eloquently played on Congressional heart-
strings by pointing out that

rents are so high in foreign capitals that only the rich can afford to take
the highest places. . . . We have boasted through all our history that
this is a country of homes. Shall the nation alone be homeless? Shall
America's flag be a tramp in the capitals of the world, protecting not a
nation's home but only the temporary abiding place of America's representatives? . . . Now, let this nation do its part. Let us either with-
draw from the capitals of the earth, or let us enable our foreign representatives to serve their country abroad on something like equal terms
with the rest of the world.

The Lowden Act of February 17, 1911—forerunner of the Foreign Service Act approved May 7, 1926—was the result: it
launched a program for government purchase of Foreign Service
buildings, a program which for years went forward at a snail's
pace, but which encouraged the hope that more would be done
later to improve living and working conditions for homeless diplomats. Improvement did take place as time went on, albeit
slowly; and a substantial measure of hope long-deferred was realized on August 11, 1964, when President Johnson signed a bill au-
thorizing the expenditure of $49.8 million over two fiscal years
for building or buying badly needed residences and chanceries

and for rehabilitating and operating existing ones. Although the architectural style and interior arrangement of some of the houses erected abroad by the United States government have been criticized as unaesthetic examples of Americana—the embassies in Dakar and Rabat, for instance, have been dubbed "motel modern" and certain others have been described in much less polite terms—the nation's flag can no longer be considered a tramp in most parts of the world. And in some places, such as Bangkok or Rome, the reputation of the United States has actually been enhanced by the character of the buildings it owns.

World War I burst upon the Department, its diplomats and consular officers like the flood from a broken dam. In the first few days, some 60,000 inquiries were received in Washington regarding the whereabouts and welfare of Americans in Europe. Ambassador Walter Hines Page in London wrote that more than 2,000 Americans crowded into his offices, ". . . crazy men and weeping women were imploring and cursing and demanding—God knows it was bedlam turned loose." In Berlin, Ambassador James W. Gerard reported that letters and telegrams from Americans in different parts of Germany seeking help or information were coming in at the rate of a hundred or more daily. To cope with the harrowing and unprecedented demands of getting Americans home, there was on August 1, 1914, a total diplomatic staff stationed abroad of 121 persons—41 chiefs of mission, 61 diplomatic secretaries, and 19 language officers; 55 American clerks were assigned to diplomatic missions; while consuls and consuls general numbered 291. Needless to say, the establishment was never the same again, either at home or abroad. When the war ended, American activities overseas—in reconstruction, trade, tourism, and investment—tremendously increased the problems of foreign relations and imposed new tasks on both the diplomatic and consular services. It was time for a thorough and sober review of existing facilities, for repairs and improvements to the antiquated machine, in short, for a complete overhaul of what was regarded as at best a dubious career, inadequately manned to fit the times.

❀ ❀

Three main defects were seen in the system after the war: (1) low salaries, (2) inexperience on the part of politically appointed ambassadors, and (3) lack of provision to transfer personnel, when desirable, from consular to diplomatic work and vice versa. The appallingly inadequate pay of diplomatic secretaries—ranging from $2,500 to $4,000 a year—made it inevitable that appointments should be restricted to the wealthy few willing to defray most of their expenses; vacancies, accordingly, were filled on the basis of a bank account rather than on merit. In fact, before the career was placed on a proper footing, it was extremely difficult for a young American without independent means to enter diplomacy. Here was good reason for complaint that the Service was un-American and staffed with dilettantes; the social gadabouts lent serious diplomacy a bad name and contributed little but their elegance to the profession. The diplomat at the top, appointed for political considerations, was at a glaring disadvantage in comparison with his foreign colleagues. At the outbreak of the war in 1914, only one American envoy in Europe had had any previous diplomatic experience, whereas the British and French representatives stationed in the principal capitals of the continent had had an average of 27 and 23 years' experience, respectively. French Ambassador Jules Jusserand in Washington had 26 years of service behind him before coming to the United States, and British Ambassador Cecil Spring-Rice had logged 31 years. In the light of America's new political and economic responsibilities, these and other deficiencies emphasized the need for a permanent career system removed from politics and with merit alone as the basis for appointment and promotion.

Such a system required still another reorganization, sanctioned by law and embracing reforms designed by State Department officials themselves with the incalculable benefit of practical experience. Representative John Jacob Rogers, that farsighted Massachusetts legislator, became the self-chosen instrument for this purpose. His keen interest in the career concept led him to introduce a series of bills—on which at first no action was taken—whose aim was "to lay the foundation of a broader service of trained men"; and to work closely with the Department in doing so. His efforts, beginning in 1919, culminated, in 1924, with the passage of the memorable Rogers Act. For the first time comprehensive legislative treatment was given to the problem of the foreign service as a career; the diplomatic and consular branches were combined into a unified Service, the members of which were accorded the title of "Foreign Service Officer"; the merit principle was recognized as the basic law because the act provided that all new appointments were to be made after thorough examination and a period of probation in an "unclassified" grade, or by transfer from the Department after five years' continuous service; each and every officer became subject to promotion on his record and to assignment in either the diplomatic or consular branch, wherever his services could be used best; salaries were set by classified grades up the ladder to $9,000, after which a separate scale for chiefs of mission was operative. Among other internal improvements, a retirement system was provided; representation allowances were authorized; and the principle of home leave at government expense after three years' service abroad was established to keep officers abreast of developments in their own country. In the case of the last provision, authorization, of course, is one thing, and appropriation of funds is another; if Congress did not see fit to pass enabling legislation, home leave was only a will-o'-the-wisp even though it was on the books. On home leave from my first post in Persia, for instance, I had to pay all my own way; but at least the intent was there—to meet the often justified criticism that American envoys remained away so long they lost the American point of view.

The Rogers Act, signed by President Coolidge on July 1, 1924, raised to an all-time high the enthusiasm, morale, and efficiency of the American Foreign Service. It opened up a vista that immediately attracted a desirable element into what was then thought of as a secure and stable profession, devoid of favoritism and made to order for those best qualified. Candidates designated for the first Foreign Service entrance examinations, in January, 1925, numbered 172, whereas but 13 applicants had appeared to fill the same number of vacancies in the diplomatic branch shortly after World War I ended. With the consolidation of both branches, the new Foreign Service had at its outset a total of 633 officers, 511 from the old consular and 122 from the diplomatic service.

Then and Now:
The Impact of World Affairs

No greater contrast can be imagined than that between the State Department of the 1920's, when the Rogers Act took effect, and the foreign affairs center that overlooks the banks of the Potomac today. The unfoldment of world events has moved at a pace just as dizzy as the advance of science in the last couple of generations. In the effort to keep abreast of developments around the globe, practically all involving the United States in one way or another, the Foreign Service has grown into an organization that bears little resemblance to the small and selective career opening up forty years ago.

Washington in the 1920's was a leisurely city of government employees who were released at four-thirty daily; of foreign embassies which in the hot weather adjourned to Manchester-by-the-Sea or some other favored spot and left the summer chores to a second secretary or less; of tree-shaded avenues uncluttered with traffic; of an ingrown society, whether official or cave dweller; of engraved cards and duty calls and long Sunday luncheons in the country. The illusion of gracious living was enhanced under the spell of Calvin Coolidge "prosperity," which kept the attention of Americans away from troublesome affairs abroad.

After the defeat of Woodrow Wilson on the League of Nations issue, not to speak of the revelation of secret wartime treaties engi-

🏵 🏵

neered by our European allies and the disappointments of the Versailles Peace Treaty, Americans were resolutely isolationist. We would observe from afar; we would scrupulously avoid injecting ourselves into the course of European history; we would write reports, but we would not participate. Americans felt no urge to explore alien trends of political thought, except insofar as they might affect our foreign trade and pocketbooks.

In the State, War, and Navy Building—that ornate granite pile at Pennsylvania Avenue and Seventeenth Street, affectionately known as the stepchild of the administration—the tempo matched the mood of the country. For all its birthday cake exterior, "Old State" was a pretty simple structure inside. Corridors were half a block long and several yards wide, along the smooth black-and-white tile surface of which one longed to speed on roller skates. Swinging doors, like those on an old-fashioned saloon, screened the high-ceilinged offices, furnished in nineteenth-century government style and equipped with useless marble mantelpieces. Anyone could walk through and place a baby on somebody's desk—as did, quite literally, the housekeeper of a Near Eastern legation who was abandoned by the departing chargé d'affaires and chose to present me with this small problem in international relations. Negro messengers made their casual rounds and tended to the "In" and "Out" baskets at unhurried intervals. The coding apparatus belonged to another era; correspondence moved at the speed of molasses; nobody bothered to put the papers away or lock the safe at lunchtime; security-consciousness was nonexistent. Critics were to say that in 1914 the Department was about ready to cope with the Spanish-American War; that in 1939 it was prepared for World War I.

Air conditioning, of course, was unheard of; when heat waves withered the city, when federal workers toppled at their desks, and bureaus were forced to close, the wheels of diplomacy stopped turning. Those who could not be spared pulled down the shades, rolled up their shirt sleeves, placed the electric fan on the floor close to the swivel chair, and valiantly shuffled their papers till sundown. It was not surprising that the British long listed Washington as an unhealthful post. Only the thunderstorms boiling out of adjacent Maryland or Virginia kept it from being worse.

In such surroundings American foreign policy was more than adequately contained. Governed by the gospel of George Washington that Europe had a set of primary interests "which to us have none, or a very remote relation" and that it must be engaged in frequent controversies, "the causes of which are essentially foreign to our concern," the entire foreign affairs machinery of the United States was comfortably and conveniently housed in the spacious building next door to the White House. And antiquated as the equipment was, the machine turned over unencumbered by procedures which now tend to smother an embryonic policy before it has a chance to be born.

Suspicion of Europe and entangling alliances had pared policy making to the point where the narrowly domestic view prevailed, rather than the broad perspective. The traditional American policy of minding one's own business and nobody else's—the sacred creed of nonintervention—had kept incipient internationalists in their place.

Besides, there were exciting developments at home. As the politicians were quick to point out, Americans had never had it so good as under Calvin Coolidge. Radio was a booming industry. Talking movies were about to burst on the ear. Motor vehicles were invading the transport field. Airplanes were opening up a vista of transatlantic and transcontinental travel. The sky was the limit in the stock market. In this best of all possible worlds for business, the Secretary of State, Frank B. Kellogg, was the idol of the wishful thinkers with his Pact to Outlaw War—a halo of good intent which outshone his disrespectful nickname of "Nervous Nelly." The "war to end all wars," the "war to make the world safe for democracy" had not only banished the bogey of crisis from the collective American mind, but had rendered it indifferent to the possible need for an expanded State Department in the future.

To be sure, there were portents, dutifully chronicled by the press and the scattering of American diplomats on the scene. In

Germany the foundations of the Weimar Republic were crumbling; the wreckage of its economic structure was being cleared away for the entrance of Hitler and the Nazis. Italy was in the grip of the Fascists, civil wars were raging in China, and Communist Russia, with help from the OGPU, was starting to collectivize the peasants. Such a messy political picture was really none of our affair; nor was the revolving door of Latin-American dictators, nor the prototype of the United Nations at Geneva—even if we did station a full-time observer at that hotbed of European intrigue and chicanery. As for the Near East, it was a dusty, musty corner for scholars and archaeologists; Africa was still the Dark Continent of Livingstone, Stanley, and a few cannibal-defying missionaries. It was the fashion to stick one's head in the sand; and few people could understand the impulse that would lead a college graduate to exchange his birthright to succeed in business for a chance to dabble in the concerns of foreign countries at a bare subsistence salary.

When Henry L. Stimson—methodical, conscientious, gallantly committed to the principle of justice under law and unjustly dubbed "Wrong Horse Harry"—assumed the title of Secretary of State under Hoover in 1929, the Department's entire staff could be assembled on the back steps for a photograph at lunchtime. This panoramic view of the home personnel included Foreign Service Officers who happened to be on duty in Washington; the total number of career men in the Foreign Service was then less than 700.

On December 31, 1964, there were close to 3,700 officers of career—3,670 to be exact. It is not altogether safe to trust government statistics because of their irresistible tendency to rise, but counting all its employees at home and abroad, including clerical staff and Reserve officers, the Department now chalks up an overall figure of 24,677 persons. Of this number, roughly 7,100 are serving within the continental United States, while 17,522 are engaged in the conduct of our foreign affairs abroad (10,508 of the latter are "locals," that is, foreign nationals recruited on the spot).

The numbers alone tell a tale of incredible change since the days when foreign service was something of a fanciful adventure.

In the relatively "quiet" period between two great wars, the Department had an opportunity to cultivate the frail flower of public interest, to acquaint the public with the omens which presaged the arrival of Wendell Willkie's *One World*, to discard its cloak of exclusivity and emerge into the light of everyday affairs. For the experts, hired and paid by the taxpayer, were neither blind nor ignorant; as they studied the ominous pattern of events, it became all too apparent that this was a time of lull, that it would be a miracle if we escaped being drawn into the maelstrom in the making.

The opportunity to unbend from its pedestal was, however, missed—partly because of the inherent dislike of "publicity" characteristic of any foreign office anywhere, and partly because of the self-sufficient go-it-alone sentiment so prevalent in the nation. A campaign of information to advertise the administration's policies, to lead public opinion into the highways and byways of statesmanship, was as unthinkable in those days as a sputnik orbiting the earth; not until the crude word "propaganda" was placed under the Department's delicate nostrils by Herr Goebbels did realization dawn that the Foreign Service and its purpose should be got across to the masses. Instead, the Department wrapped itself in the robe of anonymity, of impersonal and Olympian detachment, and lectured the ordinary citizen whenever it was deemed necessary in the traditional Aunty-knows-best manner.

Perhaps it would have been impossible, in any case, to take the bold step of educating the public to an interest in the Service, for neither the Department nor the public was ready for it. I remember trying, in my capacity as a desk officer, to persuade higher authorities to throw dignity to the winds and go in for that radical innovation—a radio program, with or without commercial sponsors. It was a vain try. Today, at regular press conferences or through an official spokesman, the Department seeks to justify its actions and to rationalize the administration's point of view; public support is desirable in an era of people-to-people diplomacy, even if it is not always obtainable.

When the storm warnings multiplied in the 1930's, the average American found ready refuge in the storm cellar; a popular cartoon of the day showed a Middle Western farm threatened by a cyclonic "European War," with Uncle Sam going down the steps to pull the cellar door over his head. Although there were those who shook their heads at the prevalent mentality of escapism, there was no disposition discernible in the Department of Cordell Hull to preach the growing importance of foreign affairs and of the need to develop and modernize the government organization devoted to handling our interests overseas.

Out on the long, crisis-laden limb of its European branch, the Foreign Service watched the gathering storm and deluged the inadequate code room with cables. The swinging doors in the Department opened more frequently as messengers struggled with an avalanche of incoming dispatches. Desk officers who drafted instructions to the field carried them around by hand for initialing and final approval by the meticulous Office of Coordination and Review. Concurrences, few and uncomplicated, could still be obtained by telephone; on pressing matters it was not impossible to confer in person with the Undersecretary or the Secretary himself. Even when the "phony war" gave way to the fall of France and the cataclysmic events which followed in its train, there was no thought to the morrow as far as the growth of the Foreign Service was concerned.

Secretary Hull's talents did not lie in the administrative field. Nor did he always have a grasp of foreign names and places—for instance, he could never pronounce Djibouti, capital of strategic French Somaliland, and always called it "Dibouchy." He was, however, a sagacious, respected, and clear-sighted statesman under whom various officials in the Department were preparing to come to grips with the strange new shape of things to come. For example, a desk was set apart for an officer to concentrate exclusively on the problems of Africa, and out of a clear sky one day I was selected for the job and unwittingly became an amoeba in the

ॐ ॐ

bureaucratic life process. Before 1938, our policy toward the col-
onized African continent was—to invoke Lewis Carroll—"a
perfect absolute blank." On taking over this task, I was reminded
of a story about Al Smith when he was running for President.
"Tell 'em all you know," yelled a heckler in the audience, "it
won't take long." "I'll tell 'em all we both know," replied Al ami-
ably, "it won't take any longer."

With the exception of independent Liberia, for whom we acted
as "next friend and attorney," we had no particular interest in
what was to all intents and purposes an appendage of Europe and
therefore a blind spot in our view of the international scene,
where even the conventional duties of protecting American citizens and promoting American commerce were at a negligible low.
But a few months before Hitler struck in Poland, I was given a
valuable close-up of the continent. No funds, naturally, were
available from the Department's anemic budget for such an
unheard-of trip, but the Navy provided me with transportation. I
was taken aboard its 10,000-ton cruiser *Boise* on an unforget-
table, pioneering, shakedown cruise and courtesy visit to ports in
West and South Africa, which brought its own rewards. Diplomatic efforts, coupled with Navy hospitality while we lay off the
port of Monrovia, deflected an iron ore concession in Liberia from
suspected Axis interests to American; an aerial survey was made
of Fisherman Lake, soon to become a landing spot for Pan American Airways flying boats; and cornerstone laying ceremonies were
held for the first American-built diplomatic mission in Africa.

As our concern with Africa heightened, the microcosm bur-
geoned. Airplanes were being ferried to the British in Cairo by
way of West African ports, Dakar was repeatedly rumored to be a
submarine base, a springboard for attack on the Americas; our
landings in North Africa opened a military and political theater
of limitless significance; watching briefs had to be established in
strategic colonial territories. The desk became a unit, the unit became a division, the division turned eventually into a full-fledged
bureau, with a separate office for each segment of the continent.
At a staff meeting I attended in the bureau several years later, be-

fore going out as ambassador to Senegal, I counted forty-seven top-layer officers. The metamorphosis was an eloquent example of what the war had brought forth, of the impact of events which changed the Service beyond all recognition.

Most of the difficulties encountered by the Service in subsequent years can be traced to the shortsightedness of the war period. Recruiting was suspended in deference to requirements of the military and for fear that would-be diplomats would be branded as draft dodgers, thereby seriously weakening the internal structure. At the same time, no real attempt was made to define the relationship of diplomacy to the war effort. Instead of forthrightly facing up to the question whether a Foreign Service Officer should be commissioned in the armed services or exempted from the draft, or whether his ranks should be fortified with new blood, the State Department evaded the issue and confined itself to halfhearted efforts at dissuading the Officer from trading his civilian status for a uniform. The Officer himself was in a quandary. For example, I was offered a commission in Naval Intelligence and have wondered ever since whether the path of true patriotism lay in a decision to remain with the hard-pressed Foreign Service instead of accepting more combative duty with the Navy.

In any case, nobody planned for the vastly greater responsibilities which were sure to descend on the leader of the Allied coalition in the brave new world. Nobody led a campaign to bolster the thin line of the career by enlisting able-bodied college men and asking for draft exemption in their behalf. Nobody visualized the need for scores of additional Foreign Service Officers when the "emergency" was over, and for beginning their training as diplomats on an orderly basis at once. Nobody opened a drive on Congress to appropriate additional funds for the handling of our increasingly intricate international relationships either in war or in the uncertainties of the days to come. Instead, it seemed that those who ran the Service looked upon the period as a nightmare that would vanish with the peace. Temporary requirements would pass; business would return to "normalcy"; all would be as before. Such unheard-of phenomena as psychological or economic war-

fare, the large-scale "dissemination of information," the gathering
of intelligence, the pre-emptive buying of strategic supplies, could
not be expected to play a lasting part in the formation of foreign
policy; as for a world political organization, on the order of the
defunct League of Nations—it was only a gleam in somebody's
eye. Challenges of the future would be met as they arose; sufficient
unto the day were day-to-day operations and improvised methods
for dealing with momentary and transient situations.

One of the stopgap measures designed to meet the desperate
wartime needs of the Foreign Service was the introduction of
"auxiliary" officers into the body politic of the professional career.
Once before, in 1939, the Service had submitted to a violation of
the career-based-on-merit principle, when more than 120 attachés of the Commerce and Agriculture departments were ab-
sorbed into the State Department's system because they had no
other place to go after their own foreign services were abolished.
Since this group was already experienced in commerce, trade, and
related problems and accustomed to living abroad, it was digested
without too great an internal upset; its members were generally
accepted as colleagues and some ultimately rose to the highest
posts in the Foreign Service. But auxiliary officers, who signed up
for the duration with all the perquisites of career men, were not so
easily assimilated. They had neither the preparation for their
duties nor the inclination to make foreign service a lifework; and
it did not help the morale of career officers who had toiled for
years on their way up to see their hard-won positions invaded by
outsiders—at what were, in many cases, disproportionately higher
salaries. In love and war, however, the end justifies the means; and
in the crisis caused by a dire shortage of help, the expedient was
recognized as a war-justified necessity.

As could have been predicted, the end of the fighting caught
the Department with its manpower down. To the pained surprise
of those who awaited a return of the *status quo*, it was discovered,
when the dust settled, that the number of available officers de-
pressingly failed to fill the void; that all posts and all positions
from vice consul up were starved for "bodies." The scarcity of

🏵 🏵

personnel led to a hasty build-up that helped deal the Rogers concept of the career a heavy blow and was the forerunner of other innovations of the same type.

To meet the gaping need, Congress authorized in 1946 the so-called Manpower Act, which attempted to graft 250 combat veterans and wartime government employees onto the career body by "lateral entry." Crises, far from diminishing, were multiplying; and to tackle the pressing problems of war's aftermath, it was essential to have a bigger staff immediately and to rush officers abroad wherever they were most wanted. The manpower entrants were unlike the auxiliary officers in that they were admitted, after an examination, on a permanent basis; the auxiliaries were temporary incumbents only. At the same time, it was realized that the Foreign Service would have to be brought up to date if it was to function at all in the rapidly changing world, and a catchall Reorganization Act was passed, which attempted to combine the best features of previous legislation with several new ones. The device of the "side-door" entry into whatever grades and salary groups were considered appropriate to the age and qualifications of the applicants attracted more officers into the badly depleted Service, but at the same time ensured the destruction of the original career principle. No matter how able and willing the newcomers might be, they lacked the background and experience of those who had passed highly competitive examinations and had begun to climb from the lowest rung of the ladder.

Those provisions of the Foreign Service Act of 1946 which permitted lateral entry were the prelude to fusion of the permanent home staff with those who had chosen to serve abroad. Opening the gates at different levels, as well as from the bottom, is useful when a particular niche needs to be filled, but an individual who starts his "career" at the top, or at a point attained by others only after twenty years of conscientious work, is scarcely a "career officer" in the sense contemplated by Mr. Rogers.

On the home front, bright young men of the New Deal or like persuasion, popped up in sensitive policy-making units or became "special assistants" without benefit of foreign experience or pre-

vious government service. There was no problem getting into a
department suddenly confronted with momentous global developments and sorely in need of extra hands, but it is problematical
how much some of these junior brain-trusters contributed to the
sum total of the Department's knowledge. Again, it was no boost
to morale when seasoned employees saw themselves surrounded by
fresh faces from out of town. Foreign affairs, it appeared, required
no aptitude test; "special assistants" came, saw, and—if they did
not exactly conquer—left when something better appeared on the
horizon.

One of the more calamitous by-products of the Department's
failure to bolster the position of its trained personnel and to aug-
ment its ranks was the loss of political expertise, temporary
though it proved to be. Franklin D. Roosevelt cordially disliked
the Foreign Service; he bypassed it whenever possible and, insofar
as possible, assumed personal charge of America's foreign affairs,
entrusting the most important missions to hand-picked envoys
such as Harry Hopkins or General Patrick J. Hurley, without
reference to the State Department. One notable exception was
Robert D. Murphy, who was plucked from the Foreign Service as
the confidential executor of Roosevelt's policy toward Vichy
France. Whatever the President's reason for rejecting the professional diplomats—some say he was prejudiced against "un-
American" or "undemocratic" holdovers from the dilettante
days—it is difficult to understand why he had so little respect for
the promising new career launched in the name of an honored
congressman from Massachusetts. Undercutting Cordell Hull,
Roosevelt's one link and channel of communication with the foreign affairs experts across the street was Sumner Welles, a boyhood
friend he had appointed to the post of Undersecretary. At the
Casablanca Conference of 1943, the President discussed independence with the Sultan of Morocco without any of the policy
makers in the Department being the wiser. At the Big Three meetings in Teheran, our ambassador, who had given up his residence
to accommodate the American delegation, was not even kept informed of the momentous conversations taking place. At Cairo,

🏵 🏵

Presidential diplomacy dispensed with trained experts except for interpreters.

Whether a determined effort to put the Foreign Service into its own, to build up its reputation as a strong right arm of the war effort and gear its activities into the coming of the peace could have overcome Roosevelt's aversion will never be known. There is good reason to believe, however, that it might; for on countless occasions, beginning with the blitzkrieg on Warsaw, the career had distinguished itself by bravery and devotion under fire. Throughout the Nazi invasion on the Continent officers stayed at their posts to destroy codes and burn confidential documents; narrow escapes were an everyday occurrence; in England, air raids demolished the consulates at Plymouth, Bristol, Liverpool, and Manchester; in Belgrade, a bomb smashed half the minister's residence, killing a legation employee a block away. In Greece, as in Yugoslavia, Foreign Service personnel stuck to their posts and carried out their duties without regard for personal danger. It was a miracle that casualties did not take a heavy toll of the ranks.

When we entered the war, officers in neutral Switzerland helped hundreds of Allied airmen, interned in Swiss camps, to liberty. Many a Foreign Service Officer, overrun by the tides of war, was himself interned by the enemy. One of my colleagues on the embassy staff in Oslo was a quiet and modest man named Walter W. Orebaugh, born in Wichita, Kansas, who had just opened a consulate in Monaco when Axis forces occupied southern France in 1942. Orebaugh was interned by the Italians, but after Italy signed an armistice on September 8, 1943, he determined to escape in order to avoid falling into the hands of the advancing Germans. With the help of friendly officials, and by hiding in the homes of peasants, he made his way to the mountains near Perugia, where he became the acknowledged leader of a band of partisans. To the Fascists and the Nazis he became known as a "very dangerous person to be kept under closest observation"; nevertheless, he managed to direct guerrilla raids against truck convoys and supply depots, as well as to aid and organize escaped

British and American prisoners of war. Orebaugh's operations, culminating in a voyage down the coast in a leaky fishing boat to Allied headquarters, scarcely satisfy the image of the striped pants diplomat but present a good example of the courage, patriotism, and resourcefulness of the breed.

Heroism—whether physical or moral—is so much a part of Service tradition that it does not need to be advertised; but it might have helped to bring the Foreign Service respect if someone had spread the word and fired the imagination with true tales of its behavior under bombardment, in evacuation, or with governments-in-exile.

The leadership to which the Service was entitled by virtue of its professional experience went by default. Ignored in the war planning, the Department could only carry on its routine diplomacy, unable to make its voice heard, or to exercise its initiative at critical policy junctures.

Spinoza said that "nature abhors a vacuum," and this can be a diplomatic or political vacuum as well as any other. Military advisers stepped into the breach and their views prevailed over those of the diplomats; military recommendations and military decisions took the place of policy planning that might have changed currents of history. The civilians bowed to the inevitable. As Kaiser Wilhelm II is reported to have said, "Politics must keep its mouth shut during the war till strategy allows it to talk again."

It has long been conceded that hindsight is better than foresight, and it is probably an oversimplification to say that America should have anticipated the manner in which the mantle of free world leadership would descend on its shoulders. If the public had been prepared for the advent of the Cold War, if it had known that the British would hand over the torch of freedom in Greece, if the breach to be filled by the Marshall Plan had been perceived far in advance—in short, if the reasons had been apparent and clearly understood by the public why Uncle Sam could never crawl back into the storm cellar—it might have been possible for us to meet our postwar responsibilities with something like assurance and resolution. But we were not prepared; we were not at first even willing; and we have given the impression of riding off rapidly in all directions to contend with unwanted situations.

All this is, of course, an indication of the distance we have traveled as the main bearer of the Free World's burden since hostilities ceased. It makes one wonder, however, what the establishment will be like a few years hence if its development and growth are projected along the present lines; if the balloon of bureaucracy continues its ascent; if administrative complexities continue to increase in response to widening demands, or whether, with an aptitude born of experience, we shall learn how two can do the job of three quite well.

🏵 🏵 🏵 🏵 🏵 🏵 🏵 🏵 FIVE 🏵 🏵 🏵 🏵 🏵 🏵 🏵 🏵

What Is a Foreign Policy Anyhow?

"What's a foreign policy anyhow? I don't know—nobody knows —what a foreign policy is."

This classic remark was made at Miami, Florida, on February 17, 1964, by an officer of the International Longshoremen's Association. The dockworkers had decided not to load ships with wheat for the Soviet Union; the administration in Washington had determined that it was in the national interest to dispose of surplus grain in this fashion. When spokesmen for the government charged that the ILA's refusal to go along was "in contravention of our foreign policy," a rousing speech in rebuttal was the result.

To hundreds of thousands of Americans who heard or saw the speaker on radio or television, the question "What's a foreign policy anyhow?" was not wholly rhetorical. Regardless of individual sentiment on the sale of foodstuffs to the Communists, few members of the audience could have explained how a foreign policy is made. Even less could they have told what a policy is made of— whether in this open society which is the United States, it represents the will of the people, or the will of their leaders, or both. Like the perennial problem of the chicken or the egg, it is a puzzle to many which comes first. Whether this is an acceptable state of affairs or not, whether it represents the best, or most workable sys-

73

tem we have found for our particular brand of democracy, it behooves us to examine some of the processes by which a foreign policy, with or without the backing of the people, is brought into this world.

In doing so we must take for granted that despite a high degree of ignorance on the subject, foreign policies do exist. The difficulty lies in pinning down the precise origin or source of a "policy"—in describing concisely how the decision to put into motion a plan of action comes about. We know that the President is the master architect, or at least the responsible designer of the blueprint that outlines our major aims; that the Secretary of State and his workmen must lay the bricks and provide the straw for the policy structure; and that the people, in sundry democratic ways, such as through Congress and the press, exert an influence on the choice of building materials. Filling out this rough blueprint involves numberless hours of discussion, little and big decisions, improvised questions and answers; negotiations and pressures between different government offices and the resolving of intragovernmental differences; as well as overriding departmental priorities weighed against perfectly valid personal preferences. It is the despair of the conscientious official to spell out in exact terms how a foreign policy takes form; even textbooks on the subject fail to satisfy either the Department or its critics. The best we can do, while admitting the elusiveness of a clear-cut definition, is to say that policies in general represent a desirable goal or action and that foreign policy is above all subject to unpredictable—and often totally unexpected—ramifications, both external and internal.

Merely to keep track of the everyday relations between the United States and its friends—not to speak of its enemies and those who profess to be neither—is in itself a complicated affair; the interests of one country may impinge on or conflict with those if its neighbor, while the policies of all are likely to affect our own sooner or later. It is all very well for our Air Force to have a strategic toehold in Libya, with the consent and good will of the

Libyan government, but it is a different matter when Libya, as a member of the Arab League, is called upon by Nasser's Egypt to follow a policy of eliminating foreign bases. Or, we want to be on friendly terms with Morocco and no less so with the Islamic Republic of Mauritania, whose territory Morocco openly and insistently covets. Again, as a member of NATO, Portugal is entitled to our close friendship and support, yet we are constrained to vote against her in the United Nations Security Council in order to retain the favor, and the votes, of the African nations, which violently object to Portuguese policy in Angola. In the tangled web of world politics there is scarcely a strand that does not contain a knot; issues are seldom uncomplicated; problems must generally be weighed in a delicate balance—pro and con—to find out just where the advantage lies for the United States.

Clouds no bigger than a man's hand are forever blowing up into storms, and minor incidents in distant places have a way of developing ominous proportions overnight. Being neither clairvoyant nor infallible, the Department regrettably cannot advise Congress of all crises in advance, as some of its members seem to expect.

But the objectives of a government agency exclusively devoted to the subject of foreign affairs are plain: to put to the best possible use a highly specialized knowledge, an experience and an expertise, a considered judgment—not only in the normal give and take of diplomacy but in the sudden emergencies that feature current international life. Some years ago a newspaper cartoon showed the ship of state plowing through an Arctic sea, menaced on every side by ice floes labeled "crisis"; in the bow was Uncle Sam the sailor, trying to fend off each floe with a long pole. That is still symptomatic of the manner in which trouble is met, for the United States is not a monolithic power steaming ruthlessly toward its destination regardless of the consequences. The picture, however, fails to illustrate the comprehensive background which the Department has at its disposal and which is at the command of the Chief Executive in charting his course. How often the captain, his mates, or other members of the federal crew take advantage of the accumulated know-how of the diplomatic navigators is, of course, another matter.

Although the Department of State, its Secretary, and the President are the principals in the drama of policy making, anyone who studies the script closely will find they are neither the sole producers nor the sole managers of the play. If State is not fully master in its own domain, then who is in charge? If the Secretary is not the only one to dictate decisions, who does have the power? If the President is not always the single arbiter of foreign policy, who exercises authority?

The answer to these questions is, primarily, the politicians; in one form or another, they and other outside elements, as distinguished from the experts in foreign affairs, influence the running of the Department and the forging of policies to an extent unrealized by the general public. One has only to read the papers, however, to see who or what organized pressure group is applying the pressure. The degree to which those with political connections help call the tune is not quite so evident.

Since the President is charged by the Constitution with the conduct of foreign affairs, it is obvious that the policy line, in the first instance, runs directly from the White House. The President, of course, has neither the time nor the knowledge to devote himself exclusively to that vast and ever more complex subject; hence, according to his own temperament and taste, he depends to one degree or another on advisers—who are not only at his elbow to give him advice but whose word is as good as a directive at the State Department. In the time of Woodrow Wilson, Colonel E. M. House was sufficient. In the days of Franklin D. Roosevelt, the ubiquitous Harry Hopkins was always there. Eisenhower had his Sherman Adams and, as a high priest for disarmament, Harold Stassen. John F. Kennedy brought McGeorge Bundy from Harvard and kept an intimate group of noncareer counselors on foreign relations, a practice continued by Lyndon B. Johnson.

What is it that makes an outsider more useful to a President than a Secretary of State with all the background of the Foreign Service at his command? That is something of a mystery; yet the outsider flourishes, to the detriment of professional morale. An amateur politician sitting in the precincts of the White House, where his personal views are accepted in lieu of analysis in depth from State, holds a power that is hardly commensurate with his experience. He may learn a good many things about the game in the course of his turn at the table, and he may learn to play the cards correctly; but at best his presence is an equivocal one—and one that is bound to stir conflict in the breasts of the experts. As anyone will testify who has visited a foreign country for the first time, direct contact with the land and its inhabitants sheds new light and opens up new avenues of understanding; the academician and the theoretician—no matter how brilliant—who try to be wise about such matters lack comprehension unless they have drunk deep at the source.

The shoe would be on the other foot—and might fit a good deal better—if a Foreign Service Officer who had made foreign service his career were stationed in the White House. There he would be able to offer the skills, knowledge, and experience of his profession to those whose task it is to call the shots; he would also enjoy the confidence of the State Department by reason of his close association with it. We assign a high-ranking officer as Deputy Commandant to the National War College, where his experience with foreign affairs is on tap to help shape the course of the studies; similarly, political advisers from the State Department are stationed at other armed services institutions. Why not employ the talents bought and paid for by the taxpayer in the most responsible office of all—that of the President?

What certainly was not contemplated by the founding fathers in allotting to the State Department its position of seniority in the Cabinet is the increasing frequency with which Congress tries, or gives the impression of trying, to usurp the leading role in the handling of foreign affairs. As in the case of other departmental heads, the Secretary of State is accountable to Congress for the proper discharge of his duties; our system of checks and balances sees to it that he does not have unlimited authority to act as he may please. But Congressional hearings take up more and more of his valuable time. At every change in the Cold War's temperature, at every denouement in the perennial theatrics of world affairs, at every foreign flare-up involving American interests, the hard-pressed Secretary or one of his aides must be summoned to show cause why State might not have been able to alter the course of untoward events. Moreover, this has become a form of double interrogation; since both House and Senate insist on separate hearings, the same ground must generally be covered twice. One would think that the Constitution of the United States was a parliamentary model, which required the Secretary of State to appear in person either with or without notice on Capitol Hill; but even in England, where the prime minister is occasionally asked searching questions, the opposition does not abuse the privilege.

How many man-hours of labor are spent in preparing statements and replying to the inquisitors nobody knows. It may be an extreme suggestion to imply that the Department is intimidated by Congress, that it pulls its policy punches because it is afraid to make mistakes, but it is no exaggeration to say that it hates to tread on Congressional corns. No matter how tedious or irritating or time-consuming it may be, great pains are always taken to present the facts for the benefit of those who hold the purse strings, more pains and more rationalization than it seems worth sometimes.

The time, in fact, might be better employed these hectic days by grappling with the problems at hand or working toward solutions by transatlantic phones or cables. When called on the carpet, not because a policy may be wrong but because it conflicts with the policy of the opposition, the difficulties of the diplomats are compounded. In the democratic tradition the chosen representatives of the people have "a right to know," and perhaps it is necessary for them to sit exhaustively in judgment on our foreign operations in order to be adequately informed. But even then there is no assurance that information carries conviction; riders are tacked on to bills or special legislation is passed to express an "intent of Congress" that runs counter to administration policy. Congress may have one policy; State another. In October, 1962, for example, Poland and Yugoslavia, in the foreign trade bill, were deprived of most-favored treatment in spite of meticulous documentation and lengthy expert testimony in their favor. Arguments that this slap in the face might have the effect of pushing the two Communist countries closer to Moscow made no impression at all. Likewise, Congressional foreign policy in February, 1964, forced the administration to cut off military aid to France, Great Britain, and Yugoslavia because they did not respect our economic boycott of Cuba—an unnecessary diplomatic irritant in light of the insignificant amount of aid being furnished.

It is understandable that the House should give vent to its emotions when the United Arab Republic, in the person of President Nasser, tells us to jump in the lake with our economic aid, or when a mob is permitted to sack the United States Information Service library in Cairo, but voting a ban on the surplus food we had agreed to ship to Egypt goes far beyond a demonstration of displeasure. Such an act, even if reversed later, takes foreign policy out of the hands of the Executive and puts Congress in the position of assuming primary responsibility for the conduct of foreign affairs. It is all the more frustrating to administration policy makers when the legislative body casts a vote in haste, without bothering to discuss the consequences—whether other American objectives might be affected or whether retaliation might result.

Second only to the Presidential Assistant, then, as an influence in our international affairs is the senator or congressman; moreover, as the unwitting sower of confusion—not only among the State Department specialists but in the minds of friend and foe alike—he is unique. The Secretary of State, speaking for the administration, may be saying one thing; but from Capitol Hill comes a burst of oratory rivaling the rockets on a Fourth of July which detonates a totally different line of thought. When John Fitzgerald Kennedy, the Democrat, was a senator, he caused shivers to run down the administration's Republican back by broadcasting suggestions for a proper French policy in Algeria; the other side of the aisle is always a target for political attack— and let the chips fall where they may. But the fireworks often come from within the same party: Senator Mike Mansfield, an un- inhibited Democrat, warmly approved the de Gaulle scheme for neutralization of Vietnam in direct contradiction to the policy of a Democratic administration. Democratic Senators J. William Ful- bright, Hubert H. Humphrey, and Albert Gore on more than one occasion have contributed resounding declarations, completely at variance with the administration's official positions, which must nevertheless be reckoned with at the policy-making level in the State Department. For that matter, explosive and controversial commentaries have issued as well from the mouths of brass cannon at the Pentagon, until damped down by orders to submit remarks for censorship in advance. And whenever off-the-cuff speech mak- ing takes place abroad, by touring legislators or itinerant members of the military, the confusion is compounded.

To those who clearly understand the way our government operates, such verbal shrapnel may be dodged or disregarded; but too often it is necessary for our embassies to explain to protesting governments that the opinion they represent is solely that of the marksmen. It is both disconcerting and burdensome to those who are responsible for our foreign relations when bewildered repre- sentatives of a friendly power must listen to diametrically oppos- ing viewpoints expounded by influential members of the official community in America.

If independent policies illuminating the skies were as harmless as they are made out to be, the State Department would have no concern. However, they are indicative of a more subtle tendency: the growing urge of the legislative branch to make a sounding board of itself in foreign affairs, to throw its weight into policy making, and to crowd the Executive in doing so. With more and more at stake—such as the massive sums involved in foreign aid —this type of intervention must perhaps be expected in our dem- ocratic system; but it further splinters the decision-making power of the State Department. Vocal members of Congress, whether singly or in groups, have never been known to hesitate in laying down a barrage of recommendations; as in the case of admitting the Chinese Communists to the United Nations, the Department may become a prisoner of the partisan domestic question, "Who lost China?" and regardless of more pragmatic considerations, be compelled to twist the arms of delegates at every international meeting to vote our way.

The Central Intelligence Agency, while openly acknowledging no pretense to political orientation, is nonetheless inextricably involved in the act of foreign policy making. We have come a long way from Colonel William J. ("Wild Bill") Donovan's wartime Office of Strategic Services, as well as Admiral Roscoe H. Hillenkoetter's strictly fact-gathering CIA which immediately succeeded it. As I had cause to know during our operations in North Africa, the old OSS was regarded chiefly as an instrument for implementing policy, not for designing an exercise with such far-reaching connotations as the Bay of Pigs. Today the CIA must be considered a factor in policy operations, whether the State Department likes it or not; and Foreign Service Officers sometimes fear that its actions may short-circuit the official policies they are trying to carry out. It is one thing to combat subversion in the name of national security; but quite another for the honest and straightforward American who is our fond ideal to conduct clandestine operations aimed at the undoing of a foreign society. We can scarcely believe that Secretary of State Henry Stimson once declined to countenance such *sub rosa* activities as code breaking on the ground that "gentlemen don't read each other's mail"; and it still goes against the grain of many Americans to think that we must employ spies in peacetime. To attempt to reconcile cloak-and-dagger doings—undesired products of the Cold War—with a Wilsonian concept of open covenants openly arrived at is a hair-raising operation in itself for a State Department already harassed by coaching from the sidelines on the part of Congress and the White House.

Other organizations slice the authority of the Department still thinner. The National Security Council, with the President presiding and the chief departments and agencies actively represented, is a great determiner of policy. Here the State Department is listened to with respect, but so are other voices. From the working level to the top, position papers present measured opinions and advocate certain courses; the danger is that they may cancel each other out and produce a sterile compromise. An NSC decision naturally binds the State Department, and it may not always be a decision relished by the diplomats. If a problem is not thrown into the NSC hopper, there are many other government "shops" that will cheerfully share the load of policy making in State. Whenever the chance can be seized, trade promoters from Commerce, protectionists from the Tariff Commission, balance-of-paymenters from Treasury, and so on around the family circle, are in evidence—as well as organized pressure groups that plead and press for their particular causes and must be given a hearing, if not a say, in policy formulation.

One of the developments that disturbs the Service today is the fact that politicians—those brought in from the outside, rather than career men—are increasingly found in command posts of the Department. Political appointees, if they do not wholly dominate the organization, at least occupy the influential positions; their tenure is based on friendship at the White House, or on useful connections with the powers that be, rather than on technical background. Not so very long ago it would have been virtually impossible to imagine an Assistant Secretary in charge of a geographical area, much less his deputy, as other than a highly trained professional, steeped in personal acquaintance with his field. Thus, the early part of my own career was under the practiced eye of Wallace Murray, thoroughly schooled in the wiles of Near Eastern psychology by service at Teheran—who was first an office chief, then a political adviser, and in modern nomenclature would today be an Assistant Secretary. His principal assistant was an outstanding specialist in the area, careerist Paul H. Alling. So it was with the European, Far Eastern, and Latin-American regions —all were in the deft hands of career officers who had done time in their respective regions, had learned their lessons well, and knew the problems and the peoples from close contact. To rise to the top of the Foreign Service and be rewarded by a directorship at the home base was not only in the national interest, but made for co-operation and good morale among officers in the field.

Now the long arm of party politics reaches into the most sensitive policy-making jobs; the first act of the Kennedy administration was to name the former six-term Democratic governor of Michigan, whose familiarity with tribal customs was somewhat less than nominal, as Assistant Secretary for African Affairs. Averell Harriman, former governor of New York, one-time ambassador to the Soviet Union, came into the Department with the all-embracing title of "the President's Special Representative and Adviser on African, Asian and Latin American Affairs and Ambassador at Large," which led in turn to the post of Assistant Secretary for the Far East and then Undersecretary for Political Affairs. When Roger Hilsman, an outsider who had at least seen combat service in the Far East, resigned as Assistant Secretary for that extensive and critical region, he was immediately replaced—not by a career officer but by a civilian from the Department of Defense. Deputies to Assistant Secretaries are now also recruited from the outside. Moreover, as the establishment has grown larger, more Assistant Secretaries and Undersecretaries have had to be appointed, who not only divide the responsibilities but provide more openings for the administration's political favorites.

It is wasteful as well as time-consuming when these executives of the upper echelons, who must in any case lean heavily on the know-how of their subordinates, are swept out of office at the close of an administration and another set of political nominees comes in. The first team may have acquired some awareness of the intricacy of foreign relations and of the difficulties in running an organization that has no real parallel in either government or business; the next squad that comes to bat must begin at the beginning and repeat the process. Although there may be something to be said for a fresh viewpoint as the sides change, there is also lost motion, uncertainty, and utter lack of continuity.

For the sake of party politics, the ritual must be observed; it is an old American custom that not a single high-ranking political appointee can be expected to stay on when a new President moves in, for the jealous god of patronage is perpetually hungry for new posts. Even the Policy Planning Council, which, from the top of its ivory tower, takes the long view whenever it is not obscured by the dust clouds of immediate events, has no continuity; neither its politically appointed chairman nor the members of its staff enjoy more than temporary tenure. Formerly the need for a carry-over at lower levels was supplied by what were called the "drafting officers," the capable permanent members of the Department. At their fingertips were the precedents which used to be the warp and woof of diplomacy; they could devote themselves to becoming steadily more proficient in the practice of their profession without fear of uprooting or transfer; they complemented the Foreign Service and furnished it with a backstop on which it could depend completely. Amalgamation of the two services, as we shall soon see, changed the rules by making everyone "interchangeable"; now, whether of the career or politically favored, personnel may come and personnel may go, while interruptions go on forever in the routine of essential jobs. Temporary incumbents under the name of "special assistants" fill convenient nooks and crannies for as long as it happens to suit them. In such circumstances the development of an abiding interest in, or attachment in depth to, the work is next to impossible.

Occupants of the top spots, owing no allegiance to a career in government, need not even wait for a switch in Presidents to return to their private lives. A contrary point of view, a more tempting offer elsewhere, compelling personal considerations, may provide an excuse to resign and leave the chair vacant for a newcomer. The career man does not abandon his career; but the departure of a politician may occur at any time—including a time of crisis in the affairs of his area—without reproach. Within the space of a few months in 1964, the Assistant Secretary of Far Eastern Affairs submitted his resignation over a difference of opinion; the Legal Adviser took his departure because he could no longer afford the low salary; the Assistant Secretary for Public

Affairs said good-by because he had planned to remain in the government only two years; and the Assistant Secretary for Congressional Relations resigned to accept the position of Director of the Platform Committee for the Democratic National Convention. With them went the know-how of their incumbencies; their replacements had to learn from scratch. Yet there is not one permanent official whose memory might go back more than a few years, to dispense advice and act on the basis of his capacity to remember "when."

No "brain" exists in the Department comparable to that of the British Parliamentary Undersecretary of State for Foreign Affairs, or the Secretary General of the French Foreign Office. Not a single career professional is permanently stationed in Washington to meet the incoming team, to guide or instruct the newcomers. The top-ranking job of Undersecretary for Political Affairs is not customarily filled by a Foreign Service Officer; the incumbent is changed with each administration, if not oftener. An officer at the ambassadorial level, with a long memory and an active brain, experienced to the fingertips, might serve as a more effective tool in these fast-moving, crisis-laden times than the multiple files, indexes, archives, and library books that make up the research and reference units.

Since costs of running a political party are steadily going up, it is not surprising that national committeemen try to tap every possible source of revenue. What does seem extraordinary is the boldness with which career employees of the State Department are approached near election time for contributions to the fortunes of the administration. In the spring of 1964, senior State Department officers were urged to subscribe to a $100-a-plate gala fund-raising salute to President Johnson at Washington's National Guard Armory. The implication was clear enough: it might be better for one's career to buy a ticket, even if there was no burning desire on the part of the Foreign Service professional to attend such a strictly partisan rally.

This was not the first time that the politicians had sought to canvas the ranks of the Foreign Service. Twice in my career I received letters from national party headquarters suggesting that I buy a hundred-dollar dinner ticket for the sake of the cause; mindful of my allegiance to the government—not to a particular party—I twice dropped the letter into the wastebasket. One of my colleagues was importuned on the telephone; when he cited the Hatch Act—designed to make the soliciting of party funds from federal employees illegal—the voice at the other end of the wire said, disingenuously, "You wouldn't let a little thing like that stand in the way, would you?"

It should be reasonably evident, though it is not, judging from the chronic criticism of the Department, that the basic objective of our diplomacy is the welfare and security of the American people. It would be preposterous to assume any other aim. The taxpayer employs the Foreign Service to conduct his foreign relations; and he complains loudly if the executors of a *coup d'état* throw out our representative in Zanzibar, if a mob in Ghana pulls down the Stars and Stripes, if Panamanians riot over the flag, if Indonesia takes economic aid from us with one hand and accepts Soviet arms with the other. What's wrong, he demands, with our foreign policy if our officers permit these horrid things to happen? Perhaps the taxpayer should put himself in the policy maker's place to find an answer.

Diplomacy has been defined as the art of the possible; and it is a truism in the State Department that decisions can be taken only in the light of prevailing circumstances. Except in the most general terms, policies cannot be cut and hung out to dry in advance, like slabs of ham in a smokehouse. We may plan for likely or unlikely contingencies; but when the contingency arises, certain aspects may differ entirely from when the plan was devised. We may base a policy on the unity of NATO, but at the last moment find that General de Gaulle declines to be a member of the team, or that Turkey and Greece—two ostensible allies—are at each other's throats over Cyprus. Policies have to be determined on their merits at the moment and a particular course of action has to be taken with due regard for its effect on other vital spheres of American interest.

One of the more striking instances of how the machinery meshes into action occurred in February, 1947, when the British, without warning, divested themselves of their obligations with respect to Greece and Turkey and left it up to us whether we would assume the load. I was taking a Saturday morning off at home when the telephone summoned me to an emergency meeting at the Office of Near Eastern and African Affairs. The British ambassador, acting on instructions of the Labour government in London, had handed in a note explaining that Britain's depleted resources no longer permitted her to underwrite the cost of anti-Communist operations in the Mediterranean—an area that the British had long considered a British lake, but which had never been of primary concern to Americans. Churchill, it seems, had agreed with Stalin that Greece should be part of a British sphere of influence, but the Kremlin was now encouraging guerrilla bands based in Yugoslavia and Bulgaria to undermine the Athens government. Furthermore, Moscow had been terrorizing Turkey with a demand for base rights in the Dardanelles and the Bosporus, and for what amounted to dismemberment of Turkish territory—the cession of two eastern provinces and a slice of land on the Black Sea. Never had the Communist threat appeared in starker or bolder simplicity, never had abdication of responsibility been more complete, and never had the United States been faced with the precedent-shattering question of picking up the torch of resistance to communism in an area so far from home.

Under Loy W. Henderson, Director of the Near Eastern Office, the deep-seated and sobering implications of the problem were debated. All that day and far into the night, work went forward on memoranda summarizing the political situation, analyzing the various factors involved, and suggesting possible ways to proceed. The European office which handled Soviet Affairs was consulted; so was the Pentagon for the military aspects; so were the economic specialists for estimates of the cost of economic aid to both coun-

tries. What ran principally through the thoughts of the desk officers, like a red skein of danger, was what would happen to Europe
and the Free World if Greece and Turkey went under, and how
the independence of both those countries could best be preserved.
With the dismantlement of our large armies after World War II,
we were obviously in no position to think of force, nor would
American opinion have tolerated that; but what could be considered was large-scale economic aid, which the public might support.

The next step involved the two nations concerned: contact
with Greek Chargé d'Affaires Paul Gouras and Turkish Ambassador Huseyin Ragip Baydur. Both were quick to appreciate the
possibilities, and formal requests for help from their respective
governments were soon in the cables. Over the weekend, Undersecretary Dean Acheson was briefed with the details, so that on
the following Monday morning he could go to Secretary Marshall
with the draft of an answer to the British note. Despite the awe-
some challenge, the unpredictable consequences, the incalculable
costs of bolstering these bastions of anticommunism, the answer
was never really in doubt. When President Truman was presented
with all the facts, he acted without hesitation. By March 13 the
famous speech enunciating the Truman Doctrine had been carefully put together from a series of State Department drafts; at a
joint session of Congress on that date the die was cast when the
President asked for authority to embark on the proposed program
for economic assistance. It remained only for Congress, after due
discussion, to give its assent, and for officers in the Department to
supplement, by a round of personal appearances, the official explanations to press and public.

Foreign policy in a world as interdependent as ours means more
and more a meeting with these crises and emergencies, practically
all of which have a relation to some other situation, far or near.
Uncle Sam is busier than ever fending off the ice floes, and beyond
using to the utmost his skill in navigation, there is not much he
can do to prevent their coming on. No two ice floes are exactly
alike or are handled in the same way, for they come from different

quarters, are borne by different currents, and have different depths below the surfaces.

When a decision is made, it may be the sole decision possible in keeping with traditional American concepts of "peace with honor," or it may be one of several equally appropriate courses of action. Alternate courses, like the ice floe, do not always show below the surface; they may be considered and discarded for any number of reasons that are not visible to the naked eye. Like the individuals who formulate it, a chain in policy making is no stronger than its weakest link. Two men may possess equally high I.Q.'s and be equally able, but the man with experience is the one who counts in the pinches. That is why trained diplomats should be put in charge of diplomatic decisions; even with the best intentions, undoubted sincerity of effort, and a desire to serve the American people to the best advantage—all of which may go into their policy making—the men who lack the professional background may prove to be less effective than they should be in the vital decisions. Naïveté has no place in international relations any more than a Pollyanna viewpoint, a do-gooder complex, or an unquenchable eagerness to apply Jeffersonian principles to untutored masses in Africa or Asia. In analyzing a many-sided problem, it should be obvious that the career officer, with a reputation built on experience and good judgment, is much more to be relied on than one who is brought in from some other line of work and who bakes a policy on the basis of a short-order cooking course. The danger in the latter case is that the policy will be half-baked.

One common mistake is to think that a clean sweep in Washington is all that is needed to stave off the ice floes that beset every administration. To attack existing policies, to assert that a different approach would be more successful, is of the essence of campaign oratory; for example, "liberation for the captive nations" was a stirring substitute for the policy of "containment." But attempts to pour the wine of new policy into the bottles of old problems are more often than not failures. An incoming administration shortly discovers that in this explosive world it must, to some extent at least, take into consideration the strong and insistent views of other sovereign nations—such as the France of General de Gaulle—and that the only solutions which are practicable are very much the same as those worked out by its predecessor. Solutions advocated by sections of the public not fully informed of all developments are even less likely to be practicable. For example, leading American Negroes, worried by the image of a chaotic Congo, addressed a letter to President Johnson and Secretary Rusk urging them to support initiatives by the Organization of African Unity to halt the fighting. At the same moment it was reported that President Leopold Senghor of Senegal, a respected leader of African opinion, had rejected as "inopportune" a suggestion that the Organization of African Unity meet to discuss the situation, saying this was a matter for African foreign ministers instead.

Sometimes it happens that an officer in the State Department or the Foreign Service cannot agree with a given policy any more than the critic in the street. He may question the logic by which the policy was arrived at, he may have doubts and reservations about the judgment of the individuals responsible for the decisions. Not everyone in the Department, for example, was in agreement with the objective of forcing Katanga to unite with the rest of the Congo. But once the policy is decided upon, the officer must hold his tongue and help to carry out the policy as a loyal supporter of the government he serves. If he cannot bring himself to do that, he has three alternatives: with the consent of his superior, he may submit a minority report; he may ask for a transfer to another area of work; or he may hand in his resignation.

It is not always a simple matter to obtain a transfer when in disagreement, for if that were a rule universally applied, only chaos would result. I did once succeed in getting to a completely different part of the globe when I was in fundamental opposition to a policy in another; in that case it was a question of a specialist declining to defer to political expediency and so for the time being the specialty was forgotten without harm to my career. It might be appropriate here to discuss certain courses of action which have been, might have been, or are now being pursued by the United States with varying degrees of success. To set forth one's personal views, to criticize specific policy decisions, however, would be outside the scope of the present work; such observations belong in another book.

We have seen some of the tangible difficulties which the State Department is up against in its endeavor to function efficiently as the diplomatic arm of a great power; there is an intangible problem that makes for even more difficulty—the moralistic, even messianic, outlook of the nation as a whole. Henry Adams said a couple of generations ago that Americans dealt with a world they wished to see, rather than the world as it actually was. The United States, if pressed to define its elemental ideals, is in favor of peace, justice, freedom, and democracy: it is opposed to violence and bloodshed, it favors the solution of problems by peaceful means, and supports the "legitimate aspirations of people" all over the globe. Naturally we are not in favor of war, injustice, dictatorship, violence, or the suppression of human rights. We are altruistic, philanthropic, inclined to be religious; and when we project these qualities on the international scene we are apt to irritate others by the high moral tone and sometimes, the legalistic nature of our lecturing. It was, in large measure, pressure from the United States that fostered the independence of India, pushed the British out of Egypt, forced the Dutch to let go of Indonesia, and badgered the Belgians into granting premature nationhood to the Congo.

If Americans who advocated these high-minded measures could have foreseen the blood bath that accompanied the split-up of India and Pakistan, the rise of a Nasser and a Napoleonic Sukarno, the dangers of a tumultuous, ungovernable Congo, they might have tempered their eagerness with second thoughts.

The conviction that our domestic society should be a model for the rest of the world, that other people should respect, love, and admire us as a matter of course—in other words, that we can make the world over in our image—creates a fundamental handicap in carrying out a successful foreign policy. It does not follow that our goals are attainable within the limits of practical politics.

❦ ❦

Sir Percy Spender, Australian ambassador to the United States for seven years and later a member of the World Court, gave us some frank comments in a farewell interview. Because of its "conjuncture of religion and idealism," he observed, the United States has a hard time dealing with other governments who may not necessarily share the beliefs of the American people; if we had more experience in the ways of the world, he said, we would be more realistic, for "we live in a world where one must sometimes compromise."

America's traditional idealism prevents ready acceptance of "realistic" solutions. We say that all men are born equal, that all sovereignties are equal, that we do not intervene in the domestic affairs of other nations. We cannot understand why other governments, who have their own way of looking at things, fail to conform to our concept of what we know to be "right." Instead, we look for total answers—seeing everything in black or white instead of the grays that shade most troublesome questions. The contradictions in adhering to the rules as we make them, and in dealing with the world as it is, make it trying to evolve policies that will satisfy everybody.

Unfortunately, when external policies are an extension of internal politics, the State Department may find itself boxed in by domestic shibboleths. If the national interest is to be well served, frozen public attitudes should be subject to revision; but as time goes on, it becomes more difficult to tamper with issues that might provoke an explosion in the press. To be morally "right," even if the policy is outmoded, even if it is counterproductive in relations with our allies, seems of greater importance than an objective approach to a controversial question.

The "cherished myths" that endear themselves to the nation were attacked by Senator J. William Fulbright of Arkansas, in a speech that may well become historic, on March 25, 1964. As might have been expected, his reference to the "new realities" of our time struck sparks, but it encouraged the Foreign Service Officer to think in the terms which his profession demands—to search for all possible alternatives, to weigh all likely consequences or repercussions in order to find the answer which most usefully fits the framework of the American ideal.

No one would have dared to think "unthinkable thoughts" in Senator Joseph McCarthy's day; but those in the State Department who are paid to think were reinforced in their convictions by what Fulbright said:

We are confronted with a complex and fluid world situation. . . . There is little in history to justify the expectation that we can either win the cold war or end it immediately and completely. These are favored myths, respectively, of the American Right and of the American Left. They are, I believe, equal in their unreality and in their disregard for the feasibilities of history. We must disabuse ourselves of them and come to terms . . . with the realities of a world . . . in which those who move events and make history are those who have understood not how much but how little it is within our power to change. . . . American policy has to one degree or another been less effective than it might have been because of our national tendency to equate means with ends and therefore to attach a mythological sanctity to policy and practices which in themselves have no moral content or value except insofar as they contribute to the achievement of some valid national objective. I believe that we must try to overcome this excessive moralism, which binds us to old myths and blinds us to new realities and, worse still, leads us to regard new and unfamiliar ideas with fear and mistrust.

The planning of long-range, over-all policy, insofar as that may be practicable in a period of revolutionary change and unexpected events, is the special preserve in the Department of the Policy Planning Council. This small body of less than a score of area specialists in political, economic, and politico-military affairs has the advantage of being free from the daily pressure of telephone calls, "managerial" problems, and countless interruptions which are the lot of any desk officer in the geographic divisions. In this rarefied atmosphere the planners address themselves to some of the major questions confronting the United States. They represent the core of the foreign policy "planning community," co-operating closely with other government planners in the National Security Council and, of course, the Department of Defense. One should never forget that a diplomatic move which, in a showdown, might have to

🏵 🏵

be backed up by force must have the acquiescence of the military establishment: do we have the capability and to what lengths would we be prepared to support with arms the initial step?

The council strives to be pragmatic: "practical results are the sole test of truth." In doing so, it endeavors to point up and to clarify all possible issues in a problem, on the basis of which the Secretary of State is, theoretically, better able to decide on a course of action.

Obviously, the council is no Delphic oracle; nor can it be expected to draw up a foolproof plan. What it can do is to assemble and assess all relevant factors from the political and military points of view which would aid in obtaining perspective—to see where we are, how we are doing, and where we are going. Its recommendations are not policy until adopted at the highest level, which means that first they must pass through a barrage of critical fire from every bureaucrat within sniping distance. To take an example from my own service on what was then the Policy Planning Staff: In 1946, the United Nations, showing displeasure at the ideology of General Franco, passed a resolution calling for the withdrawal of all ambassadors from Spain; we had no choice but to go along, even though there seemed little to gain. Two years later I was assigned the question of re-evaluation; there followed weeks of study and consultation with desk officers—the "operators," as distinct from the planners; careful weighing of the anti-Franco views of the British Labour government, and the even more strenuous opposition in France; public opinion in this country; the strategic value of the Spanish peninsula to the Western alliance; and the strong pro-American sentiments of the basically friendly Spanish people. As approved by Secretary George Marshall, the staff's recommendation was that we should restore our ambassador to Madrid. Under our leadership, the United Nations resolution was reversed—a decision we had no cause to regret, for it paved the way for our present Spanish bases.

Not every policy promulgated through the council turns out as planned. Its ideas may not always be so good, in the long run, as those of the day-to-day operator, who meets each crisis as it arises and who sometimes develops a sixth sense in the process; its contribution may be lost in the rush of current events, which cannot be evaded or retarded. It does, however, afford a ready vehicle for the exchange of thought which may evolve into action on the broad policy front.

In any democracy public opinion bears a close relation to foreign policy. No simple course, however, has ever been charted for a ship of state between the Scylla of "news management" on the one hand and the Charybdis of "freedom of information" on the other. Whether the press should reflect the thinking of the public, or public thinking should be shaped by the press; whether an editorial should express the opinion of its readers or directly attempt to mold their views; whether a columnist should be the channel for a government viewpoint or should influence others by his independent commentary; whether a newspaper should "give the public what it wants"—whether murder or mayhem or a comic strip—responsible reporting as an adjunct of diplomacy is of immense concern to policy makers.

If Americans are to make intelligent judgments about their foreign affairs, they obviously must possess as many facts as can be made available. To keep citizens constantly informed, when situations change from one day to the next, requires more than a Roosevelt "fireside chat" or a "Meet the Press" program on TV. The people must know what's happening if they are to form an opinion; but trouble arises when all the facts cannot be divulged because of possible international repercussions. "The day secrecy is abolished," said the French diplomat Jules Cambon, "negotiations of any kind will become impossible." This may not square with the democratic tradition of covenants openly arrived at, so that when the consequences of publication may adversely affect a newborn policy, the diplomat becomes the opponent of the reporter.

In the sparring match that follows, each side is in the right. On the one hand, the press has the triple duty of creating better understanding, of promoting useful debate, of interpreting the background for government action. In its search for "news" it does not consider itself bound by the limits diplomacy would observe.

The diplomat, on the other hand, is not inclined to talk freely, because he fears the premature disclosure, the unwitting inaccuracy, the wrong emphasis in a front-page story—any one of which might spell embarrassment for him and for the United States. Journalism, with its passion for informing the public, is an impatient craft, always inquisitive and sometimes careless in its handling of the facts. Diplomats, by the nature of their profession, are reserved, defensive, instinctively evasive, and cautious about divulging matters on which the fortunes of a nation may depend—such matters, for instance, as might interest Soviet intelligence. They are also mindful, when brought to bay by reporters, that the object of most newspapers is to sell newspapers, and that "news" by definition is not the delivery of a routine diplomatic note but something that can be made to seem well out of the ordinary.

No better exponent of the diplomat's view could be found than Robert J. Manning, who served on the firing line for two years as Assistant Secretary of State for Public Affairs. In a valediction in Boston on May 5, 1964, Manning remarked that the press "wants to know more than do the people in whose name it acts. The freedom of the press to print without fear or reprisal . . . can, if improperly or unwisely used, run contrary to an equally basic part of the public interest, namely, the ability of the government to carry out the people's business of defending our interests abroad and guarding the nation's security."

To reconcile the right to know and the need for discretion is difficult but not always impossible. When based on mutual confidence, the relationship between the journalist and the diplomat can be mutually profitable. Abroad, the foreign correspondent and the Foreign Service complement one another, for each has access to sources of information usually unavailable to the other—the one where grass-roots sentiments grow, the other where high official policies take root. At home, proper co-operation between the two can help in educating the public. And the public, I have found on more than one occasion, is more willing to listen than is

commonly thought when the speaker speaks frankly and with
authority.

In the last analysis, it is the personal relationship between the
President and his Secretary of State that is of paramount importance in policy making. Different Presidents and different Secretaries produce different practices; and the manner in which our
foreign affairs are conducted reflects these differences. Few Presidents have so clearly stated their intentions on the subject as
President Eisenhower, on June 1, 1953:

> I seriously wish to emphasize that I shall regard the Secretary of State
> as the Cabinet officer responsible for advising and assisting me in the
> formulation and control of foreign policy. It will be my practice to em-
> ploy the Secretary of State as my channel of authority within the Exec-
> utive Branch on foreign policy. Other officials of the Executive Branch
> will work with and through the Secretary of State on matters of foreign
> policy.

Eisenhower hewed consistently to this line of reasoning and
delegated much of his authority to Secretary John Foster Dulles.
The latter, in turn, made almost a personal regime out of the Sec-
retaryship; although he could not ignore the elaborate apparatus
at his disposal, he used it less than most of his predecessors in recent history and assumed more than most the role of chief negotiator and arbiter of American relations with the rest of the
world. What he did ignore were the bothersome duties of leadership devolving upon a commander in chief of the Foreign Service
legions. As a result, morale was poor in the Department; but the
Dulles period bore the unmistakable stamp of Dulles—not Eisenhower—on foreign policy, carried out by tens of thousands of
miles of personal airplane travel to some thirty-three countries.

As the reader may have gathered, the methods of Franklin D.
Roosevelt were exactly the opposite of Dwight D. Eisenhower's.
While Roosevelt was more concerned with domestic than foreign
affairs in his first term and part of his second, and therefore reasonably receptive to advice from Secretary Cordell Hull, he

quickly took matters out of the State Department and into his own hands when World War II came. As Clemenceau once said, "War is much too important a matter to be left to the generals"; but no one ever requested the considered views of the Department on where best to strike at the "soft underbelly of Europe," on the decision to let Soviet troops take Berlin, on the political aspects of "unconditional surrender," or on the fateful agreements at Yalta.

Most flagrant in its disregard of the professionals was the Roosevelt policy of collaboration with Communist Russia. The President not only brushed aside the warnings of men who had given their careers to the study of communism, but declined to tolerate the presence in the State Department of those who differed with him on this policy. The Division of Eastern European Affairs was abolished, its experts disbanded and its chief, Loy Henderson, who had learned the foreboding score by heart, was banished as minister to Baghdad, where he could no longer be a thorn in the side of the administration's Russian policy. It was akin to mutiny, in White House eyes, to impugn the motives of our Soviet shipmate and a barely pardonable sin for a Foreign Service Officer of career. The cost of Roosevelt's reliance on his own rather than on his Foreign Service's judgment in dealing with Stalin would be difficult indeed to assess today.

Working closely with his Secretary of State, President Harry S. Truman displayed courage and understanding in crises such as the Communist threat to Greece and Turkey and the Korean War. Dean Acheson brought wisdom as well as tact to bear in White House discussions; his indisputable loyalty to the President allowed him to make a convincing case when State Department views were presented. But President Truman did not always trust the experts either. The foreign policy of the United States, he wrote later, "is the policy of a people—not a person. A President expresses it and directs it. But it is not willfully imposed by any President upon the nation and, under our system, it can never be imposed." In his published memoirs of the climacteric year 1945, President Truman recorded a policy—a Presidential policy—on the burning question of Palestine. The Secretary of State, then Edward Stettinius, Jr., had sent him a "special communication" expressing the attitude and thinking of the State Department: "The question of Palestine is . . . a highly complex one," the memorandum said in part, "and involves questions which go far beyond the plight of the Jews in Europe. There is continued tenseness in the situation in the Near East, largely as a result of the Palestine question, and as we have interests in that area which are vital to the United States, we feel that the whole subject is one that should be handled with the greatest care and with a view to the long-range interests of the country."

No more agonizing problem ever dropped into the lap of the State Department than the problem of Palestine. Sympathy for the Jews was widespread—the horrors inflicted by Hitler had wrung the hardest heart. But although the Balfour Declaration of 1917 had mentioned a "homeland" for the Jews in Palestine, no Arab took that to mean unlimited Jewish immigration, or an outright amputation of Arab territory. Roosevelt had promised the king of Saudi Arabia that he would make no move hostile to the Arab people, nor assist the Jews as against the Arabs. But in the face of unstemmed violence, the complications grew: the British administrators of the Palestine mandate resolved to wash their hands of responsibility for the troubled land; the Western stake in the strategic oil fields of nearby Arab territories was an important factor in the eyes of American military authorities; and as David Niles, protégé of Harry Hopkins and White House spokesman for minority affairs, took pains to emphasize in private, the Jewish vote in the New York elections was crucial to the Democratic party. In the Near Eastern Division, which handled relations with all the Arab states and their peripheral lands, a hundred thousand letters on the controversial and emotion-laden subject of Palestine reached literally from desk to ceiling.

On the basis of their experience in the Arab world, the specialists had sounded a carefully worded note of caution; if it was taken into account, it went unheeded. "I was skeptical," relates President Truman, "as I read over the whole record to date, about some of the views and attitudes of the 'striped pants' boys in the

State Department." Ridiculing the views of the "striped pants" boys, he left no doubt "as to who made the decisions and whose policy would be followed" on a course that led to the Caesarean birth of Israel and its simultaneous recognition by the United States. After years of bitterness and bloodshed, the question is still a complex one; the tenseness is still there; we still have interests in the area vital to the United States; and the whole subject is still one that must be handled with the greatest care and with a view to the long-range interests of the United States.

To what extent the people—not a person—made the policy on Palestine may be left to the fine hand of the historian; but the Truman memoirs are a useful commentary on the role of State Department experts in policy formulation. He noted:

The difficulty with many career officials in the government is that they regard themselves as the men who really make policy and run the government. They look upon the elected officials as just temporary occupants. Every President in our history has been faced with this problem: how to prevent career men from circumventing presidential policy. Too often career men seek to impose their own views instead of carrying out the established policy of the administration. . . .

I wanted to make it plain that the President of the United States, and not the second or third echelon in the State Department is responsible for making foreign policy, and, furthermore, that no one in any department can sabotage the President's policy. The civil servant, the general or admiral, the foreign service officer has no authority to make policy. They act only as servants of the government, and therefore they must remain in line with the government policy that is established by those who have been chosen by the people to set that policy.

In other words, a Secretary of State may advise, but a President decides on foreign policy. A physician may offer advice, but the recipient is not obliged to take it; the physician, however, may be forgiven if he has a feeling of frustration and futility when his views are publicly rejected.

Those who tend to ascribe to the boys in the striped pants the major share of responsibility for the making of foreign policies might do well to ponder the remarks of President Truman on this interesting subject.

❦❦❦❦❦❦❦❦ SIX ❦❦❦❦❦❦❦❦

Let Them Eat Crumbs

Some ten years ago, when the Secretary of State was trying to find the funds to run his department properly, the *New York Times* was moved to comment:

> That an American Congress . . . is still unable to appreciate the vital importance of its diplomatic corps to the security and future of the United States is surely extraordinary. . . . We are the greatest of all the nations of the democratic world today. Our needs and our commitments have never been greater. It is as important for us to have a first-rate diplomatic corps around the world as it is to have warships and air bases. . . . What we need in these critical times is a better State Department, not one crippled by a penny-wise policy of economy.

Somehow or other, concluded the *Times*—itself a perceptive supporter of the professional career—"popular and Congressional awareness must be created of the danger of weakening the Foreign Service."

Unfortunately, the views expressed by the editors of the *Times* are as cogent and as applicable today as the day they were printed. It surely seems extraordinary that an American Congress is "still unable to appreciate the vital importance of its diplomatic corps to the security and future of the United States," and that it deems it its duty every year to cut down on the already inadequate funds budgeted for the State Department. No matter how many times the record is played, however, nobody seems to be listening.

It is axiomatic among political scientists and historians that no form of government is more difficult to run than a democracy. In ours, no doubt, it is unavoidable that sectional interests should prevail over external concerns, and the House of Representatives has many proponents of this order of priorities. A congressman owes his living to those who elect him, and we are seeing ever more evidence that he is keenly aware of that fact. To do for his constituents what they have done for him is an elementary application of the golden rule, and a regional cause can easily tip the scales against something as hard to define as the national interest. Nothing illustrates the point better than the relative merit, in Congressional eyes, of a federal dam and, say, salaries and travel allowances for the Foreign Service of the United States.

The Senate, as befits that distinguished body, is generally more tolerant and understanding than the House in its approach to the needs of the State Department. Some of its members have even been known to rise in protest when, as Vice President Hubert H. Humphrey, then a senator, once said, "Attempts are made to rip the Foreign Service to pieces—to downgrade and attack and criticize it unfairly." Humphrey aptly observed that this was not "the way to recruit good people for the Foreign Service," and vigorously objected to unproved charges that the Service "is incompetent and wastes millions of dollars." On the other hand, senators are no less averse than congressmen to home politicking at the expense of foreign relations. Senator Karl Mundt once sent back this folksy report to the voters in South Dakota: "Oahe Dam is paid for! . . . I made . . . one promise—namely, that as a member of the Senate Appropriations Committee I would try to find ways and means of cutting the over-all appropriations of the Government sufficiently so that this eight and a quarter millions would not 'upset calculations.' " On motions made by the senator, $8.3 millions was cut from funds already approved for—guess whom? —the State Department. "Thus," proclaimed Senator Mundt triumphantly, "Oahe can go forward without the American taxpayer slipping backward."

Astronomical appropriations for Agriculture, for Defense, for the National Space Agency, boggle the mind as they soar into the billions; by comparison, the drops meted out in the budgetary bucket for such indispensable diplomatic exercises as those of representation are infinitesimal. Agriculture alone spends regularly, mostly for price supports, more than twice the expenditures of the State, Justice, Interior, Commerce, and Labor Departments combined. The Pentagon gets almost anything it wants from Congress, and sometimes, as in the case of the XB70 bomber, what it does not want. "For the good of all men and to become the world's leading space faring nation," as President Kennedy said in a speech at Rice University on September 12, 1962, we are in for a breath-taking ride as taxpayers—more than $5 billion a year at the present rate of expenditures. Foreign aid, without which no self-respecting nation can call itself a friend of the United States, still commands $3.5 billion annually.

To put a man on the moon by 1970, we expect to spend some $20 billion; over-all costs of the Ranger program, to take photographs of the lunar landscape, are placed at $269.5 million. But in the fiscal year 1964, we could spare less than $325 million to conduct relations with the inhabitants of this planet. For the fiscal years 1962–1965 inclusive, appropriations for the National Aeronautics and Space Agency came to just under $16 billion: the State Department received around 6 per cent of that amount to deal with earthly problems. Guided missiles or nuclear submarines, costing many millions apiece, are provided without question for our defense; yet for the sudden and unpredictable emergencies that arise in our diplomatic and consular services throughout the world, the State Department in any fiscal year has never been allowed more than $1.5 million. In the total estimated government expenditures for the fiscal year 1966, the State Department's share comes to only $4/100$ of a cent out of each dollar.

Although some of the funds allotted to the Department might be diverted to better use than expanding office space and, in the fashion of all government agencies, hiring more personnel, it seems well-nigh incredible that the ways and means for diplomatic negotiations in the thermonuclear age are restricted by a budget that has utterly failed to keep pace with events since the defeat of Hitler. The age, moreover, is noted for its many international conferences; we cannot refuse to participate; they stud the scene in ever greater number and variety—about 380 a year in which the United States is represented. Conferences cost money and they are worth it, for no one can deny that at the very least they let off live steam; yet less than $2 million was appropriated for "International Conferences and Contingencies" in the 1964 fiscal year.

For years the United States Delegation to the General Assembly of the United Nations was quartered in a downtown hotel which, if not second or third rate by European standards, had long since seen better days. On the upper floors, bathroom water was scarce; it was a mere trickle in the critical morning hours, when early meetings were the order of the day, while at night the antiquated machinery could be heard groaning as it labored to replenish the roof tank. Service was poor, and the first signs of a genteel shabbiness were beginning to settle over the rooms—but a bargain rate had been struck for State Department personnel. I learned to avoid the top floors on periodic assignments to New York if I wanted a shave and a shower before breakfast; but it was embarrassing to exchange visits with members of the foreign delegations who had suites in the swank hotels uptown.

A special allotment of $30,000 is authorized for representational activities at the seat of the United Nations, but that does not tell the whole story. The American ambassador to that organization is provided with a suite at the Waldorf Towers, and he is entitled to a staff that is not only agile and alert but has a flair for the UN type of business. Here is multilateral diplomacy in full swing, facing multilateral demands in times of crisis like those on a telephone switchboard. Yet the high cost of living in New York is a serious deterrent to able and qualified officers who are asked to accept an assignment at the United Nations. Foreign Service Officers are given no housing allowance when stationed in this country; and so far, despite repeated pleas from the Department, neither the Senate nor the House Appropriation Committee has seen fit to designate New York as a "foreign" post. The average officer is understandably reluctant to accept such an expensive tour of duty; for the married man with children to educate it is something to avoid if at all possible, and for those in the lower paid Staff category life is even harder.

Abroad, one may or may not fare better at conferences, depending on the city, the facilities, and the size of the delegation's budget. But one factor remains constant: the *per diem* allowance —carefully calculated and adjusted to minimum requirements in each country—is never enough to cover the full cost of room, meals, laundry, tips, taxis, and the sundry other expenses of associating with fellow delegates. It is standard practice to pay at least something for the privilege of representing the affluent United States.

I had this demonstrated for me in Paris in the summer of 1945, when an incident occurred that had its element of humor. To my delight, as chairman of the United States Delegation to the Four-Power Conference on the International City of Tangier, I was assigned to a luxury room at the Ritz, which had been "liberated" by the Americans and was run by the military as an officers' club at purely nominal prices. There I basked high in the esteem of my British, French, and Soviet opposite numbers, as became the representative of a great nation which had led the wartime coalition to victory on two widely divergent fronts. But my pleasure was short-lived. The day hostilities ended in the Pacific, the hotel reverted to private ownership—and to Ritz prices. No funds, of course, could be obtained from Washington to prolong my stay; I was transferred to an ancient, much cheaper and noisy hotel on the Rue de Rivoli, facetiously known as the "Rabbit Warren." There I found sleep practically impossible. So I went back to the Ritz and made friends with the manager; at a modest rental, he gave me a quiet little chamber under the eaves, one of those reserved for the private valets, chauffeurs, or personal attendants of wealthy guests. As far as the American government was concerned, I had moved to the "Rabbit Warren," but to my foreign colleagues, I was still residing at the Ritz. This face-saving arrangement worked perfectly until some well-meaning friends,

🏵 🏵

dining at a gourmet restaurant and unaware of my double life, sent a box of snails to my official quarters, where they remained unclaimed for days. Not until an inexplicable and overpowering odor filled the air—and a thorough but futile probe was made of the plumbing—did the real source of the aroma come to light.

Comparisons do not reflect credit on the United States, but they are nevertheless made every day in some part of the world. To the untraveled or the uninformed, it may seem only right that the old Pilgrim virtues of frugality and restraint should grace our style of doing business with foreigners. Disagreeable as it may be, however, the fact is that these admirable attributes count for little in the war of ideologies; "status," even as in the democratic United States, is what wins friends and influences people. It is a quibble unworthy of this country not to give the Foreign Service all the tools it needs to carry out the crucial task of representing the nation abroad, to implement American foreign policy, and to work incessantly for the preservation of peace and friendship in a world that could literally blow up in our faces.

"The military mind at work" is the butt of many jokes. The Congressional mind at times seems even more obtuse in failing to grasp the significance of personal relations in the realm of diplomacy. That at least is the impression conveyed by the consistently stone-hearted attitude of the House and Senate Appropriations Committees to the annual plea of the Foreign Service for money to represent the United States at official functions abroad.

It could be that there is rooted in the public consciousness a puritanical tendency to associate diplomacy with wine, women, and song in a foreign setting and little else; or a deep abhorrence, dating from the early days of the Republic, of "havin' truck with furriners." If that is the case, it may explain the thumbs-down gesture of the House Subcommittee on State Department Appropriations toward repeated requests of the budget planners for a meaningful increase in the Department's representation allowance. But it does not speak well for the breadth of view or maturity of the American people that such primitive concepts are allowed to stand in a nation that is looked to for world leadership.

The essence of the diplomatic business, whether we like it or not, is the cultivation of contacts with foreigners; a diplomat without contacts might as well go home and take up stamp collecting. Negotiations prosper in direct ratio to the degree of understanding between the negotiators; more business is transacted, more information is gleaned over the coffee and cigars than at a formal meeting across a green baize table. As Abigail Adams wrote in the year 1784, when her husband was ambassador to France, "More can be accomplished at one party than at twenty serious conversations." In that respect times have not changed.

It should not be difficult for Americans, whose businessmen assiduously promote their business by providing clients with food and drink, not to speak of other forms of amusement, to understand that the transaction of foreign affairs at luncheon or dinner is a logical custom and likely to pay off. To cultivate good will with the aid of a highball is standard operating procedure in the marts of trade and a legitimate practice even in the cost-conscious eyes of the Internal Revenue Service. It should be equally so in the give and take of diplomacy—for the simple reason that the wheels turn more smoothly when oiled with the proper lubricant; but no career officer in his right mind would permit his picture to be taken with anything stronger than a glass of orange juice in hand.

For the Foreign Service, however, even to think in terms of an expense account such as is maintained by any well-run corporation seems close to original sin in the flinty view of Chairman John J. Rooney of New York, and the other forty-nine members of the House subcommittee. We like to think of ourselves as the richest, the most generous, the most powerful, and the most friendly country on earth; yet nothing belies that self-created image quicker than the size of what congressmen jocularly refer to as the State Department's "booze allowance," or "whisky fund." This is the annual allotment for official representation, an item Rooney and his associates find as hard to swallow as a cup of hemlock.

Outside Washington and the Foreign Service, the name of John

🏵 🏵

J. Rooney is not well known; he is not a national figure, like some congressmen who spring into print at the drop of a controversy. But as *Time* magazine reported: "In 300 U.S. embassies, legations, consulates, and special missions throughout the world, nothing is more likely to cause hot blood and cold sweats than the mention of [Rooney's] name." The Rooney rulings on how the State Department spends its money—and how much it gets—are absolute. None of his colleagues cares to cross him; there is no appeal from his decisions; and no one actively connected with the Foreign Service would dare to offend him for fear that the State Department's budgetary requests might be adversely affected.

While the hard-pressed Foreign Service Officer is plagued by many other nightmares besides the mention of Rooney's name, it is undeniable that the chairman of the appropriations subcommittee wields more influence on the course of events than any individual at State, as far as expenditures are concerned. Estimates, down to the last cent, pass under what *Time* called Rooney's "harsh eye and hard thumb"; his occasional nod or more frequent frown affects everything from the quality of the broomsticks in a minor consulate to the scope of an ambassador's social activities; he has virtually made a career out of curbing the career officers' perennial quest for the wherewithal to hold up their heads in official circles. It is also a fact that Rooney has supporters; beginning in 1944, he has been elected consecutively to Congress by the voters of a district which must see little point in spending tax money to foster foreign relations and which doubtless approves the "economies" he promotes, many of them obtained at the expense of American prestige.

Any politician who exercises such unopposed and autocratic power deserves a short biography. According to the *Congressional Directory*, Rooney, a Democrat, was born in 1903 of immigrant parents in Kings County, Brooklyn, New York, where his family has lived for more than ninety years. Educated in parochial schools, a graduate of Fordham Law School, class of 1925, he began with the practice of law; as an assistant district attorney for four years, from 1940 to 1944, he may have acquired the training reflected in his acid handling of the State Department's budget hearings. Rooney has a string of titles: Knight Commander with Star, Ecclesiastic Order of St. Gregory the Great; past exalted ruler of Brooklyn Lodge No. 22 B.P.O. Elks; past New York State Vice President of Ancient Order of Hibernians in America; past president, St. Patrick Society of Brooklyn; life member, Columbus Council No. 126, Knights of Columbus; honorary member, Sgt. Harry Wm. Starbuck Post No. 601, Veterans of Foreign Wars. As a member of the Committee on Military Affairs, he visited the Western and Italian fronts in 1944; he was an official observer at the first Bikini atom test and at the Japanese Peace Conference of 1951. Despite these forays into scenes with political overtones, Rooney owes his fame chiefly to a Scroogelike control of the purse strings whenever our mechanism for conducting foreign affairs is concerned.

In the election of November 3, 1964, Rooney was returned to power over the editorial opposition of the *New York Times,* which characterized him as the "entrenched foe of adequate appropriations for the Foreign Service" and called for his retirement to private life. But Rooney, ironically enough, found a stanch supporter in the Deputy Undersecretary of State whose duty it is to administer the funds allowed by Congress for operation of the Foreign Service. William J. Crockett immediately replied with a letter to the *Times,* in which he deplored the newspaper's criticism, denied that Congressman Rooney was a "foe" of the Foreign Service, and praised the Rooney record as one of hard work and strong support for the Service. The reader may draw his own conclusions regarding the reasons for this startling contradiction in viewpoints: the fact is, however, that there are a number of officials in the Department who believe that without the personal attentions of Rooney—hard-boiled as they may be—the Foreign Service would fare even worse, if that were possible, when it comes to extracting funds from Congress for essential purposes.

For the fiscal year 1964, the Department estimated it would need $996,000 for representation purposes—a wholly inadequate sum, considering this would have to be distributed among all our diplomatic missions and many consular offices throughout the world—excluding the United States Mission to the highly gregarious United Nations in New York. The Department knew from previous experience that it could not expect more; the figure actually allowed by House and Senate conferee action was $973,000. That was the high-water mark so far permitted, $23,000 less than the amount requested, but $23,000 more than that granted the previous year. In fiscal 1965, the sum allowed edged up to $993,000. For our diplomats to play host around the world, a million dollars would seem a modest sum, with total annual expenditures of the federal government in the last few years running over $100 billion. For reasons best known to Rooney, however, attempts to crack the million-dollar fiscal barrier have invariably failed. It seems to be a fixed idea of Congress that the prestige of the United States is not worth more.

Comparisons, while not always exact, are revealing. In a recent year the American embassy in Bonn received $19,325 for representation and personal expenses; West Germany, a defeated nation, spent three times that much in Washington. In Rome, our ambassador was given $15,540; the Italian ambassador to the United States received some $45,000. In Paris, the American embassy was allotted $15,170; in Washington, the French embassy had an estimated $50,000. In Moscow, the United States operated on $12,400, while the Soviet embassy in Washington spent approximately that much on one party. It is much easier on the pocketbook to be a British diplomat than an American; the "personal expense and representational allowance" of the British ambassador in Washington is $100,000 a year, more than double what the American ambassador in London gets in salary and expense allowance. In an interview with the *Wall Street Journal* toward the end of 1964, ambassador in London David K. E. Bruce, who paid most of his bills for official hospitality out of personal funds, made the rueful statement: "I find that I'm out tens of thousands of dollars at the end of the year."

Shakespeare has taught us, in *Much Ado About Nothing,* that "comparisons are odorous." He could have proved his point in a later day by citing the official representation allowance for the United States delegation at the International Telecommunications Conference in Buenos Aires not long ago—$600 spread over a period of two months. So scant were the funds that when the delegation gave an official dinner at the exclusive Jockey Club, the American members were required to pay for their own food; in comparison, the International Telephone and Telegraph Company spent some $50,000 to entertain its guests and provided its officials with credit cards to take care of the extras. As everyone knows, parties cost money, whether official or unofficial. The reception given by Ethiopia's ambassador when Emperor Haile Selassie I made a state visit to Washington in 1963 is said to have cost his country more than $9,000.

To illustrate further the theory of billions for defense, but not enough sandwiches to go around for cooky pushers, mention might be made of *Time*'s account of the traditional Fourth of July celebration in Bonn a short time ago. There, "able U.S. Ambassador Walter C. Dowling, a careerman, could afford only $287 —enough to give 360 visitors a pass at trays of simple canapés and a sip of cheap German sparkling wine," whereas the Soviet embassy, to mark the anniversary of the October Revolution, hired the city's best club and entertained 500 guests with vodka, champagne, and caviar. Humiliating episodes of this kind are by no means exceptional; the nadir, however, was reached in the Netherlands, when a group of influential Dutch editors was brought in for a seminar by the United States Information Service. "After the first day's lectures," said the *Time* story—aptly entitled "Let Them Eat Crumbs"—"USIS hosts explained that guests could have two beers or two glasses of Dutch gin at the embassy's expense. That night at dinner, waiters began serving two slices of meat to guests, but stopped halfway through to take one slice away from the plates already served. Under John Rooney's representation allowance, the budget for the dinner permitted one slice of meat per man, and not a calorie more."

Not so extreme, perhaps, but typical of what an ambassador must stoop to if he wants to do the right thing by official circles and at the same time give the nod to the American colony on our national day, was the practice when I was in Norway. At high noon the diplomatic corps and leading officials were invited in to drink a short toast to the United States; later in the day American citizens and some of their friends were received with cokes, cookies, and lemonade. Although the Soviets had no comparable colony in size, the contrast when they held forth was impressive: cold salmon, lobster, ham, turkey, salads, sausages, deviled eggs, and all manner of similar delicacies—and of course mounds of caviar with vodka and other potables on the side.

Statistics always leave Congress cold. From the vote-getter's point of view, presumably, it is better to save the government money by letting a diplomat pay for his own social obligations. James J. Zellerbach, the paper king, is reported to have expended $200,000 of his personal fortune to meet official representation expenses during the five-year period he was ambassador to Italy. Publisher John Hay Whitney, when ambassador to the Court of St. James's, found it necessary to spend more than $100,000 above his allowance every year. General James Gavin, who assumed the post of ambassador to France without private means, is reputed to have gone in the hole $20,000 for the eighteen months he was in Paris. The well-heeled amateur who, in our undemocratic fashion, becomes a diplomat by virtue of his pocketbook, can pick up the tab any time and pay for the privilege. That is not so easy, however, for the career man, who rarely has a bankroll of his own. Two of our ablest professionals, one the deputy chief of mission in Paris and the other in London, asked Secretary of State Herter to relieve them of their assignments a few years ago because they could not stand the financial strain; the higher one rises, the greater the strain.

It would be naïve to assume that government-sponsored functions are a source of joy to the participants. That indigestible luncheon, that boring banquet, that reception to honor a visiting potentate, all constitute hard work—work with a serious purpose. To operate as the eyes, ears, and sometimes the mouth of the United States government, which means to enlarge one's circle, to ferret out facts, to act as the expounder of American policy, an exchange of amenities is as indispensable as operating tools to a surgeon. Invitations may crowd his calendar, but the representative of a great nation can never turn one down—he may risk slighting a friendly country or start speculation as to the reason for his absence; he may miss a morsel of intelligence that might find a place on the wide-vision screen of foreign policy at home. No matter how sated with official society, he goes on tilling the soil of fresh introductions, reaping the harvest of friendships already made, and storing away in his mental files the items of information he will incorporate in tomorrow's report. Eventually he must repay his obligations. Until a better method is found for cementing ties—or fencing with the opposition—a sizable portion of the affairs of state will continue to be handled with the assistance of cocktails and canapés. A handicap, perhaps, but a handicap that is shared by all the nations of the world.

Especially ironic to the American diplomat is to see his meager "whisky fund"—of which 70 per cent, incidentally, goes for food and 30 per cent for drink—depleted by dinners for congressmen. The law forbids the Foreign Service Officer to entertain his countrymen at government expense, unless foreign guests are also present, but the junketeers who descend on his post are not bashful about meeting the local bigwigs. Like a swarm of inquisitive bees, members of Congress buzz off for foreign parts as soon as the gavel falls at the end of a session; that does not, of course, preclude special "studies" or "surveys" at other times—like the famous night club tours of a well-known congressman from New York, which were an embarrassment to even his colleagues. These happy travelers fly in planes supplied by the Air Force, they feast on counterpart funds—local currency that is made available to the United States in amounts equivalent to our dollar expenditures—and their wives, daughters, secretaries, and other freeloaders go along for the ride. With obsequious care, their slightest whims are catered to by the local staff; and the whims may include anything from a booze allowance for the men—perhaps a bottle or two from an officer's private stock—to such luxuries as

Kleenex and soft toilet tissue for the women. Congress does not appropriate funds for its own enjoyment; but woe to the career diplomat who fails to offer hospitality to congressmen on the loose abroad.

Not all these tours are frivolous, of course. I have been impressed many times by the serious purpose of Congressional visitors who try to find out for themselves what makes a foreign economy tick or why there is no labor movement in an authoritarian country. Back in Washington, their views contribute to policy discussions and promote better understanding of the State Department's difficulties. If the diplomat always succeeded in producing such results—by bringing an inquiring mind into contact with the proper officials, for instance—his efforts would be well rewarded. The reverse, however, may sometimes be the case. I can recall particularly one member of the House who came to my post on a circuit of the world, courtesy of the Military Air Transport Service, whose advance billing advertised an interest in agriculture. A few hours before the dinner which I had arranged in his honor at a local hotel, in order that he might meet the officials most concerned with his subject, he begged off on the plea of a headache and an early start next morning; but when the party moved afterward into the bar for coffee, we found our indisposed guest on the dance floor with a lively, co-operative, redheaded companion of the evening.

A Foreign Service Officer must draw upon his "booze allowance" for other purposes besides accommodating congressmen who hold it in such disdain; for the care and feeding of VIP's—including those with letters of introduction from congressmen; for observing the national holiday; for fostering friendships for the United States and returning official invitations at the buffet or the bar. Social formalities govern life in the international community as strictly as the rites and ceremonies of protocol crystallized at the Congress of Vienna in 1815, even if they are not particularly dear to the heart of the homespun American. If the allowance granted him to represent his country is not enough, a Foreign

Service Officer has no recourse but to dig deep in his pockets and make up the difference.

In these days of multinational diplomacy, cut-rate representation is not appreciated; although it may reflect the ideas of constituents in the corn belt, it is hardly convincing to other nations in the face of Communist competition around the corner. Bargain-basement tactics—when we hold back on the appetizers, water down the drinks, or, as Ambassador Claude Bowers once threatened to do in Chile, serve hot dogs and beer; when officers' wives, to save expense, make the sandwiches themselves for an embassy reception and, to save catering charges, serve them as well—do not pass unnoticed. Rightly or wrongly people expect America to act the role in which it is cast, not to seduce the guests with groaning board or to ply them with strong drink, but simply to make the hospitable gesture in a manner befitting its greatness. As a cabinet minister in North Africa remarked to me with disarming frankness, when I was forced to admit that the State Department lacked funds to acquire an official residence or a chancery, "How can we respect a nation that does not respect itself?"

"For want of a nail, the shoe was lost; for want of a shoe, the horse was lost; for want of a horse, the rider was lost; for want of a rider, the battle was lost." It may be farfetched to imagine a parallel in modern terms, but the day may come when a battle was lost for the Free World for want of a caviar canapé.

Major reductions from estimated needs are made as a matter of course when the time rolls round for the appropriations committees to hold their annual inquest on requests relating to the Foreign Service. Just as the "booze allowance" dries up under the astringent scrutiny of Congress, so such regular items as salaries and expenses—which finance all normal operations of the Department and its overseas posts—shrivel to skin and bones when laid open for dissection. Although the ax might profitably be wielded on some of the ever-spreading branches of the bureaucratic tree, and steps might reasonably be taken to limit the population explosion in the Department, this does not mean that important activities should be curtailed, that commitments should not be met, or that emergencies should not be provided for. To move the Foreign Service Officer and his family around, to provide proper housing, post allowances, home leave and urgent consultation, the need for funds invariably exceeds the allotted supply, and at the end of each fiscal year a spokesman for the Secretary of State must tread the well-trod path to Capitol Hill, hat in hand, to beg for a supplemental appropriation.

In common with other departments, State is a frequent victim of Congressional delay in the passage of appropriation bills. To cite perhaps an extreme example, it was not until December 15, 1963, that the Appropriations Committee of the Senate got around to reporting out the State Department's bill for the fiscal year which had begun on July 1. Still to come in December were the Senate vote on the bill, a meeting of House and Senate conferees to adjust differences, and final action by both houses on the Conference Committee's recommendation. By that time alarm had spread lest the Department would not have enough money in the till to pay its way through the June 30, 1964, fiscal deadline; only a "voluntary turnover" of personnel within the ensuing weeks, it was thought, could keep it in business. With the spirit of Christmas finally in the air, the bill cleared the last barrier on December 18, although not before the conferees had succeeded in chopping off a tidy $37,025,000 (more than one tenth) from the $359,721,000 requested by the Department.

State's total budget for the fiscal year 1964 thus stood at $322,696,000. With the stated objective of saving the taxpayer money, $8,875,000 had been sheared from the estimates for "Acquisition, Operation and Maintenance of Buildings Abroad"; $13,350,000 from the estimates for "Mutual Educational and Cultural Exchange Activities"; and $9,800,000 from that life stream of the Service—"Salaries and Expenses." The latter was the unkindest cut of all, since every dollar in this vital category is invariably stretched to the snapping point and cuts in the vital organs always hurt more than elsewhere. For one year's "Salaries and

Expenses" the amount asked was $162.8 million, which did not seem excessive compared, for example, with a $300-million aircraft carrier; yet the drastic reduction of this item to $153 million —it had to be supplemented later by $5 million—ignored the fact that wages and prices had been rising overseas, that automatic salary increases had been provided by law, that new posts had to be opened in crisis areas, and that extraordinary and unforeseen contingencies, such as occurred in Panama, Zanzibar, and Tanganyika, were likely to arise without the consent of Congress.

What, one may ask, became of the "saving" of $37 million from the total proposed outlay to conduct the foreign affairs of the nation? It certainly did not inhibit the birth of new cells in the departmental honeycomb, which continue to reproduce themselves in obedience to Parkinsonian laws. Project Mohole, which aims to bore a hole to the center of the earth, is one yawning chasm down which the dollars might have been poured—$47 million of federal funds have already been spent on a mobile platform from which to carry out the planned drilling through the ocean floor. Projects such as the new office building for the House of Representatives, which cost more than any government building in history, including the Pentagon, might have used a few extra millions. So might the manned lunar landing program; NASA had a mere $5.4 billion program for the fiscal year 1965 with which to establish relations with the moon.

"The Department must exercise stringent economies to live within the amount currently available," admonished Assistant Secretary for Administration Dwight J. Porter—a familiar refrain sung by a long line of his predecessors and which will no doubt continue to be sung practically word for word by a long line of his successors. The Service, said Porter, "must take every possible action to reduce costs to the minimum and to exercise economy in the conduct of day-to-day operations. . . . Action by the Congress on our budget requests . . . leaves no alternative but to cut the pattern to fit the cloth. We are in for a very tight year financially."

The cloth was indeed cut to fit John Rooney's pattern one year in Geneva, when he disallowed a request for funds to provide the consul general and his family with a house instead of the cramped apartment to which his rent allowance entitled him. "That sounds like a nicety we cannot afford with the highest debt in history," he declared, "as far as I am concerned it is . . . out the window."

The Assistant Secretary for International Affairs, Francis O. Wilcox, attempted to explain why it was important for the representative of the United States to have the kind of quarters in which he could entertain adequately in Geneva, headquarters of the European office of the United Nations and many other international organizations. "I would say two things, Mr. Chairman," began Wilcox, "the first is that in a great many posts of this size and stature, it has been felt desirable to have an official residence for the United States representative. He has many, many functions to perform. He has many, many people to entertain and his work would be facilitated greatly if we had this kind———." But Rooney was not interested. "You certainly did not manage this situation very well when you now come along and ask the taxpayer to pay $700 a month rent that you did not have to pay previously." Case dismissed.

Not only was the house rent denied, but the Department was specifically directed "not to devote any other funds for such use," thus closing all possible avenues of approach to the acquisition of more presentable quarters. Flabbergasted, and perhaps hurt, that a city which all Switzerland is proud of should be singled out for such treatment, the Swiss ambassador to Washington, Henry de Tôrronté wrote a letter to Senator J. William Fulbright of the Foreign Relations Committee, asking why it was that the United States felt unable to provide its permanent delegate with facilities comparable to those of nearly every other foreign government at the busy international center of Geneva.

"I am afraid I cannot remember why this action was taken," was the apologetic response, "I believe Congressman Rooney . . . is probably the only man who is likely to recall what the circumstances were."

Senator Fulbright was right. Only one man had the answer. But it was the State Department that had to draft a reply to the prominent American resident in Geneva who saw his country's representative squeezed into an undersized flat and who complained that, by contrast, the British, French, and Soviet representatives were all happily living in the style to which diplomatic households are accustomed.

Thrift in government is a noble experiment, as President Lyndon B. Johnson dramatically demonstrated by shutting off the lights at the White House. By wielding the pruning knife, exercising administrative self-control, and nipping bureaucratic offshoots in the bud, it should be possible to effect economies that would gladden many a taxpayer's heart. But when economy lowers the prestige of the United States, as it did so strikingly in Geneva, it is false economy. Prestige may be difficult to evaluate in dollars and cents; yet most Americans would probably feel that with a booming national economy, the United States could afford to keep its representative at least as well housed as that, say, of Ghana.

When it comes to paying out for prestige, however, Rooney is adamant. The American ambassador to Germany inherited Nazi Hermann Goering's special train and used it to make trips from Bonn to Berlin, to the discomfiture of East German Communists and a corresponding boost in status for the United States. But it cost money to run the train; its political and psychological value were ignored and, like the house rent at Geneva, out the window it went.

To compensate for the opening of new Foreign Service offices where urgently required by American interests, Rooney has exacted his pound of flesh by pressing for the closing of others. In the summer of 1963, the Department announced the termination of consular services at thirteen cities, among them Basel and unfortunate Geneva, although the latter continued to support our quasi-diplomatic Mission to the European office of the United Nations. More effective administration of overseas operations and a contribution to balance of payments savings were the announced objectives of this action, which transferred the multiple services at the closed posts to distant embassies or other consulates in the countries involved. The move, it was claimed, would save about $500,000 annually, presumably in local rents and services only, since no dismissal of American personnel was contemplated; and, according to the Department's statement, the action did not "reflect any change whatsoever in United States relationships with the countries or areas" in which the posts were to be closed.

A contrary opinion, however, prevailed among the Swiss. In a front-page editorial, the influential *Neüe Zürcher Zeitung* strongly protested that although it might be a matter of little concern to the United States, the "senseless" closing of Basel—one of the oldest American consulates in Europe—and of Geneva, which served 300 American firms and 8,000 American residents, could be regarded only as "an expression of disrespect or want of comprehension" and that it would "hurt the good relations between the two countries." That inhabitants of both cities would henceforth have to travel to the federal capital of Bern to transact consular business was the least of the resulting resentment; because of the cantonal structure of Switzerland, with its small local "capitals," the elimination of two long-established consular offices flouted economic, social, and historical traditions, aroused sectional jealousies, and severely wounded the *amour-propre* of the Swiss populace.

"It can be well imagined," the Zurich paper said with unconcealed sarcasm, "that in far-off Washington in one of the many thousand offices of the State Department a team is occupied with the rationalization of the consular service. A computer is fed with the number of inhabitants of Basel and Geneva and perhaps also with the indication of the distance in miles from the capital of Bern, as well as maybe with other useful data, such as the number of visas issued in the past few years, consumption of electric current, the age of the consul, etc. The computer sets to work and promptly supplies the answer that consular services in Basel and Geneva are superfluous."

The *Tribune de Genève,* reminding its readers that barely two years had elapsed since American consular facilities in Geneva were expanded under the press of new business and a site sought for a permanent building, chose to look at the closing as a "perfect illustration of the instability of American policy." The right hand probably did not know what the left hand was doing, concluded the editor charitably; "that is what so greatly discourages the friends of America and, what is more serious, gives an unstable appearance . . . at a time when . . . security is being sought."

Whether or not the reaction was so outspoken in other places, such as Salzburg, Venice, Manchester, or Le Havre, when the respective consulates were shut down, the Zurich editorial undoubtedly summed up the general feeling: "Certainly, no one will make a drama out of it. It is an administrative measure. In the trend of rationalization. In the interests of an improvement of the consular services. These are the bloodless formulae with which such measures are explained. But they do no justice to the psychological aspect of the matter, which should be reconsidered in Washington."

It would be too much to expect that an administrative measure would ever be reconsidered in Washington on the grounds of its psychological aspect, particularly when "bloodless formulae" are the mark of the machine age. One can only hope that the annual saving to the taxpayer was worth it when weighed against the loss in good will. To some misguided patriots concerned with American prestige in countries where Communists vote regularly in the elections, as in Switzerland, it might even appear the part of wisdom to assert the American presence in a few additional places, flying the flag where it could be prominently seen, rather than hauling it down where it has flown for generations.

Sometimes the day can be saved by unabashed foreign intervention. During one of the recurrent economy waves, the consulate at Malta was earmarked for sacrifice, its services to be transferred to my offices at Tripoli on the North coast of Africa. Malta was not only a source of immigration to the United States, an attraction for American tourists, and a naval station for NATO—including units of the Sixth Fleet—but the oldest post to fly the American flag in the Mediterranean. When I called on Admiral

❦ ❦

Lord Mountbatten, British commandant of the naval forces, to break the news, he exploded in wrath: "Tell your government that if it hauls down the flag here I'll take it as a personal insult!" I telegraphed his remarks verbatim; the consulate at Malta was spared, and today it is an embassy in the newly sovereign country of that name.

Bareboned austerity in the American diplomatic way of life is particularly noticeable when applied to motor transport. Although the job requires daily attendance at the functions which round out their ten- to twelve-hour workday, upper brass of the State Department at last accounts had a total of nine sedans—two of them assigned, and most of them old—at their disposal. As one of the drivers in the Washington merry-go-round succinctly observed to Betty Beale of the *Washington Star,* the State Department handles top diplomats and royal parties and gets the worst cars. Princess Grace of Monaco, for instance, was taken around in an aging Plymouth sedan; some of its stable companions were six-year-olds.

To make an invidious comparison with the Pentagon, it was revealed in 1964 that the defense establishment had a pool of 150 cars for general service, and 36 individually assigned cars with drivers for top-layer personnel. To each according to his needs, perhaps; but the generals and the admirals, not to mention lesser grades, have a housing allowance as well, access to commissaries and service clubs in town and country, and government-paid servants—none of which is available to their poor relations in State. All this, with car and driver too, makes for the good life on Washington assignment for the military. The lack of a housing allowance at the home base is cause alone for the diplomat's dread of Departmental duty. Even the retired military have it over their State Department counterparts; provision was made in Public Law 87-793 of October 11, 1963, to give them the benefit of an automatic cost-of-living increase—not extended to those who retire from the Foreign Service.

From the point of view of our balance of trade, nothing is more important than Detroit's foreign sales; nothing can advertise the American manufacturing genius better than the automobile. Across the seven seas, American cars are like the national emblem, a source of pride and a symbol of free enterprise. For a few hundred thousand dollars a year the Foreign Service could be supplied with a fleet of late models—no rent-a-car agency would be satisfied with less than the latest—and the world would have a constant reminder of American productivity. Just around the corner, too, would be an American sales outlet. Yet the motor pool at many of our embassies is a collection of secondhand vehicles, cast-off limousines from another federal agency in Washington, overworked sedans, used floor models, or manufacturer's specimens donated at a discount. It is not unusual for an ambassador of the United States to make do with a venerable model flying the American flag from the fender, while the minister of a country chiefly supported by our economic aid rides around in a shiny, air-conditioned Cadillac.

In 1953, when I was our first envoy to Libya, I met Secretary Dulles and Harold Stassen at the airport and placed at their disposal the official Chrysler limousine. Since I knew the transmission might fall out at any minute, I followed them in a borrowed car. The Chrysler did not break down. But Charles E. ("Chip") Bohlen, when ambassador in Moscow, was not so lucky as Dulles and Stassen. His ancient vehicle—no funds were available for a new one—collapsed on a trip to the Kremlin. It was no help to the American image that an imposing Soviet-built limousine sped past at that inopportune moment, carrying the ambassador of Outer Mongolia.

Cutting down expenses may be a desirable aim in itself, but it is often a detriment to morale and hinders the Foreign Service in the discharge of its professional obligations. On May 29, 1961, President Kennedy addressed a personal letter to all chiefs of mission, which included the following:

The practice of modern diplomacy requires a close understanding not only of governments but also of people, their cultures and institutions. Therefore, I hope that you will plan your work so that you may have the time *to travel extensively* [author's italics] outside the nation's capital. Only in this way can you develop the close, personal associations that go beyond official diplomatic circles and maintain a sympathetic and accurate understanding of all segments of the country.

With these sentiments every diplomat would emphatically agree. Not only the chief of mission but all members of his staff would consider local travel a most desirable, if not essential, part of the job. Unfortunately, in addition to time, extensive travel takes money; the chief of mission may be able to afford both, but those who would familiarize themselves with the country and who cannot write their own checks are often confounded by that depressing warning, "No funds available." If our envoys are to get around a country, Congress will have to stop paring the travel allowance and raise it instead; it is a subject in which every Foreign Service Officer is directly and deeply interested.

This lack of travel money is, of course, chronic and of long standing. My introduction to the phrase "No funds" was at the very outset of the career, when I was notified of my appointment and invited to report for duty in the Department of State. It was near the end of the fiscal year and the travel appropriation, as usual, was exhausted. I could travel to Washington at my own expense, it was explained, or wait till the following fiscal year to have my way paid. I chose the former. It was the first, but by no means the last, out-of-pocket expense I had in the service of my country.

When costs are counted in nickels and dimes instead of in dollars, the Foreign Service Officer gets an inferiority complex; when repairs and furnishings for his embassy are held up or postponed, he gets red in the face; when ambassadors of other countries have air-conditioned offices—as I did not—in Africa, he is hard put to explain; when the lack of modern office machinery such as dictaphones and electric typewriters slows down output, he is frustrated; when outmoded or inadequate equipment for the code room impairs its efficiency, as disclosed by testimony from Ambassador Foy Kohler in Moscow, he becomes concerned for his country's safety. Only when the situation becomes critical, as in the case of the Moscow embassy, can Congress be persuaded to replace the antiquated facilities: in the fiscal year 1965 the ante was raised by one million dollars—earmarked for urgent improvements in the communications setup for the sake of our national security.

We have long since given up erasers on pencils; reports are mimeographed on both sides of the paper; a fifty-dollar prize was awarded for the suggestion that extra "courtesy copies" of all letters be abolished. When Alaska and Hawaii were added as States to the Union, instructions went out to our missions to use up the old forty-eight-star flags before ordering new ones. (At last accounts, according to the press, the embassy in Oslo was still trying to wear out its largest and most durable flag.) Economies, foreseen and unforeseen, hang over the head of the Foreign Service Officer like the sword of Damocles. He must travel on American ships wherever they exist and he cannot exceed the minimum first-class fare unless he pays the difference himself, as I quickly learned when I sailed from New York on the old *George Washington* en route to my first post—my cabin was inside, below the water line; and although American flag vessels are now the soul of courtesy to our diplomats, the purser then was unimpressed with my consular credentials as a passport to better accommodations.

Even on transatlantic airplane flights, the Foreign Service Officer parts company with foreign diplomats at the ramp, sitting five abreast with the economy crowd while the representative of an emerging nation lounges in the section ahead. If funds run short, as they often do, and his travel orders are canceled, his home leave given up, or his transfer to another post suspended, he resignedly readjusts to life in Bongo Bongo. When I arrived in Senegal as ambassador in 1960, I discovered that my residence had picture windows in the bathroom, so I appealed to the State Department to furnish curtains or frosted glass. I appealed in vain, until this telegram finally brought results: "Have magnificent view of Dakar from my bathroom and vice versa."

Such penurious policies are no secret to our foreign friends. The United States, they have been led to believe, is a big country, inhabited by people who think big in business, finance, industry, and so forth. Too polite to laugh aloud, they read the printed records of Congressional committee hearings—as the Swiss ambassador did—and wonder at the incomprehensible Americans who bolster their military might with billions, but who shrink from voting the minimum to back up their worldwide diplomacy.

Foreign Service, at Home and Abroad

"The trouble with the Foreign Service is that you have to live abroad." This belated discovery was made by a colleague of mine after we had passed the entrance examinations and were about to leave for our first posts. Today my friend might not have been so dismayed, for all foreign affairs personnel of the Department and Foreign Service are now obligated to serve both at home and abroad; and an average of 40 per cent of his time would probably be spent in Washington. But in a moment of truth, the newly commissioned vice consul realized it was a long way from his home in Missouri to the post where he had been assigned—in Cali, Colombia; and he confided to me with regret his decision to abandon a deliberately chosen career before it had started.

Anyone who is not prepared to forgo the comforts of American plumbing, the hygiene and the medical facilities taken for granted as part of the American heritage—or the daily sustenance of a cup of "real American coffee"—had better not try for the Foreign Service. He would find himself in the company of many an American tourist, disgruntled at the lack of amenities, unadjusted and unadjustable to his surroundings, swearing that the town was a good place to visit but that he'd hate to live there. He would do much better as an armchair traveler, content with the fireside or the TV, while someone else incurred the hazards to health—even to life itself—to protect his interests in foreign lands.

The cooky pusher is nothing if not adaptable. He must be on his toes, levelheaded, capable, and resourceful, to keep the flag flying in steaming jungle, in desert outpost, or in teeming cities; to take the inconveniences and the irritations in his stride. He is in the front line when trouble starts, whether it is a mob bent on attacking his office or burning the USIS library, a crowd shouting, "Yankee Go Home," a fellow citizen jailed by the police, or an act of God by earthquake, hurricane, or tidal wave. In foreign calm or in foreign strife, he is the refuge and the recourse of Americans —many of them literal innocents abroad, and some not so innocent—who have to be extradited to face charges at home. He may be caught in the ceaseless swirl of big-time embassy functions, or he may be stuck in the muddy backwaters of a lonely post in the tropics. Wherever he goes, he must face a challenge to living; a sharp break with the habits and routine to which he has been accustomed; seldom will he find a land where he has had it so good. If curiosity about the world has got the better of him, if his sense of adventure is greater than a fear of the unusual or the unknown, if the immense, indefinable, inner satisfaction of serving the government of the United States pervades his soul, he will gladly give up Missouri for the discomforts of living abroad.

The work of the diplomat, said Bismarck in 1877—and the work has remained essentially the same ever since—"consists of practical intercourse with men, of judging accurately what other people are likely to do in given circumstances, of appreciating accurately the views of others, of presenting accurately his own." To handle the complex mechanism of foreign affairs, the United States needs highly qualified men and women—in this time of tension and ideological combat, only the best-qualified men and women in the land will do. This, of course, is the avowed aim of the Department; to hire the personnel and to staff the organization in such a way that a top-notch corps of civil servants is in charge and keeps the engine running smoothly on all cylinders.

The taxpayer usually gets what he pays for; if the employee of the people, the hired hand, as it were, fails in some way to measure up to expectations, if he functions less than enthusiastically with an albatross of deficiency appropriations around his neck, if other, more lucrative, jobs attract the best talent, that should not be a cause for astonishment. Those who criticize the Foreign Service Officer should put themselves in his place; they would not go to some of his posts for ten times the pay; and if they think they could do the job better, they might explain why. When all is said and done, the Foreign Service as a body gives the taxpayer far more than his money's worth; the techniques and skills of its officers, derived from a variegated career, added to the departmental storehouse of precedents from the past cannot be equated with modest salary scales, niggardly representation allowances, and penny-pinching allotments to implement policy decisions. The Foreign Service, like other professional organizations, is a group of individuals who, the longer they pursue their elected career, the more expert they become in their work. Any flaws in the picture are not necessarily the fault of the individual; the cause may lie elsewhere.

Previous experience is not a requisite for entering the Foreign Service, for there is no experience exactly comparable to that of the career. A well-grounded student, over twenty-one, just out of college courses in history, government, economics, political science, or related fields of interest, may be an ideal candidate; so may the mature man—up to age thirty-one—with a graduate degree in journalism or foreign commerce, or one who has had a few years' experience in business or the law.

At the outset of his life as a Foreign Service Officer, Class 8, first-step salary $6,050 under the federal pay bill of 1964, the neophyte is ushered into the classrooms of the Foreign Service Institute for a basic eight weeks' course in the mechanics of his calling. His wife, if any, is eligible for a two weeks' briefing, to assist her in meeting "new situations of living in different parts of the world." The salary is more than twice what it was when the enabling legislation for the career was passed forty years ago, and the grants and allowances are much greater. As in the old days of his introduction to the Department, though on a more formal footing, the young officer learns about the problems he will have to face, about America's relationship to world affairs, about the Department's relationship to other government agencies, and about the services he will perform for Americans abroad: notarial fees, the repatriation of stranded seamen, his right to interview fellow countrymen after arrest—and get them out of jail if he can—the promotion of American trade, the issuance of visas, and a dozen different other do's and don'ts written or not written in the regulations. His first post is more likely to be as vice consul in sweltering Tropicana than on London's Grosvenor Square. As he progresses upward through Classes 7 to 1, competing at each step with his colleagues through the annual scrutiny of Selection Boards, avoiding the shoals of Selection Out, he may serve successively as secretary of embassy, consul, counselor, minister-counselor; he will traverse half the globe and be exposed to a variety of languages, climates, races, and customs. On the way he may be selected to attend the Institute for a midyear course of twelve weeks, or a senior course lasting twelve weeks in foreign affairs and policy problems.

As an officer of Class 1 his basic salary is now $22,650. By the time he is eligible for the grades of career minister and career ambassador, he should have a fine intuition for the ins and outs of diplomacy, a well-rounded sense of how to do business with others in the same profession. If he is one of the few to be appointed chief of mission, he may receive a salary between $26,000 and $30,000 according to the classification of the post.

A Foreign Service Officer of career receives three commissions: one, as a Foreign Service Officer, one as a diplomatic secretary, and one as a vice consul. In another category belong the 1,300 members of the Foreign Service Reserve Corps—a group never contemplated by the Rogers Act but which, under the pressures of an expanding service, now serves to accommodate temporary appointees with special skills, or as a way station for Departmental employees and lateral entrants who have their sights set on a "career" in the Foreign Service Officer Corps. Reserve officers serve for a limited period, ranging from two to five years, and their classes and salaries correspond to those of the regular service.

If a college classmate had paid a visit to the first post at which I served—Teheran—he would have observed the workday of a diplomat, or a vice consul as I then was, and the living conditions in one of our farthest flung posts at the time. He would have followed the same route as I did in getting there, by steamer to Beirut, over the mountains to Damascus with the daredevil driver of a secondhand automobile, and twenty-six hours across the trackless desert to Baghdad in a Pullman bus of the Nairn Transport Company. From that point, a choice: Three dusty days through the Persian mountains and plateaus by car, or, by preference, a six-hour air jaunt—by single-motor German Junkers plane—ceiling ten thousand feet. A quarter of a century later, the whole trip from Washington would take less than a weekend by jet; a quarter of a century earlier, it was an ordeal by horse and buggy for which the Department allowed forty-five days in transit.

Unencumbered by family or furniture, I took over the faded glories of a short-lived Armenian legation which housed the consulate on the ground floor and the vice consul in a quadrangle of empty rooms above. From my predecessor I acquired the bare essentials of domestic life; from a departing British diplomat, a vintage Buick roadster; and from the first rug peddler to cross the threshold, enough carpet to cover the bare expanses underfoot. A bathroom had no tub and no running water, but the garden behind high compound walls entranced the eye with almond trees, swaying pines, and geometric designs around the goldfish pond. A gardener, a gatekeeper, and a bicycled messenger whose French consisted of the one word *peut-être* ("perhaps") were paid by the United States government; a faithful retainer named Hossein, and a ferocious-looking cook who seemed always to have a meat cleaver in hand, served at my expense.

I could have put up my classmate if he had been satisfied to sleep on a cot in what used to be the dining room, where the melancholy tinkle of a glass chandelier advertised each vagrant breeze; to keep the coal stirred in the grate for winter warmth; and to bathe in a tin tub ceremoniously brought to his monklike cell with buckets of hot and cold water. At that he would have been better off than in a Teheran hotel; there was a saying that the city prison, the most modern in Asia, was designed for tourists, whereas the jailbirds belonged in the hotels. He could have breakfasted on Persian melons, and caviar from the Caspian Sea, fed the Persian alley cats, and then accompanied me down the grand staircase to the offices of the American consulate below.

The staff at the time I assumed charge consisted of a dark-haired, studious and bespectacled clerk named Aminzadeh, who knew practically everything there was to know, or could find out from friends in the tea houses and bazaars; a young Assyrian who kept the accounts and, after a fashion, typed correspondence; and another American vice consul who did not arrive until the day of my departure. The United States legation, in a different part of town, was headed by Charles C. Hart, a former newspaperman from the Far West, whose household effects had just been pillaged by bandits en route; as a diplomatic mission it was better equipped than I to receive the infrequent American callers, and although the liaison between us was good, we vied with one another to see who would be the first host.

I never failed to have a feeling of expectancy as I turned the page of a new day, for the morning was sure to bring forth a varied succession of callers: a Presbyterian missionary reporting that a woman teacher had become unbalanced—would I kindly persuade her to get on the first plane for Baghdad?; a couple of boys from Northwestern on a world tour whose motorcycle had broken down and who were out of funds; an archaeologist from Chicago whose passport was lost, strayed, or stolen; a Levantine dealer in automotive parts, demanding action on a pending immigration visa; a Belgian businessman seeking to authenticate a set of documents for use in the New York courts; an engineer from Idaho, reporting the death of a fellow worker on the railway project. Only the stranded seaman could be excluded from the list of visitors; since Teheran was not a port, the services prescribed by law for American ships and shipping were outside our operations.

By noon, mail from the States might arrive: requests for information on the market for shoelaces, on getting a lawyer to handle a trade dispute, on the whereabouts or welfare of someone who had failed to write. The periodic pouch from the Department might bring instructions: to compile a report on the currency situation; to discuss the effect of import quotas on American products with the authorities; or, as once happened without notice, to proceed to Tabriz and for economy reasons to shut down the consulate there. (As a listening post near Russia, it soon had to be reopened.) At one o'clock a luncheon break: either a quiet meal upstairs, or, more likely, a formal diplomatic function in honor of a transient dignitary. If there were not too many interruptions, the afternoon could be devoted to dispatches on the changing scene in Persian commerce, industry, or finance; and before a late afternoon reception or official dinner, there might be time to squeeze in a game of tennis or a horseback ride.

Over on the diplomatic side, the day would start with perusal of the press—translation supplied by the Persian interpreter for any item remotely related to an understanding of the country; overnight cables would be digested, correspondence tackled, appointments made for calls and callers. Someone would have to go to the Foreign Office to debate a moot point in negotiations for a commercial treaty, to ask for a concession in behalf of some leading university to explore an untapped archaeological site; to arrange for a visit by a prominent New England author. Reporting and analyzing political and economic events, one of the disciplines of a trained service, had standing priority. The work of the legation would complement but not duplicate that of the consulate; each would forward to Washington the observations made from its own point of view, for however irrelevant a single fact might appear to be, one could never know whether it might prove to be the missing link in a jigsaw puzzle at home.

Fundamentally, the duties have not greatly changed over the years; the cable to Washington is still of paramount importance, as is the protection and advancement of American interests in general. But there are differences. Persia has become Iran, and Teheran is now spelled Tehran. Sharing a boundary with the Soviet Union, the country is now a strategic part of the Free World, and the United States has done a great deal to keep it so. A large American embassy with more than fifty officials combines both diplomatic and consular services; military attachés, USIA and AID staffs total three times as many. Additional consulates are maintained at Tabriz, Isfahan, Meshed, and Khorramshahr, for the American stake has grown far beyond missionaries and archaeologists. And with the revolution in air transport has come growth and a revolution in living: California-style houses, some with swimming pools, and regular embassy briefings for congressmen or other world travelers.

So it has become with other posts, in many of which the embassy and consular work are united under one roof and one flag. From small beginnings large missions grow; and where none existed before, the seeds have been planted and are bearing first fruit. Americans borne everywhere on the wings of air travel, colonize the towns, the cities, the country districts, or pass through to see the sights. They become involved, like people of any other nationality, in personal predicaments and in threats of war or revolution; when disaster strikes on land, sea, or in the air, the Foreign Service Officer must take charge, and if, on impending hostilities, he must evacuate an entire colony in accordance with well-laid emergency plans—as duly happened in Cyprus—he really goes into high gear. In a more prosaic matter, it was estimated in the fiscal year 1964, that 1,425,000 passport applications would be acted upon by consular officers throughout the world; that 295,000 immigrant visas and almost 1,500,000 nonimmigrant visas would be granted. Whether his office is of giant size like that in Paris, a little one like Katmandu's, or medium big like Stockholm's, the responsibilities are the same and the differences only those of scale. The niche which the individual officer fills is usually, although not always, the one he fills best in the master plan of serving his fellow citizens.

As for rewards—if any are to be counted in this nomad life— they are not of the conventional variety. Security there is, of course, for no one is discharged except for cause, and only the few who fail in efficiency are selected out. The career, needless to say, takes one far out of the main stream of American life, deprives one of the conventional opportunity to become vice president of the firm, and throws one into contact with unconventional ways, novel situations, and unaccustomed lines of thought. Financially, the returns can never compare with what one may expect as a district sales manager, as an executive in electronics or engineering; a plumber, a carpenter, or a bricklayer may earn more per hour than a college-educated vice consul in the Foreign Service. The average starting salary, for instance, offered graduates in the 1963 class at the Harvard Business School was slightly over $9,000— many started work at double what they could have earned as a Foreign Service Officer. Reward comes from the spirit—the spirit of public service which, for some unfathomable reason, now and then animates a person more than money; in the opportunities for broad experience and for learning about different cultures at first-hand; in a sense of pride that one is contributing, in however small a measure, to the unfoldment of big events, and that one speaks and acts in the name of a country as great as America.

The penalties are accepted with open eyes. Although it is perfectly possible to join the Service without a private income, an officer knows full well that he will receive no encouragement to support a family in the style to which a budding tycoon might look forward. Change is the keynote of the diplomat's whole existence—those who prefer the security of a stable life need not apply here. His home is definitely not his castle; it is either government-owned or leased, and he is subject to eviction without warning by transfer to another post. His children's schooling is disrupted with every change of station, with every new tongue to learn, and with every new set of friends to cultivate.

Compared to his predecessors, however, the new Foreign Service Officer is entitled to fringe benefits never encompassed in the most rosy visions of Congressman Rogers. Gone are the days when an officer would live only off the land, when undue hardships in living were taken in stride, when lack of medical facilities and supplies were an inseparable part of life abroad. He is helped now by a solicitous government with funds for the education of his off-spring; he is given free periodic medical examinations, free hospital care, and, where needed, free dysentery pills; in some places, where the Army operates a commissary and post exchange, he is pampered with low-cost groceries and sundry American necessities sold at a discount. But on many other assignments he is hard put to make ends meet. Instead of living high on the hog, he must watch the budget when the rate of exchange goes against him. In Lebanon a few years ago, the dollar-paid American was at such a disadvantage that a newly married consul could afford meat only once a week, which moved a scandalized countryman to suggest that CARE packages be furnished by Washington. Instead of flitting from one scintillating soiree to another, as the romanticists would have it, he must dutifully represent his country at functions that are duller than ditchwater for the most part—and for a goodly share of which he pays out of his own purse when it comes his turn. Instead of pushing cookies, he is likely to be burning the midnight oil long after the ball is over, while he pushes a pencil on a dispatch concerning the latest upheaval of the local apple-cart.

It is time to discard the cliché of striped pants. In this second half of the twentieth century, a new diplomatic type is emerging whose charcoal-gray suit, black Homburg hat, and bulging brief-case are universally recognized as the symbols of his office, even in countries where the flowing robe or colorful turban used to brighten an international gathering. Decorations and uniforms are still seen on state occasions, but the American—like the proletarian Communist—still wears white tie and tails at high noon, his main concession to formality. Benjamin Franklin at the court of Louis XVI, not permitted by his government to display undemocratic finery, was authorized to carry a sword to distinguish him from a waiter. Many Foreign Service Officers have been taken for waiters, and it is a safe bet that they would prefer that mistake to being thought of as someone in a working costume of striped pants.

Officers of career from all countries share that "passion for anonymity" which is as much a part of the profession as the motives which inspire them to enter it. The American diplomat is no different from the rest. He expects no acclaim from the multitude and as a rule gets none, for those who embark on a lifetime of public service seldom attain the hall of fame or earn the thanks of those whom they serve. On the contrary, they may earn the abuse of an angry citizen who gets into a scrape at a tourist trap, or otherwise becomes enmeshed in the local laws; who may ask for a miracle in tickets or hotel rooms when none can be wrought, or who thinks that consulates exist mainly to furnish funds to indigent travelers.

I shall always remember how the efforts to rescue two American victims of an airplane crash in Venezuela were repaid by certain members of the American community in Caracas. On the inaugural flight of a mail and passenger plane to a remote missionary station near the Brazilian border, our commercial attaché, Frederic D. Grab, and a writer for the *National Geographic* were aboard. Encountering head winds on the way back, the plane ran out of fuel and disappeared without a trace in the jungle vastness.

With difficulty I managed to assemble a few planes to conduct a search, and set up camp at a primitive malarial town on the outskirts of the jungle. Every day for three weeks, weather permitting, we crisscrossed the area where the plane went down, sometimes flying just beneath the clouds, sometimes just over the treetops. But results were nil. Trees 350 feet high formed a solid carpet of foliage, which smoke signals from the survivors' fires could not penetrate. (Frederic Grab and two others died in the accident, while the rest were eventually brought out by volunteer searchers on foot.) Weary and discouraged, a state of mind shared by the entire party, I received a telegram one day from a group of fellow citizens in civilized Caracas who took us to task for not quickly discovering the site of the crash and strongly implied that not much was being done to help the survivors.

The anxiety and frustration of those at home were understandable, but that message seemed a particularly thankless method of expressing their sentiments.

No more fascinating game of roulette can be played than that of "post preference." A little transfer card, perhaps intentionally dated April first, gives you the chance to say where you would like to go. For twenty-five years I listed Geneva as a first choice —and finally got there; but no one ever paid the slightest attention to my German language qualifications for a German or Austrian post. Notwithstanding the computers and other paraphernalia of career management, post assignments are like the workings of Fate, dealing out a deck of cards face down. What you pick up can change or alter your whole life; you may draw an ace or you may get the joker—whichever it is, the card must be played to the limit of your ability.

One of the stories, probably apocryphal, with which the young officer used to be regaled concerns the vice consul who made a name for himself selling bathtubs to the sheiks in broiling Aden (fascinated by the shiny enamelware, the sheiks used the tubs not for bathing but as a kind of reclining throne). For his success in promoting American trade, the vice consul was rewarded with a change of climate. Sent to frigid Malmö he promptly caught pneumonia and died.

The moral of this fable is that an officer must have a wardrobe elaborate enough for any contingency. Linen jackets and mosquito netting may be a must in one part of the world, but superfluous in another, where furs and long underwear may be the fashion. The government thinks of many things to improve the lot of the career man, but it does not pay for clothing—even when his assignment is canceled after a special stock has been laid in; and so far, no one has set up a clearinghouse where diplomats and their families can exchange equipment when shuttling between the tropics and an arctic freeze.

A diplomat of the old school, J. Butler Wright, who wound up as ambassador to Cuba, used to say that there were two kinds of posts: the "good" posts and the "interesting" ones. It is not impossible, of course, to find a combination of both; but the world of the Foreign Service is such that the "interesting" posts far outnumber what are known as the "good" ones. Notwithstanding, fond mothers may visualize their diplomatic offspring in the chanceries and drawing rooms of Europe; but the odds are greater that a young officer today will find more scope for his abilities in Tunisia or Togo than in Brussels or Bonn.

At the so-called "differential" post—"differential" is a polite expression for the more rugged word "hardship"—one may boil the water and disinfect the lettuce at home, but protection vanishes when one goes out for dinner. Acquaintance may then be made with those obstinate little parasites which infest certain areas of the underdeveloped world. The "differential" is compensation in a cost-of-living allowance slightly higher than the norm, which, however, cannot keep even a tough constitution from showing the effects after thirty or more years' exposure.

The good posts have their hazards too. Ulcers are the occupational disease of the Service, whether brought on by the stress and strain of global politics or by the rigors of food and drink consumed for politeness' sake. Peter Ustinov, in his candid-camera satire on the breed, claims with reason that diplomats, as well as politicians, "are deserving of our deepest sympathy. . . . It is they who have to drink one another under the table while toasting one another's good health. . . . It is they who have to laugh at the unamusing, eat the inedible, listen with apparent interest to the boring . . . welcome the unwelcome, praise the unpraiseworthy." There is the sheep's eye to be swallowed in Arabia, the cold raw egg for appetizer in Iran, the paprika and spice to be downed South of the border, the bean curd flower in seaweed soup for breakfast in Taiwan, the fires of aquavit quenched by beer chasers in Scandinavia. Survivors of the searing sauces and the alcoholic depth bombs which go into their diet have a common plaint: I regret I have but one stomach to give for my country.

To Jules Henri, counselor of the French embassy, was ascribed a startling admission at the end of his ten-year assignment in Washington: "I drank, God help my digestion, 35,000 cocktails in line of duty." Jules did not survive long enough to become an ambassador; he died, in line of duty, at another post. At a Presidential luncheon in Liberia, I happened to sample a meat course of undetermined flavor, something on the order of sweet pork. Nothing more unusual than a rare specie of jungle beast; but when someone mentioned, by chance, that the banned and surreptitious Leopard Society—feeder on human flesh—had been at work again and that "long pig" was rumored on the market, I suddenly lost interest in the dish.

It is not easy to avoid what is set before you; to decline a second helping may not only affront your host but create a difficult problem in diplomacy. On a memorable trip to Sebha, capital of the Fezzan in southern Libya, I encountered a meal that taxed every resource I possessed as the envoy of the United States. The liver and cold tinned asparagus which opened the repast were followed by a heaping portion of spaghetti with meat sauce. Then came a large roast lamb with fried potatoes, and boiled spinach greens as a separate dish. That would seem enough to satiate the most ravenous appetite, but more was to come. Meat balls and tinned peas; next, fried eggs and mincemeat swimming in gravy. Sweetmeats and sticky pastry brought an end to the main courses, but candied fruits in syrup were close behind. When it seemed impossible to take one more mouthful, a bowl of tinned peach halves was served. For the honor of my country I accepted one of those halves. It was not enough; his eyes beaming politeness, the Fezzanese servant showed his knowledge of English. "Two!" he commanded. There was no escape. I swallowed the second half and gave thanks to Allah that only coffee and the ceremonial three cups of tea remained. And that evening I flew back to Tripoli to attend a substantial dinner of *couscous* given by the prime minister honoring the good relations between our two countries and attended by Libya's emancipated Queen Fatima.

The taxpayer, incidentally, gets a bargain when he hires a Foreign Service Officer; he generally gets two for the price of one, for he hires the wife as well. She is the unsung heroine of the Foreign Service saga; she not only has to manage the household and see to the children's schooling, but she must represent America at its smiling best, even as her official husband; she too has to laugh at the unamusing, eat the inedible, listen with apparent interest to the boring, and welcome the unwelcome. The Foreign Service wife is more than merely competent—she goes out of her way to perform philanthropic work or make voluntary contribution to the welfare agencies wherever she may be stationed. In the Senate she has had one articulate champion—the well-traveled Hubert H. Humphrey as a member of the Foreign Relations Committee—who, in support of legislation for benefits to widows, pointed out on January 27, 1964: "The government does not compensate that woman, even though she may be doing as much good for our country . . . as the Foreign Service Officer himself. . . . By their conduct and their sacrifices, those fine women bring honor not only to themselves and their families, but also to their country."

As a hostess, the wife of the Foreign Service Officer often deserves a medal for service above and beyond the call of duty. Take the problem of producing official dinners in a certain West African capital, where the houseboy one evening was carefully instructed how to decorate a wild boar—apple in the mouth and sprig of parsley in the nostrils. Consternation reigned when the dish was triumphantly brought in, apple clenched firmly between the houseboy's teeth, parsley protruding from his nose. Or the case of the hostess in Poland, who told the cook to open some tinned goods for a dinner of meat balls, sauce, and spaghetti. To the discomfiture of everyone, the meat balls were unyielding to fork or knife; they were, in fact, tennis balls which had come in tins and been opened with the rest. Such domestic lapses are legion; and the fortitude with which they are met by the American diplomatic housewife deserves a special round of praise from the taxpayer.

A cooky pusher may be exposed to physical danger as well as to threats to his physique. Rebellions and revolts, civil wars and civil commotion, always have been and still are potential perils. Before the bombings of war in Europe made hairbreadth escapes an ordinary occurrence, Japanese aggression in China produced the Panay incident; J. Hall Paxton, second secretary of the embassy at Nanking, was a passenger on the United States gunboat of that name, which was attacked and sunk by Japanese planes on the Yangtze River. Earlier, American consular officials had been physically assaulted by the Japanese in Mukden and Shanghai. In the Italian war against Ethiopia, Minister Cornelius Van H. Engert and the entire staff of the legation at Addis Ababa were under fire by lawless bands in a siege that lasted three days. In the Spanish Civil War, exposure to danger was frequent. In more recent times, the Congo has been the scene of hazardous duty, including the house arrest of the staff at Stanleyville by rebels who massacred many of their white hostages.

Violent death or fatal illness has been the fate of some; the memorial tablet in the lobby of the Diplomatic Entrance to the State Department is a stern reminder of that fact. Erected by members of the American Foreign Service Association—not the government which they served—by 1965 it listed seventy-three officers "who while on active duty lost their lives under heroic or tragic circumstances." In the summer of 1964, the Department finally got around to paying its own tribute when it dedicated a bronze plaque on the threshold stone of its South Court, named Memorial Court, to "the memory of those who gave their lives for the cause of peace and friendship among nations." All deaths in the Foreign Service, far removed from home and friends, are heroic or tragic; the roster would be much longer if each and every one were recorded. When a rooftop sniper put an end to the career of Thomas C. Wasson, consul general in strife-ridden Jerusalem, there was no question that his death was heroic; the bulletproof vest he had bought, in full awareness of the risk he ran in volunteering for the post, failed to save him. When Theodore Marriner, counselor of embassy at Paris, was transferred to Beirut and there shot to death by a disgruntled Armenian visa applicant, that was high tragedy. So was the case of Robert Imbrie, vice consul at Teheran, killed by a fanatical street mob after taking photographs of a drinking fountain regarded by the Moslem populace as a religious shrine. Imbrie's murder took place under particularly

brutal circumstances. Whether he was thought to have poisoned
the fountain or put the evil eye on some veiled women bystanders,
an angry, gesticulating crowd soon gathered and let fly with
stones. With an American companion and legation messenger,
Imbrie tried to escape in a cab, but the attack was joined by a
group of soldiers and officers wielding sabers and bayonets. Badly
injured, the occupants of the carriage were snatched from their
assailants by police and taken to a hospital. There the mob broke
through doors and windows and literally beat Imbrie to death
on the operating table.

I was unpleasantly reminded of this event when I followed
Imbrie to Teheran as vice consul some years later. On a visit to
Meshed, distant Persian city near the Turkestan frontier, I gazed
in awe at the magnificent mosque of the Imam Reza. I had uncon-
sciously raised my camera, with that rash American instinct for
taking pictures, when shouts and brandished weapons brought me
to my senses. Fortuitously, at that moment two members of the
local *gendarmerie* materialized from a side street; they suggested
that I walk—not run—immediately to my hotel and leave them
to handle the situation. Needless to say, I followed the advice. I
also clicked the shutter; but my picture of the mosque was spoiled
by scowling faces and clenched fists.

Those who lose their lives under relatively prosaic circumstances
do not make the honor roll; pneumonia, cancer, heart failure, a
motor accident, may be tragedy to the family but not tragic or
heroic enough to qualify for space on the memorial tablet. And no
one takes note of wives and children who succumb to illnesses that
might have been prevented if emergency care had been available.

In more primitive days it was yellow fever that exacted the
greatest toll; to preserve and repatriate the remains of one American minister who succumbed in Monrovia, so goes the macabre
legend, a barrel of rum was used. Cholera rated next as a killer,
until DDT and international sanitary regulations became effective. In addition to murder and malaria, the mortality table in-
cludes shipwreck, drowning, volcanic eruption, infernal machine,

exposure, and acute exhaustion. The most recent name on the list is that of Robert A. McKinnon, victim of an uncommon "tropical disease" in Africa.

For the bulk of their fellow citizens, the names of these officers in the Foreign Service who have sacrificed their lives, like any soldier on the battlefield, are unknown. Memorials, however, endure —inadequate recognition of a group of selfless men.

Profile of a Cooky Pusher

"Ca·reer.' A profession or other calling demanding special preparation and undertaken as a lifework; as, to follow diplomacy as a *career*."

The above definition, taken from *Webster's Collegiate Dictionary*, applied exactly to the Foreign Service Officer envisaged in the Rogers Act of 1924. He was to undertake the profession of diplomacy as a lifework, and the calling demanded special preparation. That special preparation, however, was not to be found in any hall of learning devoted exclusively to the study of foreign affairs; instead, it came from the general education, background, previous experience, temperamental fitness, and intellectual qualifications of the applicant.

A couple of private and unofficial Washington institutions did cater briefly to a candidate's aspirations for the Foreign Service; one of them was a cramming school run by Angus MacDonald Crawford, as Scottish as his name and as fond of his whisky as that implies. In a crowded ground floor room of his Georgetown home, Crawford applied last-minute aid to a faltering memory and filled the mind with a vast collection of facts; but the cleverness he displayed in spotting questions in advance led to his undoing. To avoid the repetitive or stereotyped written examinations which had made such a situation possible, preparation of the papers was placed in the hands of a distinguished and expert committee in 1931 and so remained for the next twenty-one years.

The tutoring schools went out of business; today, aspirants who wish to fill in gaps in their formal education or to polish up subjects on which they have become rusty go to Georgetown University's School of Foreign Service or take college-level courses at other formal institutions. Occasionally applicants were—and still are—successful without the equivalent of a bachelor's degree, but the overwhelming preponderance of officers in the Foreign Service, then as now, have had the benefit of graduation from one of our leading colleges and universities.

It seemed quite natural that the best preparation for diplomacy should lie in the breadth of training, the variety of courses, the opportunity for meaningful discussion, and the stimulating lectures available at the larger academic institutions. For this reason, Ivy League colleges from the start led the list of degree-holders; and the Service, accordingly, met with criticism and complaint that it was "undemocratic." Harvard in particular was indicted as the main source of recruits, for Harvard's alleged snobbishness was supposed to rub off on a career diplomat. The fact was, of course, that Massachusetts produced more intellectual curiosity per square yard than, say, Nevada or North Dakota; that the educational facilities of New England preparatory schools were correspondingly richer; that a selection could be made from among a greater number of qualified students; and that all this produced a type of candidate well suited to practice the art of diplomacy and to live with people of different cultures in lands beyond the horizon. Since a private income was still an important, though not an indispensable, asset in the diplomatic career, many graduates of Ivy League schools had this added advantage.

To meet the charge that the State Department was a closed shop for the eastern seaboard, it was soon decided that candidates had to be corraled from states not usually noted for an interest in foreign affairs. The base of recruitment was "broadened," so that "greater geographical distribution" could be shown to Congressional and other critics. Nobody could object to commissioning a Foreign Service Officer who hailed from the great open spaces or the backwoods, provided only that he met the rigorous and varied tests.

However, when the policy was consciously adopted of seeking recruits uncontaminated by the poison of an Ivy League, to prove the Service was "democratic," it opened the door to the view which prevails today that the Service should be "representative" of America as a whole. On that basis one could argue that the graduate of an eastern school such as St. Paul's or St. Mark's was no better qualified to meet with the born, bred, and trained diplomats of the Old World than a graduate of Podunk High; that the freckle-faced boy from down on the farm, the honest lad behind the drug counter, or the part-time attendant at the filling station —all American to the core—had the same inherent equipment to "represent" their country at the Court of St. James's as the youth with more worldly advantages in the educational realm. Maybe so, but without the higher academic training which would enable him to participate intelligently in the formulation of foreign policy, the usefulness of a young man, no matter what sector of the country he came from, might be a limited one.

Almost forty years after Harvard stood revealed as the chief supplier of cooky pushers, it is interesting to note that Harvard still occupies the same position. A survey by the State Department's College Relations Staff to find out where Foreign Service Officers are educated took the period from January, 1957, to August, 1962, as a sample; of the 926 officers appointed during these five and a half years, Harvard was first with 60; as in the past, its Ivy League competitors, Princeton and Yale, were not far behind, with 44 and 41 officers, respectively. The University of California, however, with 56 graduates, had forged into second place as the source of Foreign Service material. Leland Stanford at Palo Alto, it may be observed parenthetically, was in sixth position, reflecting the fact that more officers now come from the Golden State than from any other. So far, no analysis has been made of this cultural phenomenon—whether the climate develops a wider world perspective, whether the Asia-oriented shores of the Pacific are drawing more attention to foreign affairs, or whether Californians are seeking escape from their crowded paradise by joining what may seem to some like a glamorous Foreign Legion.

Not unnaturally, the British diplomatic service has a recruitment base with even greater emphasis on educational background than its American counterpart. It has been found that more than 94 per cent of British foreign service personnel come from either Oxford or Cambridge and that 70 per cent attend private schools before entering their university. Britishers may not have as wide a choice of universities as Americans but the high scholastic standards demanded of them are obvious.

Without a shadow of doubt, the base has been greatly "broadened" as far as America is concerned, not so much by effort and design, perhaps, as by the evolution in American attitudes toward service abroad. In 1928, when I took the examinations, the list of those admitted included candidates from the following states—in alphabetical, not "representative" order: Alabama, California, Colorado, Connecticut, Illinois, Indiana, Louisiana, Massachusetts, Missouri, Minnesota, Nebraska, New York, Ohio, Pennsylvania, and the District of Columbia. Today all fifty states are represented on the roster, as well as Puerto Rico, the Virgin Islands, and the Canal Zone. Moreover, of 463 junior officers brought into the Service in a recent two-and-a-half-year period, 10 per cent were women—in itself a startling change from the situation forty years ago when only one woman had received an appointment. In 1964, female foreign service officers totaled 282.

The average age of all entrants during the period 1961–1964 was between twenty-six and twenty-seven years. Whether any significance can be read into the fact or not, it was roughly a year more during the period 1950–1961.

Although much has been made of the fact that the Foreign Service was supposed to be the preserve of a picked element from the northeastern states, and that this situation no longer applies, it is pertinent to note that the seven officers at present on active duty who have made the class of career ambassador represent a cross section of the country not very different from that which entered the Service shortly after passage of the Rogers Act: one each comes from Colorado, Louisiana, Illinois, Kansas, New York, West

Virginia, and the District of Columbia. Among sixty-one active officers who have reached the grade of career minister, the spread is somewhat greater: twenty-five states are represented.

The ten institutions which stand out as the source of commissioned officers in the Foreign Service together produce about a third of all the officers appointed. In the 1957–1962 period above mentioned, the score for these ten was as follows:

Harvard	60
University of California	56
Princeton	44
Yale	41
Georgetown	28
Stanford	23
Dartmouth	22
Columbia	21
University of Michigan	15
Minnesota	15
TOTAL	325

Farther down the scale was a group of 26 other well-known colleges and universities which contribute in substantial measure to the career Foreign Service:

Virginia	13	Duke	7
Northwestern	12	Haverford	7
Wisconsin	11	Michigan State	7
Brown	11	Rochester	7
Florida	11	Swarthmore	7
Chicago	10	Texas	7
Washington	10	Tufts	7
Hamilton	9	Williams	7
Oberlin	9	Colgate	6
Smith	9	Cornell	6
The Ohio State	8	Fordham	6
Pennsylvania	8	North Carolina	6
City College of the City University of New York	7	St. John's (Brooklyn, N.Y.)	6
		TOTAL	214

Beyond this point, a wide range of lesser colleges—including such improbable institutions for diplomatic timber as Gustavus Adolphus, Carson-Newman, Houghton, Iona, and Vallejo—has added to the diversified aspect of the educational record. Whether or not he is being deliberately encouraged to displace the Ivy Leaguers, it is obvious that the typical Foreign Service Officer today does not necessarily originate in one of the larger centers of population; he may also be a small-town boy who attends the nearby college and is graduated with an ambition to see more of the world. Furthermore, with every state in the Union represented, it is of some interest to observe that the number of college graduates entering the Service from each is roughly proportionate to that state's population.

In sum, the 926 officers appointed during the selected five-and-a-half-year period came from 204 colleges and universities in the United States, plus one in Canada. In addition, three officers were appointed who were not college graduates, showing that the man who does not have a degree is indeed the exception in this career. If a count were made of all the colleges and universities, large and small, represented by the present grand total of some 3,700 officers in the Foreign Service, it would run to more than 450 institutions and include not only every section of this country, but also some foreign countries.

What do these figures suggest? Not that the big eastern colleges have lost their lead as the prime producers of officer material, but (1) that the impact of World War II on the isolationist strongholds has been profound, (2) that a whole new concept of working overseas in the international field has arisen, (3) that student interest in foreign affairs has compelled many colleges to enlarge their curriculums accordingly and, perhaps most pointedly, (4) that a vigorous recruitment drive carried out each year by teams from the State Department—which deliberately beat the bushes in search of prospective talent and thereby compete directly with banks, corporations, and other government agencies having branches abroad—is causing a whole spectrum of degree-holders to enter a field where few ventured to tread before. However, nets cast upon the waters sometimes dredge up strange fish, and it is in the quality of the catch that American policy makers need to be principally concerned.

The announced goal of those who seek the raw material from which Foreign Service Officers are made is to find "the best young men"—and women—"that our society produces" and, presumably, to prod them into taking the written, oral, and physical examinations for entrance into the Service. At one time, when a deeply interested State Department official, Joseph C. Green, was Executive Director of the Board of Examiners of the Foreign Service, a well-publicized characterization of the type of candidate desired was simply: "A highly intelligent, well-educated, versatile, American gentleman, with a gift for dealing with people." The word "gentleman," however, precipitated a long intramural argument and was finally eliminated because of the strenuous opposition of those in charge of the administrative processes. That did not wholly eliminate gentlemen from the Service, of course, but it showed the drift of the times and indicated the direction in which the standards were to be altered.

Instead of making these tests more difficult, to bring forth better, even if fewer, candidates, the reverse has been the case; less difficult tests attract from 6,000 to 8,000 a year who consider themselves qualified to try—a thundering herd of more than 10,000 applied in December, 1959. For these, the openings normally available number less than 200—less if allowance is made for lateral entrants; and two years may be involved before the successful candidate receives an appointment. As the State Department guardedly puts it, those who surmount the hurdles of eligibility are taken in at a rate "depending upon the needs of the Service and the current budgetary situation."

The examiners, by profession, are choosy, and may be relied upon to choose, if they can, "the best that our society produces." But a question inevitably remains as to how many of these thousands of candidates from varied geographical, social, cultural, educational, ethnical, and economic backgrounds—who undeniably represent "America as it is"—are attracted more by government allowances, government security, and a chance to see the world at government expense than by an unselfish desire to serve their country abroad; whether they are merely shopping around for a career in "foreign service," with the mental reservation to drop out if it does not come up to expectations; whether they are all truly gifted and talented people determined to show the best face of America abroad. It has been estimated that one in four who pass the written examination does not appear for the orals, and that one in five of those who pass the orals declines an appointment. One suspects that at least part of this army of youth poised to scale the heights of a diplomatic career may be lured not so much by the challenge of excellence as by the "no experience necessary" sign; learn while you earn—which means picking up intelligence, background, and language qualifications at the post.

No statistics are published to indicate the number and age groups of those who resign from the Service, or their reasons for leaving. However, taking the fiscal year 1964 as an example, figures compiled from the Department's *News Letter* show 55 career officer resignations for the twelve-month period, as distinct from 72 who retired for what may be assumed to be "normal" causes. In the Reserve category, the number of resignations was much higher—102 Reserve Officers resigned, while 18 were retired. Although the exact figure is as closely guarded as the rest, it is known that approximately 85 per cent of the women who become Foreign Service Officers leave the Service before their careers are up.

The old service of the Rogers Act was frankly an elite corps. A superior education, a superior intellectual approach, a superior sense of responsibility and self-reliance, a superior flair for languages, all were important requisites for admission; those who made the grade took immense pride in their abilities and enjoyed a unique sense of camaraderie, akin to that found in the congenial circles of a close-knit professional club. Examinations, administered by the Civil Service Commission until 1931, were exhaustive and exacting: two grueling days of international law, mathematics, French, commerce and industry of the United States, geography, political economy, American history, the history of Europe, Latin America, and the Far East—everything, in fact, except such topics as then-darkest Africa and the somnolent Near East. What was more important, a substantial portion of the papers had to be written like an essay in the king's English—good English usually being a prerequisite for successful diplomacy—on which a candidate was judged as much as on the answers themselves; for, it was rightly thought, the use made of the idiom was as self-revealing as any set of written questions could be.

An acceptable mark on the written tests was only the prelude to an oral ordeal. How a candidate conducted himself even if he did not know the correct answer, how he impressed the Board of Examiners in his person, how he handled himself in comparison with others, were often the criteria of success or failure; letters of recommendation, the security agent's report, fluency in additional languages, and, at length, the results of a detailed physical examination, were all weighed in the dossier's balance. There is no doubt that the first decade or so of selections under those stringent standards produced about as finely screened a body of officers as it was possible to get for the career.

The word "elite"—often wrongly regarded as the equivalent of "snobbish"—merits a dictionary definition, too. *Funk* & *Wagnalls* calls it "the choicest part, especially of a society, army or the like; the pick; flower." *Webster's New International* adds "collectively, highly trained soldiers;—applied to the Swiss first-line troops." Both describe perfectly what Congressman Rogers and the draftsmen of the act of 1924 had in mind when they visualized a corps of career officers to serve the United States abroad—the pick, the flower, the choicest part of our society, a body of highly trained men as the nation's first-line troops, much like the United States Marines. If that is still the goal of those who determine the composition of the Foreign Service, the methods of choosing the troops have been radically altered.

On the surface, the same general formulas govern the recruiting process, the same steps in selection apply. The Department, in the words of Deputy Undersecretary for Administration William

J. Crockett, is still looking for "men and women who are alert—who possess a toughness of spirit and inner fire—because living and working abroad demand these qualities." But the written examinations have undergone a significant change. To fill the vacancies in an expanding Service, the entrance requirements have been tailored to meet a lower common denominator—one which in fact represents the cross section rather than the elite of America's population. Instead of the searching inquiry into a candidate's aptitudes, and his capacity for mature thought, as revealed by written answers on various subjects, the multiple-choice questionnaire and check list—on the order of a popular quiz program—have been substituted. Instead of fluency in a modern language, candidates who are appointed are given a language test *after* they enter on duty; in-service training is provided for those who do not have any language skill at all or "whose competence is below an acceptable minimum." The present forms, to be completed in one day's sitting, were worked out by the Educational Testing Service at Princeton, New Jersey; they require the candidate to correct the grammatical errors in one English composition; and for the rest—"English expressions," "general ability," "general background" —to place a cross in one of five squares against each question where the candidate has at least a one-in-five chance of guessing right, whether he knows the answer or not.

How this compares with the old method of judging a candidate's suitability for the diplomatic career makes interesting speculation. One straw in the wind, however, may be pertinent: the State Department has been moved to add a Writing Improvement Program for newcomers in the Foreign Service to the schedule of its basic Foreign Service Officers' Training Course. When in 1963 it became distressingly evident that too many Departmental employees were verbose, circumlocutory, turgid, or ungrammatical —in short, did not know how to write—classes in clear and concise English were set up, meeting five times a week for two-and-one-half-hour sessions, and supplemented by a battery of selected reading. So great was the response, as well as the need, that the advantages of this gratuitous instruction were quickly ex-

☙ ☙

tended to AID, USIA, and Peace Corps personnel, with the expectation that enrollment would soon reach more than 1,500.

It is obvious, as Voltaire might have said, that many officers do not have the time to write short telegrams or terse reports; and that the rapid increase in personnel has not been accompanied by a commensurate rise in scholarly standards. One example, preserved for posterity in the *Federal Diary* of Washington reporter Jerry Klutz, should suffice to show the corruption that has taken place in the diplomatic vernacular: An officer in the field was authorized to take home leave before July first, before being transferred. In reply, someone sent the following telegram:

> Post unable determine whether transfer individual concerned would be commensurate with staffing requirements in absence knowledge (*a*) assignment replacement and his ETA, and (*b*) ETA individual concerned at new post.
>
> While post does not consider desire of individual concerned significant operative factor in view of exigencies of service, planning could be facilitated by knowledge of his future assignment.

What the "post" meant, in simple terms, was: Who is to replace the officer and when does he arrive? Where is the officer going and when? To frame a query in such simple terms, it would seem, is beyond the grasp of a good many latter-day officers. To pontificate used to be an ingrained tendency of the old diplomacy: "It was absolutely unintelligible," Anatole France once wrote, "because it was couched in diplomatic language." But in this streamlined era, the least one should be able to expect of a diplomat is the ability to express an idea briefly, lucidly, and in idiomatic English.

The part played by colleges in preparing young Americans for the demanding role of public servant in the new world order is worth serious study. If a college-trained mind was regarded as a requisite in the diplomatic task a couple of generations ago, it is even more decisively related to our responsibilities today. More places and more people call upon us for more effort, which in turn calls for more highly trained individuals in crucial positions, as in the Foreign Service. Our top educational centers seem to be doing everything in their budgetary power to produce graduates who can meet the challenge, but a nagging doubt remains whether the admission tests for the Service are keeping pace with the greater challenge.

The fact is that the Foreign Service no longer prides itself on being an elite corps; it seems to pride itself on *not* being elite. And, if taken literally, its aim—in the often repeated words of Secretary Rusk, of representing "America as it is"—could mean a motley crew indeed, composed of individuals from every walk of life. Without detracting in the least from those able officers who contribute so substantially to its over-all performance, the question facing an ever bigger Service is whether quality is being sacrificed for quantity. Is the recruit of today—and tomorrow—to be recognized as one of "superior" caliber rather than an average, or cross-sectional model? "Average" in most lexicons is "fair" or "mediocre." One might ask the further questions: Is the "best available" good enough? Should not the Foreign Service be composed of *exceptional* men and women, every one of whom would stand out in a crowd of diplomats, domestic or foreign? Should not the Foreign Service go all out to attract them? In a country as literate and as filled with opportunity as the United States, the choice should be legion. It is high tribute to the Foreign Service that even if it does represent America in all its highly diverse aspects, it generally excels in its work. But a drift toward mediocrity, in an age when mediocrity is mass produced, must be vigilantly watched if "the best young men that our society produces" is to be the constant rule in producing diplomats.

If there is a clue to the future it may be found in another expected change; the examination and selection process for career officers is due for further revision. The Deputy Undersecretary for Administration has cleared the way by putting forward the ambiguous thesis that "academic excellence is not the only important measure of a man." At a meeting of the Advisory Committee for the Foreign Affairs Training Program at Howard University on December 13, 1963—a program made possible by a $600,000-

Ford Foundation grant to prepare "minority group students," especially those in Negro colleges and including Puerto Ricans and
Indians, for careers in foreign affairs—William J. Crockett forecast a different type of examination "in order to get the kind of
people we need to do the job that has to be done in today's
world." Too often, he explained, young officers enter the Service
with the idea of reporting on political events, or participating in
negotiations, only to find that they are assigned to duties of a routine nature. The Department, therefore, instead of searching for
candidates trained only in political science, wants men and women
with "broad" training who can also fill positions in administration, consular activities, and economic affairs. To all surface appearances, this is not very different from the objectives of the
Rogers Act, the early executors of which subscribed to a belief
that the most effective officers were those who were versatile
enough to serve in a variety of positions, and who fully expected
to do so insofar as their capacities permitted. But the intent here is
different; specifically designed, it would seem, to meet minority
pressures. Of the 3,700-odd Foreign Service Officers in January,
1961, there were only 20 Negroes, the most prominent of whom
was Clifton R. Wharton, Massachusetts-born graduate of Harvard, who rose on merit to be ambassador to Norway. Only 5
more Negroes, all graduates of northern colleges, had succeeded in
meeting the tests and entering the Service during the period
1961–1963. In March, 1964, however, the number had reached
50; in the higher civil service jobs in the Department itself,
Grades 9 to 18, there were 25 Negro officers in 1961, and 58—
more than double—in 1964. It is clear enough that if the Foreign
Service is to be representative of Secretary Rusk's "America as it
is," it must, for instance, contain many more Negroes; and if Negroes have not hitherto had the qualifications, they must either be
assisted in acquiring them, or the entrance hurdles must be lowered a few more notches.

The taxpayer is entitled to wonder whether the foreign service
of the U.S.S.R. represents "Russia as it is," whether its base has
been broadened to include minority groups from Siberia, from the

🏵 🏵

Urals, from Kazakhstan or Uzbekistan—whether the professional career has been debased by lower admission standards and by insistence that "academic excellence is not the only important measure of a man"—or whether its educational requirements are such as to produce only the most superior examples of the new Soviet man to deal with their capitalistic adversaries.

Who Killed Morale?

If the highly selective Foreign Service of the late 1920's and 1930's was a buoyant expeditionary force in the still-limited zones of American diplomacy, the diversified army that now marches into the farthest corners of the earth has nothing like the same morale. The old corps may have had its faults and failures; perhaps it was full of intellectual snobs who felt that their success in passing the stiffest entrance tests yet devised gave them a special standing in Washington circles; perhaps it did transgress the bounds of propriety when a small clique ran the show and meted out the best posts—to themselves included; perhaps it was deficient in some of those other qualities that are an "important measure of the man" besides academic excellence. But at least it demanded, and, as we have noted, nearly always got, the finest talent the country could produce; and the members of that small and exclusive band, carrying a banner with the strange new device of promotion from the bottom as the sole badge of merit, were inspired to show that they deserved the confidence placed in them. They preened themselves on the knowledge that out of a thousand or more applicants, less than two score annually were chosen to fill the places available; and they went to work with enthusiasm and an *esprit de corps* that was notable in government service.

Morale is that "priceless ingredient" in any organization which has to do not only with the mental health of the workers as a whole, but with the attitude of the individual toward his work; it often measures the difference between zest for accomplishment and dispirited routine. The recipient of many heavy blows since the brave and promising start of the career in 1924, morale at the State Department—and particularly in the Foreign Service—is far indeed from what it should be today.

Various matters affect morale, some elusive and undefinable, some obvious and specific. Just as in other walks of life, certain factors, or certain combinations of factors, may depress or elevate the spirit of the Foreign Service Officer. But there has been little to raise the spirit in recent years and a great deal to lower it. The wonder is that anything like the high dedication characteristic of most officers has survived.

Not surprisingly, the cooky pusher smarts under the implications of that misnomer because it betokens an unjustified lack of confidence on the part of the public and the press. He feels that his profession is suspect; that he himself is not respected; that he is always a target for criticism, seldom the beneficiary of an accolade; and frequently, that his Department is bypassed, disparaged, or deprived of authority and prestige by either the White House or the Congress, or both. Perhaps it is our federal system that is at fault, but the impression prevails that the State Department is complete master in its own house and therefore fully responsible for its actions; that the Secretary of State is completely the initiator of foreign policy. The fact that they are not in no wise lessens the responsibility fastened upon them by the public. The Secretary of Defense can dictate policy in South Asia, but the State Department is a convenient scapegoat if the political situation goes from bad to worse; the administration can get the credit for economic aid to Laos, but the Foreign Service may get roundly censured if local graft and corruption taint the use of the funds.

Under the suspicious eye of Congress, a policy maker may become nervous and overcautious because of the possibility of stirring up a storm. Now and then he may take what seems to be a wrong turn; being human, he may sometimes err in judgment. Yet instead of being allowed to practice undisturbed and un-

🏵 🏵

heckled the profession for which his Department was created, he is
constantly being haled into court under arraignment of politically
motivated or ill-informed critics. It is no lift to the morale when
the sensational press runs blistering headlines about the collapse of
some pet policy, and rarely if ever tosses a verbal bouquet in the
direction of those who achieve an occasional beachhead in the
struggle for peace.

The Foreign Service has no defense against detractors, much less
the means to enlist sympathy for itself as a body of faithful and
conscientious public servants. It suffers in silence while the slings
and arrows of outraged criticism rain down upon it. For the sad
truth is that the State Department and its overseas arm, the Foreign Service, have no constituents.

Not only does the Service lack natural backers in any segment
of the population, it is totally without organized support in the
style which special interests take for granted. Congress from the
beginning has been accustomed to act under pressure from lobby-
ists. Logrollers, sectional pleaders, high-powered seekers of sub-
sidies or other benefits, all are familiar figures on the Capital stage.
Registered agents of foreign governments freely spread their propaganda, public-relations firms do a brisk business for their clients
in the very shadow of the dome. But no citizens' committee promotes the cause of the Foreign Service, no militant union demands
a higher wage scale for employees of the State Department, no
group of patriots attempts to create a favorable sentiment in Congress or the country. A career that is dedicated to the proposition
that peace is more important than war finds itself an orphan in a
wilderness of indifference.

Under the inspiration of a former ambassador, Arthur Bliss
Lane of New York, an effort was made a few years ago to enlist
support among the people for a Foreign Service League. The proposed organization was modeled along the lines of the Navy
League, which at the height of its success had thousands of enthusiastic members agitating for bigger and better battleships; the
specific objective of the Foreign Service League was to awaken interest in, and to spread information about, our department of for-

eign affairs. The theory of its founders was that, despite the growing number of Americans who now enter some form of service abroad, the duties of an ambassador, a secretary of embassy, or a consul were largely unintelligible to their stay-at-home countrymen. At best, it is a baffling business to describe the profession; but much could be done, it was thought, by imaginative private effort to convey to Americans an idea of the services rendered to them both at home and abroad by their Department of State.

The Foreign Service League was launched; the response, however, save from those already converted, was pitifully small. After spending the few donations it received, for publicity and recruitment, the infant league gave up the ghost. Its assets, consisting of exactly $1,821.18, were turned over to the only persons who cared—members of a society for retired diplomatic and consular officials, to be used for repairs to their Washington clubhouse.

The nearest approach to a concerted move for the promotion of the career is the American Foreign Service Association. To quote from the masthead of its organ, the *Foreign Service Journal,* the association is "composed of active and retired personnel who are or have been serving at home or abroad. . . . It groups together people who have a common responsibility for the implementation of foreign policy. It seeks to encourage the development of a career service of maximum effectiveness, and to advance the welfare of its members." Obviously, however, an association composed in major part of still active government workers can carry no torches that might cast an unfavorable light on policies of the administration which employs them. Through the editorial columns of the *Journal* it can and does question certain Departmental or Congressional policies and practices, but any editor of the magazine would lay his head on the block if he dared print an article that ran counter to the official party line. The party line, of course, is the line of the party in power—whether on ramifications of the Cold War, on relations with the public, or on intramural matters. As a result, the *Journal,* like the upper echelons of the Department, has one ear cocked in the direction of an invisible

censor; it says only what a dutiful government employee can be
expected to say, not what he may actually think.

To be sure, the *Journal* strives to be constructively critical
when it feels it can do so safely. It features a "Department of Dissent" for those who take exception to various administrative procedures; some of the views it has expressed over the years have
been bold enough to warrant a reprint in the daily press. But as
long as the publication is managed by those still in the Service, its
editorial staff can never escape the feeling that big brother is
watching over its shoulder. Neither the American Foreign Service
Association nor the State Department Employees Association—the
indigenous equivalent of a union for the clerical personnel—has
the money or the nerve to make an overt bid for recognition and
reward by the masses.

Tinkering with the Foreign Service has long been a habit of the
legislative branch; nor was it broken by passage of the act of
1924. The Rogers Act, as we have seen, was the foundation on
which the modern edifice was designed to rest; but it was not allowed to rest long. To be fair, the aim of the legislators has naturally been to improve and strengthen the structure, and they cannot always be blamed if their efforts have coincided with events
that have had an unsettling effect on morale. In 1931, for instance, the Moses-Linthicum Act gave the Service a boost by revis-
ing the pay and allowance schedules, which were palpably out of
step with the rising costs of living. It was not the fault of Senator
George H. Moses and Representative John C. Linthicum that the
tonic properties of this piece of legislation were immediately dissi-
pated by devaluation of the dollar and by administrative retrenchments caused by the depression. Morale in the underpaid
Foreign Service naturally suffered; a reduction in force—the first
of several "RIF's" (Reduction in Force) to come—a 15 per cent
pay cut, and the elimination or reduction of allowances caused
added distress. In December, 1934, the number of Foreign Service Officers had dropped from 762 to 688, or almost 10 per cent;
no one entered the Service for four years because of lack of funds

for recruitment. Although the Service had regained most of its losses before war began in 1939, the ingrained lesson of economy was so taken to heart that those in charge of the Department's budget continued the policy of asking Congress only for just enough to struggle along. As we have noted in a previous chapter, the wartime Auxiliary and the postwar Manpower and Reorganization Acts, all in the nature of emergency measures, did not reassure the diplomats, who saw the merit principle vitiated by entry at the middle grades. Their uneasiness was increased following a diagnosis—fallacious on two counts—by the Hoover Commission on Government Personnel in 1949, and a high-powered Advisory Committee in 1950—to the effect (1) that the home staff and the Foreign Service were not getting on well together, and (2) that every member of the Department was qualified for and desirous of service abroad. As a means of pumping new vitality into the blood stream of a starved and impoverished Foreign Service and giving it strength to carry its new load of leadership in world affairs, the board of consulting physicians prescribed a remedy: amalgamation with the Washington personnel. This was to be accomplished gradually, over a period of years—with the caveat by a wise member of the panel, Secretary of Defense James V. Forrestal, that it should "not be permitted to operate so as to destroy the morale or spirit of either group."

Service abroad and service at home had hitherto been distinct and separate, although complementary to each other. Officers in the Foreign Service could be brought back for temporary duty at home, but the home staff was permanently put, with no thought of duty overseas. Understandably, the prospect of round pegs being thrust into square holes and square pegs into round holes was not a pleasant prospect to the career. The difficulties of inducing a reluctant patient to accept his medicine need not be detailed here, but the program progressed only slowly over the years; so slowly, in fact, that its sponsors felt that the carrot, unaccompanied by the stick, was not enough.

A step was then taken which not only struck at the roots of a system supposedly based on competence and merit, but helped materially to undermine the morale of the career. The Director General of the Foreign Service, a career officer in the direct chain of command from the top, was stripped of his authority and prestige and relegated to the emasculated position he occupies today, an innocuous advisor on policy to the Deputy Undersecretary for Administration. An impartial supervisor of recruitment, promotion, field organization, and assignments, the Director General was a stalwart defender of career principles against personnel preferment or other unsound administrative practices that tampered with the integrity of the career by influence or favoritism. His independence of action did not suit those whose interest lay in an amalgamated establishment—to include not only the home service but the left-over staffs of such wartime agencies as OWI, OSS, and Lend-Lease.

It was not the first time that an attempt had been made to assault the integrity of the career. When Cordell Hull was still new to his administrative duties and responsibilities, he was shown one day a letter from Democratic Chairman James A. Farley asking that the counselor of embassy at Paris, an experienced career man, be moved out and the first secretary of the embassy, likewise of the career but contributor of ten thousand dollars to the party fund, be moved up to take his place. Hull asked the Chief of Personnel if the Secretary of State possessed the authority to grant this request, which seemed reasonable enough to him. Yes, he had the authority; but, said the chief, the Secretary could get a new Chief of Personnel if that was the way the career was to be run. To the lasting credit of both, no such change took place; and Chief Homer M. Byington gained new stature as a defender of the career principle.

However, it was one thing to stand fast against the purchase of advancement with cash; but in the move to downgrade the Director General, career officers saw an ominous sign that their profession was doomed to dilution by the incorporation of semiqualified, quasi-experienced officers lacking in the strict Foreign Service requirements of general background and education. They saw a specialist in tariff negotiations, for instance, with no more relish for living abroad than the man from Missouri, uprooted from Washington and sent to an isolated embassy behind the Iron Curtain; they saw an officer skilled in the intricacies of Korean politics ordered home to deal with the tariff question. "Interchangeability" was another word for amalgamation; and the Foreign Service, which could also foresee the managerial revolution to follow in the wake of such a far-reaching change, felt that it was in for more than its share of encroachment by the administrators. Its morale was affected accordingly.

The architect chiefly responsible for the alterations which were presently to modify the original structure was a politically appointed official named John Peurifoy, who was fond of mentioning that he had started life as an elevator boy on Capitol Hill and who, twenty-five years after enactment of Congressman Rogers' legislation, found himself with the title of Assistant Secretary of State for Administration. Peurifoy lost no time in announcing that amalgamation of the Foreign Service with the permanent home guard in the Department would be his "monument." The fact that he was prematurely and tragically killed while driving his car at a high rate of speed as United States ambassador to Thailand was in no wise to interfere with the fulfillment of that ambition.

It remained for a committee headed by Henry M. Wriston, at that time president of Brown University, to apply the shock treatment in full. Taking a long breath in its opening statement, the Wriston Committee announced in 1954 that it had been set up "for the purpose of making recommendations to the Secretary of State concerning the measures necessary to strengthen the effectiveness of the professional service to a standard consistent with the vastly increased responsibilities in the field of foreign policy which have devolved upon the President and the Secretary." One of the by-products of the New Deal was the word "gobbledygook," denoting a method of speech which expressed in official terms what could be said much more simply in plain English. What the committee could have said, quite simply, was that a decision had been reached by Secretary of State Dulles that the two types of service would have to be joined in shotgun marriage.

In making its recommendations, the Wriston Committee decided that "perhaps the most serious single contributing cause" of the decline in Foreign Service morale had been "the absence of strong administrative leadership within the Department of State and the Foreign Service—a void which has resulted in poor management of the Service." Whether that harsh criticism was justified or not, the effect of the decision to amalgamate was to shatter morale still further. By the addition of hundreds of civil servants in the Department, the preferred stock of the original Foreign Service had suddenly become watered stock; the promotion system continued to operate, but something new had been added— the possibility of promotions in a "career" that could start at any time, up to and including the pinnacle grade of Class I.

"Wristonization"—which one young vice consul's bride innocently construed as some form of "sterilization"—was a severe setback to the prideful career service; but before it was officially decreed, a much more serious development had occurred which virtually demolished morale in the Service, both abroad and at home.

On February 9, 1950, Senator Joseph R. McCarthy, Republican of Wisconsin, confronted an audience at Wheeling, West Virginia, with this shockingly irresponsible statement: "I have in my hand a list of 205 that were known to the Secretary of State as being members of the Communist party and who, nevertheless, are still working and shaping the policy in the State Department."

No purpose is served today by beating the dead horse of McCarthyism, which fortunately lies in the limbo of odious memories. For Americans, however, it is important to remember what did—and what could again—happen here. McCarthy launched an all-out attack that drove from public life such lifetime experts as John Carter Vincent and other "old China hands"; viciously slandered the astute Russian specialist Charles E. ("Chip") Bohlen, later ambassador to the USSR and France; impugned the loyalty and caused the resignation of senior officers regardless of their anti-Communist records; hounded out of the Service men who may have erred in judgment but who were never subversive; caused one officer to die of a heart attack; sent to the bonfire books mentioning communism in the libraries of the United States Information Service; and frightened officers in the field into writing colorless political reports that ran no possible danger of being interpreted later as leanings to the left. For all the bluster and demagoguery which ensued over the next few years, not a single spy was exposed in the American Foreign Service—not a single Communist, such as Britain's Guy Burgess and Donald MacLean. But it left us barren of firsthand experience in the Far East, the most critical area of the world today; and the damage to America's prestige and to the morale of the Service was nearly irreparable.

The McCarthy clean-up program was carried out in the State Department by a deceptively amiable proctor, R. W. Scott McLeod, former police reporter on the *Cedar Rapids Gazette* and onetime FBI agent in Concord, New Hampshire, who owed his appearance on the Washington scene to the extreme right wing Republican Senator Styles Bridges. In 1953, McLeod was installed in a paneled suite on the fourth floor of the State Department, in undisputed control of Security, Consular Affairs, Inspection and—indirectly—the sacred, hitherto untouchable Office of Personnel. There he began what the *Reporter* magazine has called "the most intensive intramural investigation undertaken in the history of our government—a 'full field' study, within the space of a year, of every single member of the Department's . . . eleven-thousand-person complement, from ambassadors down to supply clerks, in Washington and scattered among 267 diplomatic and consular posts abroad."

Flying teams of investigators fanned out across the globe to interrogate chiefs of mission and investigate their staffs on the slenderest suspicion of having leftist connections, of drinking too much or too often, of deviation in sex habits. Whispers of secret dossiers, of denunciations, of the "development of derogatory in-

❦ ❦

formation"—to use McLeod's expression—filled the corridors of the government's No. 1 civilian agency at home. Instead of frank observations based on personal familiarity with the Communist menace, many officers in the field began to feed into the pipelines a bland mixture of what was thought acceptable and in conformity with the temper of the times; those who fearlessly continued to report the truth risked unpredictable consequences. Foreign diplomats in Washington complained that they could no longer obtain an opinion or a policy statement from their customary contacts in the State Department. A cartoon in the *St. Louis Post-Dispatch* caught the fear-ridden atmosphere with a row of wooden dummies in striped pants stashed away against the wall of a "Career Officers' Club."

Senator McCarthy presided over the disintegration of Foreign Service morale with a persistence and determination worthy of a less ignoble cause. As his assistants, Roy M. Cohn and G. David Schine, grubbed around the back yards of our European posts for incriminating gossip, the McCarthy name became as well known as Eisenhower's; in some circles abroad McCarthyism superseded the Statue of Liberty as the symbol of America. Almost, it seemed as if Lenin's prophecy had come true: "When the American bourgeoisie, having completely lost its head, seizes thousands and thousands of people on suspicion of bolshevism and creates an atmosphere of panic, spreading broadcast alarming stories about Bolshevik plots . . . we must bow and thank messieurs the capitalists. They are working for us."

Torn between career and conscience, Foreign Service Officers debated whether they should compromise their futures by reporting what they saw or heard without inhibition or mental reservation, or whether they should resign to seek fields where their talents would be less circumscribed and their personal conclusions on Communist policies less likely to condemn them as loyalty risks. "If there are disloyal members among us," pleaded the *Foreign Service Journal,* "no one will resist their removal forthwith, but if the rest of us are loyal, let the Department have the courage to defend our loyalty and to reaffirm a creed of the Foreign Ser-

🏵 🏵

vice . . . to know our enemies as well as to cultivate our friends."
Unhappily, this appeal fell on ears that were at least partially
stuffed with politician's wax. For reasons of political expediency,
the rule of McCarthy and McLeod was permitted to proceed un-
checked; courage was lamentably lacking in the highest places;
and, saddest of sad, Secretary of State Dulles himself failed to go
to the defense of his officers at any time, either individually or collectively. Dulles, in fact, had got off to an inauspicious start as
Secretary in 1953, when, instead of greeting the Service with
words of encouragement or praise, he demanded a "positive loyalty" to the Republican administration and its policies after, as he
phrased it, twenty years of allegiance owed to another party. Such
an astonishing misconception of the role of the Foreign Service,
whose loyalty, of course, is solely to the United States government
and not to any political party, had taught its officers they could
expect no cudgels to be taken up in their behalf at the top.

As morale fell to an all-time low, confidence in the Service as a
career sank correspondingly. In the three years preceding Mc-
Carthy's charge that there were traitors in the State Department,
the number of candidates who took the Foreign Service examinations averaged around 1,200; in 1950, at the very moment when
the need for new recruits was greatest, the number dropped, like
a barometer falling before the storm—to an ominous 807; in 1951
to only 758. In this extremity, recruiting teams were organized
for the first time, to take to the hustings and deliver sales talks to
the graduating classes of colleges and universities—a fixture ever
since, and one which the Service could scarcely do without today
in its competition with private industry.

As the *New York Times* put it, McCarthy

and some other leather-lunged committee-room brawlers have raised at
least two questions in youthful minds: first, is the Foreign Service so
infested with sin and error that no high minded young man should join
it; second, even if the Foreign Service is as pure as the driven snow and
as right as the Ten Commandments, is it worth a young man's while to
expose himself to the insolence and the insults, the snooping and the

gum-shoeing that are inflicted on those who seek responsible jobs in the so-called "sensitive" federal agencies? . . . The State Department can be, and sometimes is, stuffy and inefficient. The remedy for that failing is a higher standard of intellect and performance all along the line, which means making the Foreign Service attractive to gifted and devoted young men.

Not only were gifted and devoted young men put off by the hazard of having their careers blighted, should they happen to disagree with McCarthy, but—in contrast to the wholesale study of English promoted by Moscow after the war—prospective students were afraid to sign up for courses in the Russian language, in the sources of Soviet communism, or in Russian literature. The mere attempt to learn might be interpreted as a leftist orientation; even to ask for a copy of the *Communist Manifesto* by Karl Marx and Friedrich Engels was enough to raise a wary eyebrow in the library of the State Department.

Although no one who earned his living from the government dared to speak out against the hysteria, the collective voice of five distinguished former diplomats was at length raised in behalf of a demoralized Service. Former Ambassadors Norman Armour, Robert Woods Bliss, Joseph C. Grew, and William Phillips, and former Assistant Secretary G. Howland Shaw valiantly attacked what they called the forces working for "conformity from the outside." In a letter to the *New York Times* on January 14, 1954, which made front-page news, they warned that the State Department's personnel and security policies were "laying the foundation of a Foreign Service competent to serve a totalitarian government rather than the Government of the United States as we have known it." The five experts, none of whom was identified with a particular political party, pointed out that the normal conduct of personnel affairs was being subordinated to exaggerated notions of security. "When any such tendency begins its insidious work, it is not long before accuracy and initiative have been sacrificed. . . . The ultimate result is a threat to the national security." Attacks on the Foreign Service were characterized as "so flimsy as to have no standing in a court of law or in the mind of any individual capable of differentiating repeated accusation from even a reasonable presumption of guilt."

The authors of the letter predicted, only too accurately, that an officer who in good faith recommended actions he believed to be in the best interests of his country might subsequently find his motives challenged and be forced from the Service, discredited in the eyes of his fellow citizens. Before the year was out, John Paton Davies, a career diplomat of twenty-three years' standing, was dismissed from the federal government by Secretary Dulles—not for being "soft on communism" but because in the judgment of a specially convened Security Board, he was "lacking in judgment." Dulles tried to sugar-coat the verdict by saying that although he did not doubt the personal loyalty of this officer—who in the best traditions of a police state had been investigated and cleared eight times previously—he agreed with the finding of the board that the continued employment of Davies was not "clearly consistent with the interests of the national security."

Davies was found guilty of thinking what Senator J. William Fulbright would today call "unthinkable thoughts"—of a daring in dissent which led him to express doubts about the ability of Chiang Kai-shek to hold China against Mao Tse-tung. This led him into conflict with official opinion as to the proper American policy on China. He was also convicted of making contact with known or suspected Communists in order, as Davies explained with elementary logic, to obtain information about communism. Although close collaborators of Davies on the Policy Planning Staff, headed by the Department's top Soviet scholar, George F. Kennan, had placed on the record a memorandum testifying to Davies' integrity, inventiveness, and insight—qualities without price, one might think, in a diplomat of career—the action was unavailing. Davies' dismissal dimmed still further the all-but-extinguished flame of Foreign Service morale. It made mincemeat of President Eisenhower's exhortation to the Service a few days earlier when, ironically enough, he had spoken of the "glorious opportunities ahead" and the need for "the highest morale based firmly on . . . [the Service's] . . . own convictions as to the importance of its work." To a dismayed and discouraged career, these fine words were a mockery in view of what McCarthy had done to the Service.

"An ounce of loyalty is worth more than a pound of brains" was the Elbert Hubbard motto that graced the desk of Scott Mc-Leod's chief secretary, a former woman athlete named Gwen Lewis. The witch hunt which McLeod carried out not only eliminated some of the ablest men in the Foreign Service, but, if it proved anything, showed that for every ounce of brains so employed there existed a good deal more than a pound of loyalty.

As if the McCarthy-McLeod inquisition was not enough to break the spirit of the Service, the Wriston Committee in the summer of 1954 issued its decree that the career henceforth should be indivisible with the Department's home staff. "The Foreign Service has been retarded in its development," announced Chairman Wriston, "by a persistent belief that promotion from the bottom is the only true incentive and that incursions of elements from the outside into the higher grades would seriously impair both incentives and morale." With these words, the bell tolled for Congressman Rogers' career principle. Like other career chiefs of mission who had spent the better part of their lives in the "persistent belief that promotion from the bottom" was the only sound way to reach the top, I was offered a chance to speak out before the forcible marriage was consummated. I might have saved my breath—or the time spent in submitting a written opinion—for the ceremony had already been rigged. Most members of the career believed that more time should be allowed for the nuptials, five years at the minimum, or preferably ten, as the British were taking to reach the same ends. Further, it was feared that morale could only be damaged if individuals joined the Service on an involuntary basis. But logic and reasoning had no effect; every argument of the career was summarily brushed aside. The outraged Executive Secretary of the Foreign Service Association expressed the sentiment of many with a story about the pupil in the fourth grade who worked hard on the ten problems of his mathematics test, was the last to turn in his paper, and got every answer wrong. "Don't you think," began the teacher, "if you had worked a little harder . . . " "Sorry," the little boy interrupted, "but I had to work like hell to make that zero."

Only the threat of a fate worse than "interchangeability" offered some measure of consolation, for a scheme was afoot to abolish the separate identity of the Foreign Service and prepare it for absorption—and thus for obliteration as a distinctive career—into the greatest bureaucracy on earth, the United States Civil Service.

The mandatory merger of those who had no training or inclination for service abroad with those who had both, but no desire to serve at home, was a radical remedy for whatever was wrong. With nearly 1,500 "career" positions suddenly presented to Washington officeholders, those middle-aged homebodies who did not choose to accept a change of life were invited to seek other employment. There were at that time 1,285 regular Foreign Service Officers on duty; the act of integration designated 1,450 positions in the home office and 2,239 at overseas posts—a total of 3,689—as Foreign Service Officer positions, so that the size, but not necessarily the strength, of the Service was nearly tripled overnight.

Whether the Service had been "retarded in its development" or not, Wriston was right in one respect; incursions of outside elements seriously impaired morale. Regardless of the question of individual qualifications, as between regular Washington employees and career men, the cherished concept of a professional career based on promotion from the ground up went by the board. What was the point of working your way up from the bottom when you could enter, without much trouble, in the middle or near the top and take up your "career" from there? It was found advisable to brief stunned members of the corps by word of mouth in order to obtain prompt "understanding" of the far-reaching decision. High-ranking officers carried the message to Latin America, Europe, and distant Asian posts. In a report dated October 12, 1954, the Wriston Committee concluded that this "expression of the Department's interest" had had a "beneficial" effect on morale, but conceded that resistance to the program persisted "among some segments of the personnel." Resistance, of course, is futile against a bureaucratic steam roller; it was soon stamped out entirely by further "explanations" of personnel policies and actions under the Wriston program.

Time heals all wounds; but it will be many more years before the generation that remembers the old career has died out. Despite the injury to its self-esteem and its morale, the Foreign Service has doggedly carried on; being a versatile and resilient body in the first place, its powers of recuperation are extraordinary. It has adapted itself to the facts of life. The "Wristonee" is now part of the same team, and, in most cases, an accepted contributor to the development of the Service.

But of late the rich old blood has been further diluted. At a White House news conference on October 3, 1964, President Johnson announced that the vast majority—some 900—of the United States Information Agency's Foreign Service Career Reserve officers would henceforth be "an integral part of the Foreign Service." These men and women, to be known as Foreign Information Officers, will carry the specialist's art into still another realm—"public affairs" with all which that connotes in respect to press, radio, television, films, exhibits, libraries, and cultural contacts. Although most of the agency's personnel stationed abroad have been of high caliber, and as devoted to the interests of the United States as the most conscientious career officer, it would have stretched the imagination of Congressman Rogers to the limit if he had been asked to consider the integration of those who made propaganda their profession with the exclusive Foreign Service of the Department of State, or told they would be designated as diplomats overnight, carry diplomatic passports, and be eligible in due course for promotion to the rank of ambassador.

As in the case of Wristonization, the adulteration of the original Rogers Act by large doses of extraneous personnel cannot be expected to improve the morale of purists who have thought of diplomacy as one of the stricter disciplines. They see themselves inundated—yesterday by the home staff, today by a formidable information corps, and tomorrow, no doubt, by those who have made a career out of foreign aid. In fact, the last two steps were presaged in the report of the Committee on Foreign Affairs Personnel headed by former Secretary of State Christian A. Herter, which a few years ago made a comprehensive study of State, the United States Information Agency, and the Agency for International Development, and recommended the development of a "family" of "compatible services."

Whether the "family" will prove "compatible" or not, the tinkering has gone to even greater lengths. On March 15, 1965, Congressman Wayne Hays of Ohio introduced for the Johnson administration a bill, H.R. 6277, to establish an entirely new foreign service personnel system. This bill would transfer some 19,000 civil service employees of State, USIA, and AID to a "simple," "unified," "uniform" foreign service system designed to serve the needs—domestic as well as overseas—of *all* agencies engaged in the business of foreign affairs. In other words, all foreign service employees would be interchangeable, and Foreign Service Officers of the United States, instead of serving State alone, would be available for duty in whatever agency where the need might happen to arise. A more radical departure from the distinctive concepts of the Rogers Act could scarcely be imagined.

Only the future can tell if the high degree of elasticity now applied to the term "diplomat" will in the long run strengthen the morale of the Foreign Service or the reverse. Meanwhile, however, other factors, such as the growing bureaucratic jungle and the difficulty of finding reward at the top, tend to prohibit complete restoration of the spirit. The former has already been discussed; the latter will be considered in the next chapter.

American Ambassador

"I have in my pocket the key to the back door of the White House," quipped the ambassador under whom I was serving in Norway, "and it's worth more than thirty million dollars." C. Ulrick Bay, president of Bay Petroleum, majority stockholder of American Export Lines, senior partner of A. M. Kidder and Company in Wall Street, and inheritor of the fortune made by Bay's Bandages, had contributed a part of his thirty millions to the Democratic National Committee; in return, he had been nominated by President Truman for a post which a career officer could have filled with distinction. The Senate had given its advice and consent without questioning the competence of the nominee as a diplomat; and Ambassador Bay was free to spend months at a stretch in New York and Palm Beach, or racing his yacht in Norwegian waters. In Oslo, incidentally, he was known to the diplomatic corps as the "ambassador ad interim."

William Howard Taft was the first, and may go down in history as the only, President to decry publicly a system that lets the rich pay for the privilege of representing their nation abroad. "We boast ourselves a democratic country," he told a National Board of Trade Meeting in 1910. "We say that there is no place within the gift of the people to which we may not elect the most humble inhabitant, providing he be fit to discharge its duty, and yet we have an arrangement which makes it absolutely impossible for anybody but a millionaire to occupy the highest diplomatic post."

Nothing has ever been done to change the "arrangement" whereby expensive posts are filled by the "fat cats"; it has always been possible to purchase an embassy for cash on the barrel head. Congress could alter the situation at any time by appropriating the funds to run diplomatic establishments which are beyond the means of a career man and insisting that career men should fill them; but no congressman has ever tried to force a showdown in the notorious 'arrangement"—neither Democrat nor Republican.

From time to time lists reach the public of donations to the party treasury by ambassadorial appointees. Such a list was compiled by the Senate Subcommittee on Privileges and Elections in February, 1957; it showed that nineteen individuals who had acquired the title of ambassador had given a combined total of nearly a quarter of a million dollars to the 1956 Republican campaign fund. Among the subscribers was Maxwell H. Gluck, who, in effect, had bought the post of ambassador extraordinary and plenipotentiary to Ceylon for $21,500. Since Gluck's appointment became a *cause célèbre* at the time, it will serve as well as any to illustrate what happens when a diplomatic post is awarded to one who, without any other recommendation, has helped to replenish the coffers of the winning party at the polls.

When Gluck—"it rhymes with luck"—head of a large clothing chain in Ohio, breeder of race horses in Kentucky, and resident of New York City, appeared before the Senate Foreign Relations Committee for confirmation of his appointment, he was unlucky enough to run afoul of the first objection in decades to a diplomatic nomination. Singled out for more than rubber-stamp approval, he was asked to name the prime minister of the country to which he was about to be accredited; it was an uncommon name, Bandaranaike, and he flunked the test. Further, Gluck had never heard of the fact that Ceylon was one of five signatories of a highly topical United Nations report on Hungary; and he demonstrated an abysmal lack of knowledge concerning the affairs of the strategic area where he was to serve as a principal representative of the United States. The quiz period in this instance was conducted by Senator J. William Fulbright of Arkansas, who cast a solitary vote in disagreement with the nomination; but despite this embarrassing performance, Gluck was confirmed, went to Colombo, entertained pleasantly, left the work to the trained members of his staff, and when he departed, barely a year later, made an indelible impression on local sensibilities by allowing his wife to dispose of her surplus clothing at public auction. The Ceylonese are a polite people and held their peace; but they quietly underlined the State Department's chagrin by sending as ambassador to Washington one of their most brilliant personalities, as admirably fitted for public life as Ambassador Gluck was not.

Although the Gluck episode exploded into editorials and ignited a train of indignant press comment about amateurs who were unprepared or unfit for the demanding role of ambassador, it proved a dud as far as curbing such nominations was concerned. The Republicans under Eisenhower received the blame; and Senator Joseph S. Clark of Pennsylvania, a Democrat, took the lead in deploring the appointment of persons "utterly without qualification" merely because they had made large contributions to the Republican campaign fund. Such protests, however, have a hollow and partisan ring, for Congress knows perfectly well where the remedy lies. In 1962, it was the Democrats' turn. Matthew H. McCloskey, the party treasurer, was named ambassador to Ireland; and less than two years later, to the well-concealed blushes of the administration, the Associated Press carried a dispatch that began as follows: "The Federal Government today filed a suit for $4.9 million against a Philadelphia construction firm headed by Matthew H. McCloskey, and two Boston firms, for alleged defects in construction of the Veterans Hospital in Boston. McCloskey, long prominent in Democratic Party affairs, resigned recently as Ambassador to Ireland to help the Democrats raise funds for this year's election campaign." McCloskey might better have remained in Ireland, for the Washington stadium-Bobby Baker scandal was to blazon his name in the public prints only a short while later.

Politics being what they are, the Foreign Relations Committee seems able to forget quickly whatever it learns about diplomatic qualifications for diplomatic posts. When President Kennedy sent up the nomination of a Democratic party friend, breeder of livestock and manufacturer of serum, William True Davis, Jr. of St. Joseph, Missouri, as ambassador to Switzerland, at its politically sensitive capital of Bern, it was duly confirmed. Past president of the Animal Health Institute, member of the National Livestock Association, and other veterinarian organizations as listed in his *Who's Who* biography, Davis was supported by Missouri Senator Stuart Symington on the ground that not only was he a successful businessman, but that his sister was married to a successful businessman. Nor was there any difficulty in obtaining approval for President Johnson's special assistant Ralph A. Dungan as ambassador to Chile, whose recommendation lay in the fact that he came to the White House in 1961 as special assistant to President Kennedy. Or for Virginia horse breeder Raymond R. Guest as ambassador to Ireland, who, in response to a question from Senator George D. Aiken of Vermont, undertook to explain Ireland's role in NATO. The only trouble with his answer was that Ireland is not a member of NATO.

As we have seen in Chapter V, the Department is continually put upon to take into its fold the politicians' preferences. Just as it must assimilate the administration's candidates in its highest Washington posts, so must it accept as chiefs of mission those whom the national committeemen decide are deserving of reward. In the Eisenhower era, for example, a representative of the Republican party was assigned to the State Department for the express purpose of picking plums off the ambassadorial tree for deserving politicians. While he was about it, he picked one for himself, thereby dislodging the incumbent; it happened, incidentally, that I was the one he dislodged—and there was nothing that career officials could do about it.

To the victor at the polls, as always, belongs the spoils; and the spoils have always included ambassadorships. The Department's role is that of a passive agent: transmitting to the government concerned the request for an *agrément*—asking, in other words, whether the nomination of an ambassador is acceptable. Few countries would care to reject a nominee of the powerful United States, even if not enthusiastic about his qualifications; but once in a blue moon an *agrément* is refused. The Swiss government, for instance, balked at accepting Earle E. T. Smith, a former political appointee to Batista's Cuba, for the excellent reason that Switzerland, at our request, was handling American interests in Castro's Havana and the past associations of Smith might have proved embarrassing. In the end, notwithstanding White House displeasure, Switzerland turned down the nomination—which was more than the State Department could have done.

But political favoritism has gone a step farther. On the eve of the British elections of 1964, the deputy chief of mission in London, a career officer, was dislodged by a professor of international labor relations, who had started his career at the top as ambassador to a new African country. Although this might have been a calculated move to anticipate the victory of the British Labour party and thus to gain praise for the United States, it completely shattered all Foreign Service precedents; never before had the key number two spot in an embassy been given to an outsider. At the same time, the next most important position at London—that of chief of the political section—was also lost to the career. If the practice of naming ambassadors on the strength of their political connections should be extended to their deputies as well, the incentive to pursue a career up the ladder of the Foreign Service will be just that much less.

Although some political envoys have impressed foreigners favorably and, with a helping hand or seeing eye from the staff, have carried off the masquerade successfully, there have been others who have profaned the role of ambassador by their behavior. The gaucheries and vulgarities of Ambassador to Spain Alexander P. Moore, once married to the famous actress Lillian Russell, were legion; on television today they would appall any American who valued the good name of his country. Herbert

Hoover in his memoirs says: "During my journey I had oppor- tunity to observe the character of our Ministers and representa- tives. Some of them were 'career' men doing excellent service. But some were political appointees who were eyesores both to the countries to which they were accredited and to us."

In the unpublished, and unpublishable, chronicles of the For- eign Service are numerous examples of these "eyesores"—who have hurt the American image by their personal habits, by un- pardonable breaches in manners or morals, or by errors in negotia- tion from which they have been rescued in the nick of time by their staff. We have had an ambassador in South America who imbibed so heavily that he fell flat on the embassy floor, an am- bassador in Portugal who propelled whipped cream into a lady's bosom across the dinner table, an ambassador in the Netherlands who was known as "Herman the Hormone" because of his propensity for pinching the behind of any girl within reach. Ambassadors from the career, by contrast, are not given to such antics; they do not transgress the rules because they know they are subject to discipline, whereas political appointees who have a key to the back door of the White House are not.

Every so often the Foreign Service is beguiled by promises of reform at the top; but it has long since learned to discount cam- paign oratory on the subject. At Springfield, Ohio, on October 17, 1960, candidate for President John F. Kennedy said that "campaign contributions will not be regarded as a substitute for training and experience for diplomatic positions . . . senior posi- tions in the State Department; the Foreign Service . . . shall be filled from the ranks of career diplomats. . . . I do not want our politics colored by considerations of national security, and I do not want our national security colored by considerations of poli- tics." This moved the *Chicago Daily News* to comment, when the McCloskey appointment was announced: "We have no doubt that McCloskey is an estimable gentleman. But again the score is one for old-fashioned spoils politics and nothing for pretensions that a more admirable standard will prevail."

Because the barter of diplomatic posts so vitally affects the morale and effectiveness of the career, President Kennedy is worth quoting again. Addressing the American Foreign Service Association on May 31, 1962, he expressed the view that "there is a place for the non-career Ambassador—not for political reasons, *but when he happens to be the best man available; . . .* my feeling is we should send career men, to the maximum extent possible, *unless there happen to be special skills which a non-career officer holds*" [author's italics]. No one, however, bothered to explain the "special skills" of that "estimable gentleman, " Ambassador McCloskey, which could not have been found in a top-ranking officer of career and which made McCloskey the "best man available" for the Dublin post. Or, for that matter, of another "estimable gentleman," William C. Doherty, retired president of the National Association of Letter Carriers and a senior vice president of the AFL-CIO, who became our first ambassador to Jamaica in October, 1962, and resigned a year and a half later; or of an estimable lady, Mrs. Katharine Elkus White, chairman of the New Jersey Highway Authority, which operates the Garden State Parkway, nominated by President Johnson as ambassador to Denmark in 1964. There is no need to go on; the list of those who have sprung full-blown from the brow of a President is endless.

It is not easy to understand precisely why a politician's mouth should water at the prospect of a diplomatic plum, except, as one incumbent put it, "Because I was bored and my wife wanted to do some entertaining." To be the big American frog in a foreign puddle may appeal to the vanity of some; curiosity or a quest for adventure may spark the ambition of others; a frustrated desire to be of public service may sincerely animate a few. In his personal capacity, the political ambassador may be an upstanding, patriotic, and engaging citizen; no one can say that the course of history would have been different had he stayed at home. But the outsider soon discovers, estimable gentleman though he may be, that he does not rate as a full member of the club, whether with his own trained staff or with his sophisticated associates in the diplomatic corps; that he is out of his depth in the lingo of international politics; and that the faintly condescending foreign office with which he deals is fully aware that money or connections, not diplomatic skill, got him where he was.

Whatever he may think of the amateur ambassador, it is hardly prudent for a career man to say it aloud, for the chief of mission holds in the hollow of his hand the efficiency reports on all his subordinates; such a report, in a case of personal dislike, could be used as easily to mar as to make a career. It should be enough to mention the fate of one able careerist who had an irrepressible penchant for making puns. His chief in Bucharest, a wealthy manufacturer of dairy products, succeeded in hounding him out of the Service for an overheard remark: "All I have I owe to udders."

I have served under amateurs of various stripes, but the Hoosier novelist Meredith Nicholson was the most compatible, the most unpretentious, and the most understanding. When I was assigned to his legation in Caracas, he welcomed me with these considerate words: "I know nothing about diplomacy. I will look into your office from time to time, but I leave to you the running of the mission. You can find me on the porch, contemplating the beauty of our surroundings, when you want me to sign the dispatches."

Nicholson did come into my office one day with a chuckle. He held in his hand a letter from an old friend, another noted writer, Ambassador to Spain Claude G. Bowers. The time was a few days after the outbreak of the bloody Spanish Civil War, when all Latin America was emotionally agitated; the place where the letter was dated a week earlier was a pleasant little Spanish town where the ambassador was writing a book. "I wish you could be here," was his message, "in this lovely, peaceful spot. The scene has never been more tranquil."

Another nonprofessional under whom I served, who also liked to contemplate his surroundings but who worked hard at the job, was the rough-and-ready West Coast journalist Charles C. Hart. Hart practiced shirt-sleeve diplomacy in a literal sense, personally pounding out the drafts of his dispatches on the typewriter, cuffs rolled back to the elbow. His picturesque language enlivened the routine of political analyses back home, and his occasional report couched in lighter vein was a favorite appetizer to begin the day for Secretary Hull. One such gem was entitled "Keeping Fit in Teheran." It described the bruises and sprains and broken limbs suffered by a half-incapacitated diplomatic colony in its endless pursuit of exercise—mountain climbing, horseback riding, tennis —as well as the pneumonias contracted on fishing expeditions or long trips in open automobiles. "As for me," it concluded in words to this effect, "I sit in my swivel chair, admiring the Persian carpets that adorn my walls and the soothing view of the snow-capped Elburz range from my windows—and I am feeling very fit indeed."

The question is: Can the America of today afford the luxury of appointing amateur diplomats, however personable they may be? Walter Hines Page, one of the most gifted amateurs, wrote thus about his ambassadorship to Great Britain: "The realness and the bigness of the job here in London is simply oppressive. We don't even know what it is in the United States, and, of course, we don't go about doing it right. If we did, we shouldn't pick up a green fellow on the plain of Long Island and send him here; we'd train the most capable male babies we have from the cradle."

Diplomats of other countries laugh up their sleeves at an all-American spectacle when we make ambassadors out of butchers, bakers, or candlestick makers—for other countries stick to the principle that in foreign affairs there is no substitute for experience.

"Reposing special trust and confidence in your Integrity, Prudence and Ability . . ." begins the Presidential commission appointing an ambassador of the United States; and in those words are summed up the most urgent and desirable qualifications of a diplomat. Integrity, prudence, and ability. Although it is not always evident that such is the criterion applied to an ambassador chosen from the outside by the dispensers of political patronage, it goes without saying that a Foreign Service Officer who has reached the top of the ladder the hard way must possess all three attributes in abundance.

In another pre-election speech, at Miami on October 16, 1960, President Kennedy voiced the noble sentiment that only the "best-qualified men" should serve as ambassadors; men who "know the problems and concerns of the areas where they are stationed—who can represent the cause of freedom with credit—men who are selected for their ability and not the size of their campaign contributions." If this lofty principle were to be strictly and uniformly observed, 95 per cent of our chiefs of mission would be recruited from the ranks of the professionals—career men who have made diplomacy their lifework and have steered scrupulously clear of partisan politics. They are the men who know the problems; they can and do represent our cause with credit; and they are picked for their jobs on the basis of their records rather than for offerings on the altar of a political campaign chest. At present, 68 per cent of our ambassadors are so selected.

The remaining 32 per cent may be no less able in their own walks of life, but they belong in an altogether different category. With rare exceptions, such as Edwin O. Reischauer, who went to Tokyo from Harvard as an acknowledged expert on Japan, they have become ambassadors regardless of their aptitude for diplomacy, knowledge of the area, or acquaintance with a foreign language. Yet the man who writes a big check is not the only one to get a plush post—it may be the faithful camp follower who delivers a city or a state, who musters a foreign origins group, or in some other manner wins friends and influences voters. Or it may be an official who eventually becomes more of a liability than an asset—such as witch-hunter Scott McLeod, booted upstairs and out of the Department as ambassador to Ireland. Although the fitness of the amateurs—or as they prefer to be called, the "non-career" chiefs of mission—to preside over a post or to represent the cause of freedom varies with the individual, many of them would be literally tongue-tied in the practice of international relations if they were not backstopped by an experienced deputy with a sure touch.

The percentage of career appointments has risen slowly over the past twenty years, from a fifty-fifty balance during the Roosevelt period to the present score of roughly two thirds for the professionals and one third for the politicians. This represents a considerable improvement over pre-World War II days, when the scales tipped the other way; it is pointed to with a sort of wry pride by the State Department, which must compete with the nonprofessionals when it submits the names of its career men to the President as nominees for diplomatic posts. And like most statistics, these do not tell the whole story. The unhealthy and less comfortable missions greatly outnumber the coveted ones and, as might be expected, arouse little interest among the politicos. Kuwait, Kuala Lumpur, or the Congo would hardly be considered a fair return for the money of a millionaire—such tough spots belong to the career as a matter of divine right. Again, there are exceptions that prove the rule: career men in 1964 had Paris, Rome, and Madrid, while noncareer appointments have been made to certain posts in Africa. There are indications that President Johnson's record in appointing career men may be better than most of his predecessors.

Toward the end of 1963, the Department sent to the Jackson subcommittee for its information a study of the "typical" United States ambassador, including both career and noncareer chiefs of mission in the report. The composite mission chief was found to be in his early fifties, "to know the primary or secondary language of the country to which he was accredited," and to be prepared to spend two years and ten months in his post—this average being based on the length of service of all ambassadors who resigned or otherwise completed their tours of duty since the start of the Kennedy administration. The average age of the career chief of mission was 53, indicating a normal table of progress through the various classes to the top. On the other hand, the noncareer diplomat, averaged at 51.9 years, showed a wide range of ages, from 38 for Carl Rowan, the incumbent in Finland, to 69 for Matthew McCloskey, the appointee in Ireland. Equally varied in this particular sampling was the previous experience of the political appointees: government or public service, law, teaching, business, the press, labor unions, and foundations. The career men, by obvious contrast, came from the Foreign Service career.

All told, 109 chiefs of mission were covered in the report—106 in charge of embassies and three in charge of legations; the 109 included two women then holding posts, Ambassador to Ceylon Frances E. Willis, careerist; and Minister Eugenie Anderson in Bulgaria, noncareerist. Such figures will no doubt soon be obsolete in a world bursting with new nations and, therefore, with new posts. As for languages, it was discovered that 95 per cent of the ambassadors in Latin-American countries were "proficient or better" in either the primary or secondary language of their post; those in the Near Eastern and South Asian areas, 93 per cent; Far Eastern, 92 per cent; African, 89 per cent; and European, 79 per cent—a grand average of 87 per cent. Left unexplained, however, was the distinction between "primary or secondary." The primary language of many countries, such as Iraq, might be Arabic, and the secondary language English; or the primary official language, as in Nigeria or Liberia, might be English, and the secondary language a tribal dialect. English, therefore, might account for the high percentage of "proficient or better" in certain of these cases.

Exactly what are the duties of an ambassador in these tumultuous times? What is the public concept of a man deferentially addressed as "Mr. Ambassador," but whose title is so generally misunderstood that when a colleague of mine was introduced at Clark Field in Manila someone asked, "Who is this man they call Mr. Bastard right to his face?" For the first time in history, in November, 1963, a conference composed exclusively of American emissaries was called to discuss the role of an ambassador under the challenging conditions of the modern world. Sixty-five ambassadors, active and retired, career and noncareer, met at the Pennsylvania State University to consider a number of broad and pertinent questions: the spread of summit conferences, the increase in international organizations, advances in technology and science, the "revolution of rising expectations," and the effect of all these on the ambassador as an institution. For the statistically inclined, the gathering represented 1,500 years of United States Foreign Service experience and 300 years of ambassadorial service at 129 different posts. More ambassadors were assembled under one roof than at any time since the Congress of Vienna, and the deliberations—if they did not educate the public—at least gave the participants a rare opportunity to air their personal views on some of the problems encountered in their work.

The over-all objective of a diplomat, of course, is to cultivate and maintain friendly relations with the people of other countries; while standing up always for his own country, to see that points of friction between it and the country where he is stationed are resolved, or at least minimized—that disputes do not escalate into the use of force. A foreign ambassador who had served here long enough to learn the American idiom—Jules Jusserand of France —once called diplomacy "the art of bringing home the bacon without spilling the beans." It is always the diplomat's duty to find the key to peace, to defend the peace with advantage to his own country if possible; to promote solutions based on the concept of a peaceful world, not one of violence. In this search for the peaceful way, it is not always possible to score a clear-cut touchdown for our side; the negotiator lays himself open to the charge of "appeasement," which is another bad word for the "accommodation" actually taking place today between irresistible political forces and immovable political bodies in the shadow of the bomb. John F. Kennedy, when a senator, referred to professional diplomats as "vendors of compromise" and manufacturers of "fabricated harmony"; but if the diplomat fails, the future, as President Johnson has said, "will rest upon other shoulders; and no one can contemplate the results with a feeling of ease."

If bloodshed and war are just around the corner, the diplomat must be a man of great patience, the very virtue least understood by the uninformed and the most irritating to them. "Nothing tries the patience like stupidity," said the Indian diplomat K. M. Panniker, "but nothing is more stupid than impatience; there are times when patient waiting can be dynamic diplomacy." Naturally, patient waiting for the dust to settle can be overdone, but "dynamic diplomacy" as sometimes practiced without benefit of experience, wisdom, or maturity can be stupidity itself.

In addition to the role of patient negotiator—it took me two and a half years to reach agreement for American base rights in Libya—the ambassador of today faces demands unknown to his pre-World War II predecessors. He must be familiar with many matters directly related to his new responsibilities as chief of mission: economic, military, educational, cultural, informational, the unique problems of multilateral diplomacy. With the instantaneous contacts now common in the field of communications, he must be a better reporter than ever, keeping an eagle eye on critical events and swiftly, unerringly, interpreting their significance to Washington. He must be prepared to speak for his country in public, effectively and lucidly; in fact, to be something of a public figure in the day-to-day life of the country where he lives. This can be carried to extremes when he or members of his staff may have to face—with cool heads—an anti-American demonstration or more destructive acts.

The American ambassador is, first and foremost, the personal representative of the President, a fact that gives him special standing in the eyes of the local government, and usually gets him a special hearing as well. He speaks not only in the name of the President but in the name of the people and government of the United States. His authority extends not only to the staff of his own diplomatic mission, but to the representatives of all other United States government departments and agencies in the foreign country; in the event of disagreement, his decisions stand pending an appeal, if any, to Washington. He is the focal point in his country for all American interests—as well as all American gripes—official or unofficial; he is the solicitous shepherd to the flock of expatriate Americans in the community. Only when a military command is involved do the lines of authority run not through the ambassador but from the President to the Secretary of Defense to the Joint Chiefs of Staff in the Pentagon—so that in a military sense the military commander in the area may also claim to represent the President. A working arrangement between the embassy and the military is essential, even if the harmony is fabricated.

As a memorandum from the Department to all chiefs of mission made clear not long ago, the ambassador is leader, co-ordinator, and supervisor; his is the responsibility for success or failure in carrying out United States policies in the country of his assignment. Specifically, he is head of the country team, composed of the representatives of all government bureaus in his bailiwick, such as USIA, AID, CIA, Treasury, and other members of the official family. His object is not to knock their heads together, however much he may be tempted to do so, but tactfully and skillfully to concert their operations like the leader of an orchestra. He has to run the show—the trade and aid programs, the top-level negotiations, the treatment of distinguished visitors, to whom he is glad-hander and guide; he must be the tireless cultivator of contacts and friendly relations, the perpetual representational activist and extractor of information. He must be a stanch upholder of American prestige by the impression he makes on others; for if a man is judged by the company he keeps, so are countries judged by the personalities, the attitudes, and the actions of their chief diplomatic representatives. An ambassador is the personification of his country; just as the Italian ambassador is the embodiment of Italy or the Burmese ambassador of Burma, the image an American ambassador creates of himself is the image of America to those who observe him. Lastly, an ambassador has the responsibility of keeping a "happy ship," to borrow naval parlance; of successfully delegating authority in his mission, of giving it direction and instilling co-operation and enthusiasm among the crew. Much may depend on the reputation of an embassy; at one post where I served under a noncareer diplomat, the aide to a visiting admiral reported to Washington that morale "stank to high heaven," which was hardly conducive to respect, either inside or outside the mission. At other posts, by contrast, morale was good despite difficult working and living conditions—thanks to the personality of the ambassador.

Assuming that an ambassador is to serve his country to the best advantage and to make on foreigners the best possible—not a "cross-sectional"—impression of the United States, it may be useful to note the qualities he should possess other than integrity, prudence, ability—and everlasting patience. Integrity is implicit in "The Honorable," a title permanently affixed to his name when the Senate confirms his nomination; nothing can be of greater value to his country, nothing can do more to uphold the dignity of the United States when foreign criticism rains down upon American policies and practices than for the ambassador on the spot to be known as a man of integrity. It goes without saying that prudence and ability should be found in any diplomat worth his salt. To these fundamental characteristics, George Washington, in his instructions to John Jay as special envoy to Great Britain, added sincerity, candor, truth—and "a firmness against improper compliances."

Harold Nicolson, in a later-day definition of the "ideal" envoy, mentions experience, resource, discretion, and courage; "a man, above all, who is not swayed by emotion or prejudice, who is profoundly modest in all his dealings, who is guided only by a sense of public duty, and who understands the perils of cleverness and the virtues of reason, moderation." To an already exacting list, Nicolson added accuracy, calm, good temper, modesty, and loyalty. But, he said, the reader might object that he had forgotten intelligence, knowledge, discernment, prudence, hospitality, charm, industry, courage, and even tact. "I have not forgotten them," said Nicolson, "I have taken them for granted."

What cannot be acquired from a letter of instructions is good judgment; unless a man has that naturally, he will be unable to sift truth from rumor, separate the reliable from the unreliable, decide when and how to play the cards in his hand against many a wily opponent. A mission chief, if he is to test properly the temper of the country he is dealing with, must have the common sense to meet and judge people from every stratum of life; he must evaluate opinions in the press, analyze objectives of the local government, and cup his ear to the statements of the opposition. He should, if possible, have foresight in predicting the wave of the future. At the same time, he must be immune from the disease of "localitis"—the illusion that his own little segment of the sphere is regarded with such rapt attention in Washington that its relation to the whole may be relatively ignored.

Elementary as it may sound, the ambassador should be able to command the respect and confidence not only of his own government but of the foreign officials with whom he deals. I once served under a politician who had neither. New to diplomatic discretion, not "cleared" for top secret, he was bypassed by Washington and the foreign minister alike; and as counselor of embassy, I had to substitute for him in certain cases affecting our national security. When it came time for my transfer, I received the greatest compliment of my career: The foreign minister said he was sorry to see me go, for he could not now be sure that what he said would be accurately reported to Washington.

Along with the obligations of his office, an ambassador is often heir to some trying diplomatic dilemmas. For example, in certain countries—the non-Communist variety—the problem of relations with the opposition, which may or may not be a "loyal opposition," can become acute (the opposition in a Communist country is generally too dangerous for an ambassador to play with). One of my career colleagues in a country where the "outs" were aiming to get "in" simply for the sake of being "ins" realized that he would be damned if he did and damned if he didn't maintain contact with leaders of opposition parties. If, in order to round out his knowledge of the political picture, he associated freely with those who were against the government but who might be in the saddle day after tomorrow, he stood to compromise his position with the existing regime, losing its confidence, and forfeiting an indispensable working relationship. If, on the other hand, he refused to meet members of the opposition, he ran the risk of cold-shouldering a group whose good will he would need if they came to power. History is replete with instances where an ambassador has enjoyed the closest relationship with omnipotent chiefs of state or their prime ministers—to the profit and advancement of American interests—only to lose all influence when the "ins" were thrown out and the "outs" whom he had sedulously refrained from cultivating were ushered in. In this particular case, the ambassador was also under fire from his fellow citizens at home for not pushing aggressively for the elimination of "Fascist" tendencies in the dictatorial country where he was serving, and for not insisting on the application of Jeffersonian principles to the unsophisticated environment. How to preserve relations with those in control and with those who may come to be in control presents a problem that can be solved only on the spot, in the light of local circumstances, and, as in the case of my colleague, with the personal skill of the ambassador as a diplomat.

Another recurrent problem for the ambassador is that he must suffer the presence of others gladly in handling emergencies in his district. Ever since the airplane became a handy vehicle of diplomacy, trouble shooters, brain-trusters, bright young men or Harvard professors, White House assistants, Congressional factfinders, ambassadors-at-large, special representatives of the President, and personalities with the personal rank of ambassador, have been making flying visits to scenes of crisis, as if the ambassador and his embassy were incapable of finding the facts, incompetent to report them, and unable to handle the trouble—either with instructions or without. Neither fish, flesh, nor fowl in the diplomatic hierarchy, these highflying, high-powered emissaries tackle intricate situations with varying success and with varying degrees of enthusiasm on the part of the ambassador on his own grounds. To attempt to assess this mode of diplomacy would be to recount the chapter and verse of countless international episodes and weigh the results in the historical balance of accomplishments. But of one thing there can be little doubt: such visits tend to detract from the authority and prestige of the chief of mission who, too frequently, must stand aside like the forgotten man—asked only to provide the refreshments or other entertainment.

Occasionally, a top-level official, carrying rank and title, may be able to speak with a louder voice than an ambassador, perhaps to convey a disagreeable decision that would only render the ambassador unpopular in local circles. Or he may be able to give a push to the discussions an ambassador is patiently trying to carry on. Such an occasion arose when Secretary Dulles, and later Vice President Nixon, in passing through Libya, put their shoulders to the wheel of our slow-moving negotiations for the base agreement. The reverse occurred when Averell Harriman was drafted and sped to Teheran as a special assistant to the President to persuade the irrational Prime Minister Mossadegh to act rationally in the Iranian oil dispute of 1951. Harriman could have saved the taxpayer the cost of the trip, for he could do no more than our ambassador could do. Unless the Washington emissary has some peculiar qualification for the task, unless the issue is of such a technical nature as to lie beyond the resources of the embassy— and, above all—unless the ambassador is also present at the talks, these impromptu flights from home over the head of the man in charge are not likely to be of much help. A chief of mission, in theory at least, should be able to act, as well as report, for his government; it should be feasible, in an age of telephones, telegraphs, and television, for the denizens of Foggy Bottom to gain an adequate picture of the foreign scene without flying out for a look every time trouble erupts. Crises, major or minor, are the daily diet of a diplomat. If his star is repeatedly dimmed by others, not only is the ambassador apt to feel that his government does not trust him, but the authorities in the foreign office may begin to suspect the same thing.

George Washington was mindful of this last possibility when he sent John Jay to London in 1794 for negotiations which resulted in the treaty bearing Jay's name. The President took pains to emphasize that the regularly accredited minister, Thomas Pinckney, continued to enjoy his entire confidence, but that he desired to show a "solicitude for a friendly adjustment of our complaints" by sending an envoy directly from the United States with "a full knowledge of the existing temper and sensibility of our country."

The diplomat must beware lest the dead hand of bureaucracy kill initiative and stifle enterprise. "If a man puts himself under

🏵 🏵

the yoke of bureaucratic discipline and avoids the hazards of making mistakes," once complained Foreign Minister Yosuke Matsuoka of Japan, "he is more certain of promotion than a man who has brilliant ideas and who is not afraid of experimenting even though it involves the risk of making errors." This is an argument frequently heard in favor of appointing unrepressed doers from outside the career. It need not be, of course; for imagination and enterprise have enabled many a Foreign Service Officer to rise to the rank of ambassador by the exercise of those very qualities.

Among his tribulations, nevertheless, the ambassador is often confronted by the specter of bureaucratic restraint: Has he the power to make a decision on the spot? Can he or can he not act on his own, or must he refer every question to Washington? He may not be tightly tied to the apron strings of the State Department, but he knows that he is fenced in by regulations and by the different agencies that may have something to say in the premises. CIA or USIA or the Pentagon complex often has its own ideas about a proposed move on the diplomatic chessboard, and clearance must be obtained from all who may be concerned before the green light shines. By then events may have outrun a request for instructions. To give the ambassador the authority as well as the responsibility which goes with his position might bring anguished cries from those who batten on committee consultation in the United States; but more leeway to the chief of mission would unquestionably speed the attainment of our policy objectives.

To illustrate with an incident that had its dramatic side: During my service in Libya, the prime minister had resigned and flown off to Rome, his nerves frayed by the thankless task of guiding a newborn state. The king was ill, in seclusion; there was a rumor that he might abdicate. The whole government structure seemed about to collapse—just when I had reached a vital point in the long, drawn-out negotiations for an airbase. So when the tottering Libyan cabinet begged me to fly to Italy to persuade the prime minister to return, I cabled the Department urgently for permission to try.

Time was of the essence, yet I was bound by the Department's rigid rule against crossing the borders of the country to which I was accredited unless specifically authorized to do so. The hours ticked by without response. In Washington, the wheels ground methodically. Committee met with committee, weighing the pros and cons of my recommendation. The Pentagon had to be consulted. Policy factors had to be considered; so did tactics, in the light of progress to date on the airbase negotiations. Suggestions at a lower level had to be referred to a higher level for further discussion. I sent a second cable. No reply. Finally, in the emergency, I made my own decision. So great seemed the threat to the future of Libya—and to the security interests of the United States as well —that I boarded the plane of my air attaché, flew to Rome, and called on the prime minister at his hotel. With all the eloquence I could muster, I urged him to come back and steer the ship of state through the storm, pointing out that the fate of his country, and our crucial discussions, rested in his hands alone. He heard me in silence, still smarting from the political wounds that had caused him to resign. He would think it over; he would give me his answer that evening.

At eight o'clock I was again at the prime minister's door. His face was wreathed in smiles. He would do as I asked, and to mark the occasion he invited me to dine with him downstairs. With a load like lead off my mind, I was enjoying the repast when I spied an officer of our Rome embassy discreetly waving a piece of paper from behind the potted palms. I made my excuses, rose, and went over to receive the message—a priority cable to Tripoli, repeated to Rome for information. At long last Washington had moved. There were my orders. *Under no circumstances* was I to follow the prime minister to Rome, for that, the Department feared, might be interpreted as interference in the internal affairs of a sovereign country.

No doubt the Department was technically right, and I was technically wrong in resolving the dilemma as I did. No doubt I was lucky in that the prime minister accompanied me back to Tripoli; if he had refused, the repercussions might have been very unfortunate. But the point is that the establishment in Washington could not have sensed the atmosphere of crisis as well as the man on the ground; that it could not have gauged the personality of the prime minister as well, either. Sometimes a gamble must be taken in diplomacy, even if an occasional mistake should occur. The Jackson subcommittee has made the constructive suggestion that chiefs of mission might be entrusted with spot decisions on the level of those which assistant secretaries would have to take in Washington; and such latitude would be of enormous aid to those qualified to exercise it—although in the case of the untried amateur it might quite possibly be fatal.

A chief of mission serves strictly "at the pleasure of the President." He may be a careerist recommended by the Secretary of State, or an amateur picked for qualifications best known to the White House, but when the administration changes, an ambassador, by unwritten law, must hand in his resignation. The game of musical chairs then begins. In some cases his resignation is not accepted; in others another post is provided, making way for someone else; in still others a career officer may find the rug pulled out from under him in a position it took him twenty-five years to attain. Appointees on the losing end of the political seesaw, of course, automatically call it a day and go fishing.

The theory behind this diplomatic shuffle after every Presidential election is to give the new leader of the nation a free hand in choosing the men who are to represent him abroad. An ambassador who gained his post by contributing to the Republican campaign fund does not usually expect to be continued by a Democratic administration—although he may change his spots and become a Democratic contributor as well. One tour of duty may satisfy the politician, in any case. It is the ambassador from the career who is hardest hit by the turnover; although he can elect to serve in a lesser capacity, he may be called upon suddenly to surrender his desk to a manufacturer of kazoos from Peoria. The highest rung on the career ladder is a vulnerable perch, a fact of American diplomatic life which was responsible for the first piece

of advice given to me by an old Service hand: Don't try to climb
the ladder too fast if you want to have a long career.

The manner in which an ambassador is relieved of his post frequently leaves something to be desired, if not from the standpoint
of dignity, then at least from that of simple courtesy. Lest he forget to submit his resignation after the election of a new President,
he is given a pointed nudge in the ribs by a message from the State
Department. Whether career or noncareer, he is reminded with
what seems like indecent haste—the time lag was only ten days
after the New Frontier's Victory—and thoughtfully supplied
with a "sample letter," which he need only fill in with the name
of his country, date, sign, and forward to Washington.

When this long-established practice results in the appointment
of a politician at the expense of a trained officer from the ranks, it
cannot fail to do violence to the concept of a career that holds—or
ought to hold—that every Foreign Service Officer, if he is good
enough, should have a sporting chance to become an ambassador,
and that any ambassador who has earned his post should have an
equally sporting chance to keep it during a change in administra-
tions. But the violence is compounded when the change is announced prematurely and the public gets the news before the ambassador does, or before even the government to which he is accredited. Such a fate befell career officer Leland Harrison, who,
while walking on the golf course at Bern one fine day, was greeted
by a friend with the tidings that he was no longer United States
Minister to Switzerland. The information had just been broadcast
over the radio; when I saw him in the corridors of the State Department a few weeks afterward, the dazed diplomat was still trying to find out why he had not been notified before the Swiss.

I was a bit luckier when the post at Dakar changed hands. I had
been told in confidence that my successor, who proved to be a
political appointee, had been picked and that I was soon to leave,
but the news reached the public and the government over Radio
Senegal via a leak at the White House, not through an official announcement from the Department of State. An exasperated for-

eign minister made the most of the occasion by complaining vociferously about another American practice—that of switching its envoy before the local authorities had time to get acquainted with him, or he with them. With some asperity, the minister observed that after seven months we had barely come to know one another and to establish a basis of mutual confidence; now I was to depart and he would have to begin over again with a new man. The minister could consider himself better off than some others; for instance, the foreign minister of a South American country who had to say farewell to the American ambassador a mere four weeks after he had extended a welcome; or the foreign minister who waited in vain for an American envoy bumped from his ambassadorship by a political appointee before he had even started for the post of his assignment.

In the State Department of today, the top-ranking officer is in danger of becoming a drug on the market; dispossessed career men roam the corridors looking for employment commensurate with their rank and experience. If they are not blocked by those with political influence, by lateral entrants who start their careers near the top, they compete at a disadvantage with the favored "younger man"—one with less than twenty-five years' service by the modern yardstick. The implication seems to be that a man should feel satisfied if he can serve once as ambassador; there are too many claimants for his job to give him more than one post. One might hesitate to apply Gresham's law to this aspect of the situation; but it is paradoxical, to say the least, when experience is at a discount in a field where experience should be at a premium.

How to dispose of those senior officers who congest the upper ranks and do not choose to resign is more of an administrative than a political problem. Logically, of course, they might be put in charge of decision-making units at home or diplomatic missions abroad, but that would be against the trend. They can be left to wither on the vine, until self-respect compels them to seek new pastures; they can be invited to write a history of the country of their last assignment, as I was, or put to work preparing abstracts of ponderous economic reports, as one officer did; or they can be

❀ ❀

offered tangible inducement to retire before their statutory time
—age sixty for the Class I Foreign Service Officer, sixty-five for
career ministers and ambassadors. It is no secret that the Kennedy
administration put a heavy accent on youth; the policy of favor-
ing "dynamic" men of forty-five for ambassadorships is apparently here to stay. But this implied collision between two opposing
principles. When, in 1946, the retirement age was raised from
sixty to sixty-five for the career minister class, the plausible purpose was to retain as long as possible the services of those whose
ability had enabled them to reach the summit. The extra five years
were a sort of bonus for superior service, and those who attained
that rank generally expected to serve out the full period. In 1961,
however, an unusual device was found to hasten the exit of older
officers in order to make way for younger. For a limited period,
the bottleneck at the top was relieved when the administrators
took advantage of special legislation granting higher annuity payments to career officers who elected premature retirement. In the
fiscal year 1962, for example, 212 well-seasoned Foreign Service
Officers, including 17 career ministers and ambassadors, were induced to apply for voluntary retirement—with complete uncon-
cern on the part of those in charge for the backlog of experience
retired at the same time. In 1963, an additional 187 left the ranks,
taking their know-how and brain power with them.

A bewildered officer of Class I, aged fifty-six, was encouraged
to retire at that time on the ground that he was too old to become
an ambassador; shortly before the advent of New Frontiersman-
ship, only a few months previously, he had been told to curb his
ambition and to wait a while—he was too young to be considered
for an ambassadorial post. I had the occasion then to ask the top
administrative official appointed to the Department by the New
Frontier whether experience should not rate as high as youth in
making ambassadorial assignments. "That," was the reply, "is a
point of view—but not the prevailing point of view."

What happens when an ambassador retires? As an example of
conspicuous waste in the bureaucratic process, it would be hard to
surpass the government's failure to reap the rich harvest of inter-

national experience available for the asking. We invest hundreds of thousands of taxpayer dollars in Foreign Service careers; but on leaving the Department's payroll, an ambassador is consigned to oblivion. The end product of that long and expensive training is lost in a routine debriefing after his final post, his outstanding knowledge shut off like water from a tap; save for a rare call in some exceptional case, he is never consulted when he reverts to private life, even when problems arise in one of the countries where he was stationed. The Department couldn't care less what he does with his time, and it cares very little for the manner in which it dispenses with his services. No honors or bands or parades of colors such as are given to retiring generals and admirals; he is lucky if the Secretary of State has time to shake his hand.

How to capitalize on the know-how of government retirees is a problem not confined to the State Department; it exists in the armed services as well. Despite the fact, however, that foreign affairs is a pretty technical subject, no organized attempt has ever been made to conserve or utilize a former ambassador's know-how; no pool or reservoir of elder statesmen serves as a body of advisers, formal or informal, to the Secretary of State; no government agency recruits men over the age of sixty. In most cases the outgoing ambassador keeps an enduring interest in world events and is potentially of further usefulness to his country. He could, for example, be made available for work at the United Nations and its many specialized agencies, where the Soviet Union often succeeds in capturing key spots. Or he could represent the United States on ceremonial occasions, especially in foreign capitals with which he is familiar; again, he could help to welcome foreign dignitaries to our shores. But honorary assignments are another form of political plum to be awarded for political purposes. Instead of selecting a former ambassador as his personal envoy to the independence ceremonies of newly created Zambia—to mention one instance of plum-giving—President Johnson chose a New Jersey industrialist, Charles W. Engelhard, Jr., closely identified with the Republic of South Africa because of his extensive mining ventures; according to *Newsweek,* this appointment caused "mixed reactions" in Zambia, whose dark-skinned officials are somewhat less than enthusiastic about South African apartheid concepts.

Many former ambassadors are still willing and able; they could pay the taxpayer extra dividends. But in our prodigal country, an ambassador is expendable.

🎖 🎖 🎖 🎖 🎖 🎖 🎖 ELEVEN 🎖 🎖 🎖 🎖 🎖 🎖 🎖

Adventure in North Africa

If there is any one vice that is desirable to avoid in judging a foreign policy—and which the public is prone to indulge in—it is that of uninformed passion and prejudice. A policy pursued with passion may be, and often is, a good thing in itself; a point of view adopted by the United States government as national policy may be, quite naturally, prejudiced in favor of this country as against another. But when passion and prejudice are uninformed, when emotionalism takes over and the reasons behind a given action are not well understood or cannot be fully explained to the public, it becomes excruciatingly difficult for the State Department to serve what it considers to be the best interests of the American people.

Such a situation developed during the two years preceding our entry into World War II, and is well illustrated by the case history of an episode with which I was intimately connected from the start. Ambassador Robert Murphy, in his *Diplomat Among Warriors,* has provided a detailed account of our French "Vichy policy," a term of unexampled opprobrium in those days, and has explained the background of the North African Economic Accord under which, at President Roosevelt's behest, he came to play a leading role. More remains to be said, however, about the incredible difficulties encountered by the Department in arranging for the shipment of American consumer goods to French Africa while Marshal Pétain was in power, and of the extraordinary emotional involvement of the American people in the process.

The underlying objective of the economic accord negotiated by Murphy with General Maxime Weygand, then Supreme French Commander in Africa—who died in 1965 at the age of ninety-eight—was to keep the strategic North and West African territories of a fallen France friendly to the Allied cause; the device was to furnish the area with badly needed civilian supplies, in the hope that regular shipments would ward off economic disaster and deprive the Germans of an excuse for active intervention; the by-product was immensely valuable political, economic, and military information, systematically gathered by intelligence officers who supervised the distribution of the supplies and who were attached to the American Foreign Service with the rank of vice consul. To carry out the plan, it was, of course, necessary to preserve the façade of amicable relations with the "collaborationist" government at Vichy. No more controversial or unpopular policy could have been devised than that of dealing with a Nazi-dominated France; yet, to a neutral America, solidly determined to stay out of war, one could hardly proclaim from the housetops the advantages of cultivating good will and co-operation among the inhabitants of an area then unthinkable as the scene of our own military operations.

At first glance, the economic program did indeed look as if it might play into the hands of the triumphant Germans. Many Americans whose hearts were in the right place, but who had lost their heads over the villainies of Vichy, did not bother with a second glance and rushed to attack the Department and the Foreign Service. Secretary Hull—a liberal among liberal Democrats—was damned in the left-wing press; the extremists demanded his resignation as a "Fascist" and "appeaser." British and American economic warfare officials fought the plan tooth and nail, and government agencies in Washington outdid each other trying to block the shipments. In the face of widespread opposition, it was my unenviable responsibility to expedite the shipment of supplies, once the policy was decided on. And like other officers at State who believed that the political and strategic fruits of this far-sighted project would fully compensate for the rise of public wrath, I had to keep my mouth shut and face the barrage of the critics. Not until it paid off handsomely with the dramatic arrival of our forces on the North African beaches and relations with Vichy France were automatically severed, could the part played by the Foreign Service finally be revealed.

The idea of sending economic aid to territories under the Vichy regime was decided on in the autumn of 1940, when Prime Minister Pierre Laval, in the Churchillian phrase, "was rolling like a dog in the dung of defeat." As assistant chief in the Near Eastern Division in charge of African Affairs, I received one day the manager of the Socony Mobil Oil Company at Casablanca, Arthur G. Read, who had been asked by Emmanuel Monick, Secretary General to the French Resident in Morocco, to explore the possibility of obtaining nonmilitary consumer goods from the United States, to keep Morocco economically stable, politically quiet, and oriented to the West instead of to Nazi Europe. Other French officials with whom Read had talked were privately in favor of the scheme and were offering as bait the chance to buy minerals such as manganese, cobalt, iron ore, and molybdenum. Although little interest in the art of preclusive buying existed at that time, it did seem to those concerned that a cautious game of economic barter with the French authorities might help hold the line for the democracies in a potential theater of war and give us an entering wedge if necessary in the future.

This fitted in with reports that the fighting spirit of the French in North Africa was still high, that their military establishment, under Weygand, was still strong, and that a surprisingly small number of German and Italian armistice commissioners had been deployed to cover the vast French African territories. Such relatively favorable conditions prompted President Roosevelt to the belief that here was where the French might ultimately re-enter the war. He made North Africa his personal sphere of interest, and sent Robert Murphy, who was counselor of embassy in Paris, and later Vichy, to serve as his personal representative and to head up the economic accord in Algiers.

In doing so, it may be observed, Roosevelt characteristically

bypassed the State Department; for while Murphy gave lip service
to his own bureau, he communicated, on the President's orders, directly with the White House. Several other points may be noted:
To this day some of Murphy's most important reports have not
found their way into the Department's files; even the historian
commissioned by Secretary Hull to write the record of the Vichy
policy did not have access to White House papers on the subject;
even the Secretary of State had to say, "I wish the President would
tell me what he is doing"; and even though, as Murphy relates,
Roosevelt initiated the French-African policy of the United States
government, "kept it going, and resisted pressures against it," he
did so with Olympian detachment from the bureaucratic battle
front which centered around the supply program. Never once did
he break a bottleneck, never did he quell objections that bordered
on insubordination, never did he issue a clear-cut signed directive
to speed the flow of supplies, and never did he lift a finger to spare
his Secretary of State the mental anguish he must have endured as
the official responsible for the contentious policy.

Our North African adventure began to take form in February,
1941, with the initialing of the Murphy-Weygand agreement,
under which the French were authorized to purchase, with French
funds then frozen in the United States banks, such products as
cotton cloth, kerosene, tea, sugar, tobacco, agricultural machinery, a limited amount of petroleum; to make sure that none was
re-exported or surreptitiously transferred to the troops of General
Erwin Rommel then operating in the Libyan Desert, we demanded and received permission from Weygand to station in
Morocco, Algeria, and Tunisia a score of vice consular officers to
supervise the distribution. Paul Guérin, son of the president of
the Moroccan State Railways, who was trying to buy coal in the
American market to keep his trains running, was appointed Weygand's agent. And a shuttle service of four French freighters was
set up—two to sail simultaneously from each side of the Atlantic
—to carry the goods from the United States and bring back at
least a token of Africa's natural resources in return.

No sooner did it become known that we were contemplating a

program of economic assistance to the French than criticisms and obstructions began to multiply. With their backs to the wall, the hard-pressed fighting British were understandably reluctant to approve even the semblance of relief to territories that were to all intents and purposes under the sway of the enemy. Weeks of laborious negotiations were necessary to establish the quotas for which the British were willing to issue navicerts—documents letting civilian goods pass through the Allied blockade of French territorial waters. These quotas were based on independent studies of the normal requirements of the area, correlated with the official requests as presented by Guérin; each item on the list was minutely scrutinized by Eric Wyndham-White, a representative of the British Ministry of Economic Warfare attached to his embassy in Washington; while I acted as arbiter, middleman, and executive officer of the program. To the generally negative attitude of the British were added the polemics of the press both here and in England; such a hue and cry attended the departure of the first shipload for Casablanca in March, 1941, that it seemed as if the policy were doomed to be sunk almost before it was afloat. Even in the State Department, counsels were divided; some thought the plan too dangerous a gamble—instead of easing the economic burdens, it was urged, we should intensify the pressures, thus forcing the Germans to keep a restive population under control. To others, the mere mention of Vichy was anathema: "I'll see them in hell first!" was the initial reaction of Dean Acheson, newly appointed Assistant Secretary for Economic Affairs, in balking at the draft of a cable which approved the shipment of coal. Herbert Feis, the economic adviser, was adamantly opposed to the whole scheme from start to finish. But the political adviser for the Near East and Africa, Wallace Murray, Assistant Secretary of State Adolph A. Berle, Jr., and, of course, Secretary Cordell Hull, who knew that contact with North Africa was countenanced by the President, kept their sights unwaveringly fixed on the main purpose of the plan—to make the most of our presence in what might one day become a vitally important area for the United States. Although that day was still so remote as to be undiscernible and could not be discussed openly, it was enough that General Weygand had indicated to our representatives in Algiers that he would be prepared to facilitate an American invasion if it came in sufficient strength—in other words, if it had a better than even chance of succeeding.

Meanwhile, a dozen vice consuls had reached their posts and begun sending back voluminous reports through the diplomatic pouch or in cipher, the use of which had been authorized by Weygand. Recruited by Army and Navy Intelligence from French-speaking reserve officers, these capable American observers were under no illusions about their mission. Each reported to me for instructions before taking off for Africa. I could not, of course, tell them in so many words that they were to collect military information for the United States government—the State Department had to stick scrupulously to the fiction of neutrality as long as public sentiment was overwhelmingly against our participation in the war—but they knew as well as I what was expected of them. Officially, I explained they were to check carefully on the disposition of the supplies; to win friends for the United States by their appearance at key ports and railroad centers: and to stress at every opportunity the facts of our growing productive strength, leaving the implications to speak for themselves. They were to raise no false hopes among the French and make no mention of what we could or eventually might do to provide military support to Weygand's forces. But it was unnecessary to be explicit about the inner purport of the accord, to mention its delicacy and possible consequences, or to spell out the dangers these courageous men would run if war should envelop North Africa.

While public protests mounted at home and intramural bickerings increased, the control officers studied details of French shipping, German activity among the Arabs, political personalities and attitudes, together with a host of apparently unrelated items, such as the hours of high and low tide on the coast, the scarcity of dry goods or vegetables, and the price of American cigarettes on the black market, anything that could conceivably be of use in building up an accurate picture of conditions in the region. In addition, friendships were formed with native chieftains and tribal leaders, with disaffected French military or naval personnel, and with sympathetic business circles. Under the patient direction of Murphy from his central seat in Algiers—where he was known to the German Armistice Commission as "The Big Boss"—our investigators were welded into one of the finest groups of intelligence agents the war produced. So complete was their camouflage as they went about the seemingly innocuous business of overseeing shipments from America, that the Germans did not take them seriously. One confidential report to Berlin, purloined by the French police from the German consulate general in Casablanca, read in part: "We can only congratulate ourselves on the selection of this group of enemy agents who will give us no trouble. In view of the fact that they are totally lacking in method, organization, and discipline, the danger presented by their arrival in North Africa may be considered nil."

In the State and War Departments, we had other views. For the record, using as basis the stream of information which their activities produced, I wrote the efficiency reports of these amateur vice consuls. All received the grade of "very good" or "excellent." In particular, David W. King, at Casablanca, merited the top grade; as a World War I veteran of the French Foreign Legion, he had clandestine connections that were invaluable in organizing the cooperation of French army units in Morocco before our landing. Since he knew personally and was on the best of terms with French officers willing to impart information, he could not only furnish Military Intelligence with factual details of the resistance movement but, when the showdown came, help integrate patriotic members into plans for the American invasion. To illustrate, on the eve of our landings when General Dwight D. Eisenhower and the rest of the Allied leaders were gathered at Gibraltar, King was able to report that the French general staff at Casablanca was "entirely in agreement" with the impending operation and outlined their proposals for action in support of the landings. The close contact between Vice Consul King and General Emile-Marie

Béthouart, which encouraged the latter's friendliness to the Americans and led to his decision to co-operate, was one factor of the utmost importance in preparation for the attack.

If State Department officials leaned over backward to avoid the hypothesis of United States involvement in the war for fear that a casual word or inference might further inflame the great debate then raging, British and French visitors to Washington were not so reticent. David Eccles, sent over by Churchill as a representative of the Ministry of Economic Warfare, later a member of the British Cabinet, helped change the attitude of the British Embassy to one of greater leniency toward the economic accord; but in doing so, he did not hesitate to put down on paper his feeling that the exercise could be looked upon only as a "curtain raiser for a military adventure." Otherwise, he bluntly told Wallace Murray on June 4, 1941, ". . . unless something tangible in the form of American military assistance could be expected, the British Government was not interested in permitting economic supplies to reach General Weygand from the United States; unless there were prospects of staff talks with American participation, as well as some definite evidence that we intended to follow up the present plan with the use of American armed forces or war materials, the continuance of the economic plan was so much waste of time."

About then, too, Professor Louis Rougier, an unofficial emissary of Vichy France, who was trying to mend the shattered relations between his country and Britain, called on me to discuss the situation in North Africa. "Within a year," he prophesied, "you Americans will be sending everything you've got to Casablanca. That will then be the most important port in the world for the United States."

Whatever dreams and schemes existed behind the State Department's formal diplomatic front, only a noncommittal reply could be made to such confident assertions. Although public opinion before Pearl Harbor certainly supported the Allied cause, it was just as certainly opposed to anything "tangible in the form of American military assistance"—and it was hard enough, as I had discovered, to go against public opinion. Sympathy for the beleaguered British was matched only by the vitriol that poured from the editorial pages regarding our continued association with officials of Vichy France. A typical example of the readiness of hostile journalists to believe the worst was an outburst in the summer of 1941, when the French tanker *Sheherezade* sailed from New Orleans with kerosene and low-grade gasoline for North Africa. According to Robert L. Bendiner, managing editor of the *Nation,* the British found this example of "the American practice of violating" their blockade "too much to swallow" and seized the ship near Bermuda. The "appeasers" in the State Department, however, "were not to be thwarted," stiff representations were made, and the British, who could not afford to cross their lend-lease benefactor and potential ally, "were forced to yield," and allowed the vessel to proceed to Dakar and Casablanca with its cargo for what Bendiner chose to describe in quotation marks as "civilian purposes." The truth was that the ship was intercepted and seized by the British *at the request of* the State Department because of Secretary Hull's extreme sensitivity to a sudden shift in the political winds in France; its subsequent release was the subject of agreement, just as every move in the economic program was jointly worked out behind the scenes by the American and British governments in Washington and London.

With the United States a belligerent, the prospects for helping the French to resist a possible Axis take over in North Africa took on a different color; but the difficulties of implementing the Murphy-Weygand agreement from a desk in the State Department increased, if anything. A few weeks before the Pearl Harbor debacle on December 7, 1941, Weygand had been recalled under pressure from the Germans, who obviously were unwilling to trust him further. Nazi intentions toward French Africa or Spain were the subject of countless rumors—some planted by the Nazis themselves and swallowed by those seeking to discredit the economic accord. For example, in the spring of 1941, reports of massive German infiltration in Morocco, of 60,000 German troops poised in Spain, were later found to be plants to distract attention from the coming Nazi attack on Russia. Irresponsible press and radio stories told repeatedly of German submarines fueling with peanut oil at the French West African naval base in Dakar, each report resulting in on-the-spot investigation and laconic denial by Consul General Thomas Wasson. The British blew hot and cold. Whenever Pétain tactlessly spoke of the "New Order in Europe," whenever the Anglophobe Admiral Jean Darlan figuratively shook his fist at the British Navy, whenever the collaborationist star of Laval was in the ascendant, catcalls against our Vichy policy interrupted operation of the economic agreement. In its first nine months only 7 per cent of the authorized quotas had been delivered. Now the press campaign in both the United States and Britain, was in full swing; and the ship schedule, in deference to these pressures, was off again, on again, the sailings canceled by an edgy State Department at any time and for picayune reasons: supplies moved only by fits and starts.

In January, 1942, I was sent on a secret mission to Bermuda, to convey orally what seemed like too flammable a topic to be put in writing. When we were finally plunged into hostilities, our minds made up for us by the Japanese, the War Department would no doubt have furnished the North African subversive movement with military hardware had it been in a position to do so. However, the Army had enough problems of its own, and could spare nothing for the French territories; the best course seemed to be to bolster the French morale with general assurances and promises. Murphy had been in close touch with French officers who guardedly had talked of the ways and means by which the area could be defended with outside assistance; in fact, the whole framework of the economic accord was built out of hope that some day these men, properly supported, might be called upon to rise against their country's conquerors. To work closely with Murphy in Morocco and elsewhere and to assist him in co-ordinating military and naval intelligence, the State Department had arranged with the Navy to appoint Colonel William A. Eddy, of the United States Marines, as naval attaché to the legation at Tangier. Eddy, an expert in the Near East and fluent in Arabic, had taken off for

Lisbon in a Pan American clipper but was held by bad weather at Bermuda. At that juncture, it was determined that a stopgap message of some sort should be transmitted to the resistance elements in and around the focal point of Algiers. I intercepted Eddy at the Bermuda airport, and while the clipper waited for the clouds to lift, we conferred behind a deserted shack in the drizzling rain. On behalf of the State Department, Eddy was instructed to say to Murphy that the proposals of military and fifth-column aid, as put forward by these French elements, were of "great interest" to the Department, and that Murphy was authorized to "encourage the French to perfect these plans" for assistance to the Allies. Further we could not go at the time; the development of "Operation Torch"—the code name of our eventual North African landings—was still many months away.

Before leaving New York on this trip, I was involved in an incident that had its amusing side. At three o'clock in the morning, with the take-off scheduled for dawn, I was awakened by a phone call from Washington. Colonel William J. Donovan, with whose OSS (Office of Strategic Services) I had maintained close liaison, spoke to me in riddles and parables for security's sake. Did I recall the "place of the white house" on a far-off continent? Yes, I thought, he means *casa blanca*—Casablanca. Was I aware of an important city a thousand miles and more to the south? Yes, I assumed, Dakar. Well, I was to forward immediately, by diplomatic pouch, a parcel containing what I thought he said was a "death machine," which, to my consternation, I would find in my desk on returning to the Department. Throughout the Bermuda journey, I wondered uneasily what wild plots the cloak-and-dagger boys were cooking up now, and how I was to handle the infernal machine supposedly awaiting my attention. Not until I checked the matter out as soon as I got home did I realize that over a poor telephone connection and in my half awakened state, I had taken the word "deaf" for "death." It was a "deaf machine" —OSS metaphor for "hearing aid"—that was being sent to Governor General Pierre Boisson, whose hearing was impaired, as a tangible token of our encouragement.

In the spring of 1942, the problem of carrying out a foreign policy in the teeth of violent criticism came to a head. The Secretary of State decided that he could no longer accept sole responsibility for maintaining relations with the obnoxious Vichyites; and, casting about for some other agency to share the onus, the Department hit upon the Board of Economic Warfare (BEW). Its head, Milo Perkins, was willing to interest his organization in the shipment of American goods to North Africa as a possible lever for obtaining, in return, raw materials of value to the war effort—for the minerals offered under the Murphy-Weygand plan had been slow in materializing. To speed the accord, however, no greater mistake could have been made, for the price paid for the partnership in frustration and delay was out of all proportion to the results. Economic "warfare," of course, means just that: through the issuance of export licenses, the BEW could control, as completely as a traffic cop at a busy intersection, the movement of all items consigned to the strategic zone of North Africa—and it used that authority fully. Unable or unwilling to appreciate the subtle purpose of the Department's plan, it interpreted the rules as narrowly as possible in their application to nonmilitary supplies, shut its eyes to the safeguards designed to prevent their improper use, and created endless snafus in the clearance of waiting cargoes. The fear that Rommel's soldiers in Libya might somehow get the goods amounted almost to an obsession: tobacco, for instance, was challenged on the ground that it might fall into the hands of the Panzer divisions and give them "aid and comfort," cotton textiles were frowned on because they might be made into Nazi uniforms, and used clothing and typewriters were openly suspect. It is difficult to imagine what effect on the course of the war there would have been if a whole shipload of old clothes, tobacco, and typewriters had fallen into enemy hands. But the Treasury Department of Henry Morgenthau abetted the obstructionists by holding up the French funds for the purchases; when the press began to get wind of interagency wrangling—no new thing in government, but in this case fraught with ideological emotion—it was the sinful boys in the striped pants who got the blame while the BEW basked in a glow of self-righteous patriotism.

While the State Department smarted under charges of "appeasement," a new threat to the economic accord was developing overseas. With shipments delayed for months and all four vessels idle because of BEW's intransigent attitude, the supervising vice consuls found it next to impossible to justify their existence. French officials were under mounting pressure to expel the Americans, who had no supplies to supervise and, in the eyes of the German Armistice Commission, no other excuse for being in North Africa. The position of the control officers was indeed unique: as the representatives of the United States, a belligerent power, they were permitted by Vichy France, a country neutralized by the war, to remain on Vichy territory with the tacit consent of Germany, also a belligerent and enemy of the United States. It would be hard to discover a parallel in the history of warfare. As best they could, the French resisted the German demands, stalling, pleading that another ship would soon be on its way. Murphy, thousands of miles away from the bureaucratic struggle, would beg by cable for resumption of deliveries; but his urgings had little effect on the contradictions between concepts of economic and political warfare, on the dismaying conflicts in jurisdiction, on the critical drumfire of the daily press, and on the absence of a clearly defined power in the State Department to enforce political decisions.

On August 1, halfway point in the long, hot summer of 1942, I assembled a group of the highest officials I could find in Washington in a supreme effort to break the log jam and get the plan moving, to accomplish the purpose for which it had been conceived. By this time "Operation Torch" was in an advanced planning stage: since authority for the North African policy stemmed from the White House, an urgent appeal was directed to the President to expedite the shipments to Casablanca. Admiral William D. Leahy, who had been our ambassador in Vichy and now served Roosevelt as adviser on strategy, addressed the meeting on the President's behalf. He could not, of course, disclose the secret of the expedition soon to be launched—a secret so well kept that the Germans to the end believed that our attack would come at Dakar, nearly two thousand miles to the south of where it actually did occur. But he did make clear the President's wish that the program should proceed with speed and regularity; when BEW objectors began to quibble over details, the Admiral walked out in disgust and the meeting broke up in disorder.

Nevertheless, one would have thought any high-ranking official of a wartime agency in Washington could have sensed what was in the wind—that there were powerful political and military sanctions for promoting the modest supply program as against technical doubts from an economic standpoint. But the BEW could not, or would not, pick up the scent; the French vessels remained at their docks. On September 7, I met with the chief of BEW's blockade and supply branch in Admiral Leahy's office to discuss the matter further. No plainer language could have been used: "If a good feeling could be induced in French North Africa at this time," said the admiral, "it might save thousands of lives." Echoing Professor Rougier's remark, he added, "in two or three months we might want to send over everything we have"—or we might wish to send nothing at all; at this moment, the object was "to please the French in every way possible and remove any source of irritation, even at the risk of driblets of supplies reaching the enemy." This pointed talk was reinforced a few days later by a conversation which I had with the admiral's aide, who said that the entire question was one of "broad policy," that the White House was entirely in accord with Murphy's recommendations as to what should be sent, and that the attitude of the BEW appeared "altogether incomprehensible." But the White House, for some altogether incomprehensible reason, never succeeded in making its weight felt. It will always remain a mystery, unless future historians are able to throw light on the subject, why President Roosevelt did not break the deadlock and personally order the BEW to stop its interference with the master plan—probably the simple fact was that he did not operate that way. No more supplies moved. Whether it was the late summer heat or a fever induced by desk officer frustration, I took to my bed for a couple of days with a sudden rise in temperature.

Time ran out rapidly after that. Through Frederick P. Culbert, one of the control officers who had been flown back to Washington to accompany the invading fleet on its departure, I had confirmation that the momentous "Torch" operation had begun. To the very last, the BEW resisted all efforts to put life into a moribund economic accord. On the eve of the landings it was still deadlocked with the State Department over the export of a few tons of coal, while the senior Guérin, president of the Moroccan Railway, who had been spirited to Washington to give us priceless details of the transportation system, sat placidly in my home discussing the world situation. To the last, he and I kept up the solemn pretense that the only thing at stake was the deteriorating economic condition of French North Africa, rather than the political and military destiny of his country. And to the very last, the columnists and the commentators continued to disparage the State Department and its Secretary as the worst kind of appeasers, as defiers of public opinion, and as craven, woodenheaded bureaucrats.

On November 8, 1942, the world was electrified by the news that our forces had landed in North Africa, and the ill-conceived accusations vanished with the morning mists along the coast. Only a few thousand tons of supplies, a fraction of the amount intended, ever reached their destination. But the policy of the North African Economic Accord was vindicated to the full: thanks to the intelligence which had been gathered in advance, thanks to the friendly contacts which had been established, casualties were far fewer than they might have been. American diplomacy, by its action in North Africa, had made a niche for itself in the military hall of fame.

The bitter arguments against the project showed clearly that passion and prejudice have no place in the making of foreign policy.

What to Do?

If he had his way, the veteran Foreign Service Officer would gladly crawl back into Old State, where everything was small and simple by comparison with the "new diplomacy." In his heart of hearts he longs for an era when uncomplicated answers could be given to relatively uncomplicated questions, when the Cold War was unknown, when nationalism was self-contained, when foreign aid was remote as the Milky Way from our thoughts. Like the wishful isolationist of the storm-cellar mentality, he would like to revert to a less critical and complicated period and pull the hatch down over his head.

But such secret yearnings are futile. It is manifestly impossible to turn the clock back to those golden days, it is useless to bask in nostalgic reminiscences or bemoan the untoward events of the past. Even if the bright promise of the Rogers Act has never been fully realized, even if morale is low, even if bureaucracy reigns supreme, it is necessary to face the future with a stout heart and consider what should be done to lighten the load of distrust on the Foreign Service Officer, improve his public image, and, at the same time, increase the return on the taxpayer's investment.

The solution is not, as Congressman Samuel L. Devine's bill would have it, to abolish State and transfer to a new Department of Foreign Affairs only such employees as were determined by the President to be strictly necessary. That would be a solution of desperation, born of despair and bafflement at bureaucratic bigness.

❦ ❦

The State Department, like the horseless carriage, is here to stay.

But if State is now a colossus, and if its fantastic growth continues at the present rate, what will it look like a few years hence? If the Foreign Service is to be more and more composed of "specialists," if the Department's complexion takes on a deeper political hue, and if administrative regulation grows apace, what kind of man or woman will the future Foreign Service Officer be? The management asserts that the goal is the best possible Service that can be produced. But management, or administrative fiat, may not be the best possible way to attain that objective; if the human factor inherent in statecraft is ignored, a regiment of robot officers will eventually man our first line of defense.

Sir John Bagot Glubb—known to another generation as Glubb Pasha—who spent a lifetime among the Arabs, once pointed out that the conventional diplomacy of the West was inadequate to deal with reactions of the East; he stressed the need for more international psychologists "to study the relationships between people of different cultures, religions, and political beliefs." Foreign Service Officers who live and work with alien people in alien cultures learn instinctively to anticipate the response of others to projected moves; when those who lack such practical experience control the decisions, the United States may be the loser. Thus, when the Bandung Conference took a leaf from the United Nations and brought together for the first time all the leaders of Asia, we were left, in the words of Senator Margaret Chase Smith, a "trembling mute"—because the politically appointed Assistant Secretary in charge of Public Affairs decided it might be harmful to our side to send a word of greeting on the opening day. The Soviet Union seized the opportunity to do just that and got the credit. When, under pressure from an impatient Congress, the Secretary of State slammed the door to the Aswan Dam in the face of Egyptian sensitivities, the result could have been foretold. The Soviet Union seized the opportunity and got the credit. As long as human beings inhabit the earth and national boundaries exist, the success or failure of statesmen will depend largely on the personal element; those who are not deeply versed in the psychologies of other people have no business making policy decisions. If half as much effort were put into training our officers to look into the innermost minds of nations and to study foreign behavior patterns as is put into managing the mechanics of their careers, the American diplomatic art would be the immeasurable gainer.

To improve the present situation, a number of reforms are indicated; whether they can be put into practice depends, of course, on Congress and the public. The problems seem to fall into three categories: those dealing (1) with career Foreign Service personnel, (2) with the decision-making machinery at the top level, and (3) with the organizational structure of the Department itself. Let us consider them in that order.

1. No nation in the world is richer in human resources than the United States. Our high rate of literacy, our great educational opportunities, and our mass media of information give us advantages possessed by few others. As a people, we have ability, intelligence, diligence, and courage; we have a drive, an organizational capacity, a Yankee shrewdness; we have a way of getting on with others, and a reputation for quick, sympathetic understanding of world problems. There is no reason why we should not have, quite literally, the most effective Foreign Service on earth.

To tap this plentiful supply of top-grade ore, it is not enough to employ examinations that appeal to an "America as it is." If the Foreign Service is to represent only a cross section of America, it is by implication composed of all types of people—some obviously of high quality, some of poorer diplomatic yield, some with characteristics completely unsuited to the peculiar demands of conducting our relations overseas. A refining process that selects only the best is no less than America requires and deserves. One way to produce the best is to reintroduce the high standards formerly embodied in the tests for entering upon this highly professional career; to look for candidates among the qualified few rather than the geographically distributed thousands; and to eliminate at once those who give evidence that they are merely shopping around for the best proposition in the field of international service.

In our competitive economy, the government must compete for talent. The pages of the press are filled with descriptions of lucrative jobs for those who have decided on some form of engineering or technology as a career. Although the State Department need not stoop to the advertising columns to attract recruits, it should have the means to offer salaries on a par with those in private enterprise, such as banks or oil companies or business firms engaged in operations abroad. As a nation we should be able to afford the top talent, just as private industry considers its high-salaried executives well worth the price. With substantial pay should go a substantial expense account because of the obligation to entertain. Yet despite the 1964 raise—an election year raise—in federal pay, designed to lure and hold gifted personnel, despite fringe benefits and government aid to education, the Foreign Service Officer suffers in comparison with his business brother; private means are still a factor in what can prove to be a costly career. At the very minimum, ambitious, able young people who qualify for the Service should have the assurance that they will not have to pay official expenses out of their unofficial pockets, that they will be able to support growing families through numerous transfers without heartbreak or help from the moneylender; that they might even be able to put aside enough to buy homes in their own country on retirement. Above all, they should be assured that the expensive top posts will never be denied to them because they lack the means to run them, that even if a private foundation or philanthropic organization must put Congress to shame by supplying the funds, their eligibility will rest on their talent, not on their purses.

Once selected, the officer should be given every possible chance to develop and to increase his usefulness, to enlarge his acquaintance with other government agencies, to learn about his own country, and to sharpen his professional skills and techniques. How best to achieve these ends?

One of the more controversial suggestions that crops up from time to time is that for a "Diplomatic Academy"—a West Point of the Foreign Service—which would drill into the minds of its men all manner of knowledge relevant to their work. This hardy perennial has been cultivated by congressmen and others who are inclined to throw up their hands at foreign policy setbacks and are bemused by the idea that expert instruction under government auspices would create full-blown a corps of officers qualified to handle the most complex situation. At the request of Secretary Rusk, a Committee on Foreign Affairs Personnel was set up in 1962, chaired by former Secretary Christian A. Herter, which recommended, among other things, the establishment of a "Foreign Affairs College." Simultaneously, a Presidential Advisory Panel, headed by James A. Perkins, vice president of the Carnegie Corporation, proposed a "National Academy of Foreign Affairs." These institutions were similar in purpose; they would provide training not only to State Department personnel but to other government officials, and a restricted group of private individuals as well; meanwhile, on the premise that this did not go far enough, sentiment bloomed on Capitol Hill for a "Freedom Academy," which would extend the instruction to businessmen and civic leaders. Draft legislation for a "Foreign Affairs Academy" was prepared by the State Department at the behest of President Kennedy and a bill was introduced in Congress in 1963, but so controversial were the opinions it excited that it failed to pass.

Although it is easy to understand Congressional interest in providing more lore about foreign affairs, it seems, on balance, undesirable to regiment the thinking of individuals with the disciplines of a West Point or Annapolis. The Foreign Service as a profession is unique in purpose and intent; its most successful officers are those not with military minds, but with liberal educations, imagination, energy, and a capacity to work and learn. Private educational institutions, especially those that offer courses related to foreign affairs, fill the need without undue difficulty; a graduate or postgraduate of one of the large colleges or universities who has studied history, economics, or the social sciences has the basic qualifications for a career in the Foreign Service. The government has begun to recognize this fact by assigning an occasional Foreign Service Officer to a year of specialized study at certain top centers of learning, such as Harvard.

In the government framework itself are the Department's Foreign Service Institute and the high-level National War College, both of which admit officials from different agencies for cross-fertilization of thought. The Army, Navy, and Air War colleges accept a handful of representatives from State, as do the British, Canadian, and NATO defense colleges. All these provide expert, advanced instruction in world politics and policies, with special attention to the Communist problem; an expansion of these facilities, and more assignments to the universities, could do whatever a "Diplomatic Academy" could do, and at the same time avoid the disadvantage of a stereotyped government training. It might also nip confusion in the bud—the confusion of another bureaucratic excrescence.

Much more can be done to increase the capabilities of an officer by posting him for a tour of duty at another department, such as Commerce, Treasury, or Defense. To widen his horizon still further, he could be given a sabbatical year as teacher at one of the smaller colleges, say in the Middle West, where he would not only be brought into contact with grass-roots thinking but would be in a position to impart some of his knowledge of the world; or as a member of the staff of a Middle Western or Far Western newspaper, with the same general aim.

Along these lines, Representative Paul D. Schwengel of Iowa introduced a bill in 1964 to provide for sabbatical leaves for Foreign Service personnel, during which officers would not only attend grass-roots educational institutions, but work with trade, commercial, or agricultural institutions, and the like. When I proposed such a plan years ago to the Director General of the Foreign Service, I was told that the Department could not spare the valuable time of its employees for the purpose. The same objection might be made today; but the result would be an increased competence on the part of the officer, a better understanding of American views, and added appreciation of what his country stands for.

It might also supply an answer to those who charge that Foreign Service Officers, by reason of their protracted absences abroad, are intellectually isolated from current American lines of thought.

For the career officer, proficiency in at least one foreign language—preferably French—should be a must. Under the imperatives of the Wriston program, language requirements were discounted, because newly assimilated officers from the home service had no language qualifications at all; it was simply decreed that a foreign language could be picked up overseas and was not necessary for admission. Realization has since dawned that although no language test is required for the recruit, the ability to converse in a foreign tongue is one of the principal tools of diplomacy, and crash programs in everything from Finnish to Swahili are now available at the Foreign Service Institute. The ability to communicate with the cook in Hindi or Pushtu, while often productive of good will, is not the same, however, as an easy command of French, Spanish, German, Russian, or Arabic in which to discuss points at issue with government officials, diplomatic colleagues, and the leading local citizens. Specialization in one of these is indispensable to an officer making his career in these linguistic areas. One should be rational about the matter of exotic languages. It is, no doubt, useful and deserving of the extra pay it earns, for members of an embassy to learn the language of the country, especially for those who have cultural duties and who must develop people-to-people contacts. It is not so clear, however, that this applies equally to Foreign Service Officers who are subject to frequent transfer: Rumanian laboriously acquired over a three-year assignment in Bucharest is of little use in Malaysia, and I soon learned that pidgin-Persian did not help me in Oslo or Dakar. Nor would Persian have been essential to do business in Persia even if I had mastered it; it is increasingly obvious that English has become the common denominator of conversation everywhere and that those who do not know English speak French, Spanish, or German.

R. H. Bruce Lockhart, British author-diplomat, once wrote that too proficient a knowledge of language is sometimes a pitfall. The greatest diplomatic polyglot that I have met is Mr. John D. Prince, the former American Minister in Belgrade. He could talk to nearly every one of his foreign colleagues in the colleague's own language. Albanian, however, defeated him, but not to be outdone, he once talked to the Albanian Minister in Turkish at a large reception. The effect was not quite what he intended. After the conversation the Albanian came to the British Minister and said in halting English: "What a strange, what a silly, are these Americans. They have a Turk for their Minister to Yugoslavia."

2. If the State Department enjoyed the freedom to function only "in such manner as the President may from time to time direct," without the gratuitous assistance of others, it is conceivable that more success might be ours in the field of foreign relations. If the authority of the State Department were fully recognized in the policy-making process, if the top layer of officials employed and paid by the taxpayer was composed solely of qualified experts, its task might be considerably easier. If the Foreign Service as a whole were recognized as a group of dedicated public servants and not shrugged off as a corps of cooky pushers, its morale and therefore its efficiency might be raised to unsuspected heights.

Short of a change in the Constitution, however, the Department must accept the intervention of a President or his White House aides, of members of Congress representative of both parties, and of Congressional committees which may have ideas of their own, whether constructive or unconstructive by professional Foreign Service standards. It must also listen to zealous policy pushers in other branches of the government, to the uninhibited promoters of mass movements, and to unsought advice from the daily press. It would help if the White House not only appointed career men to all top-level policy positions, but if it refrained from exposing them to the winds of political change, and if it restrained academicians and do-gooders from imposing their theories on hardheaded planners and policy makers. On its part, Congress could refrain from putting busy officials on the witness stand every time there is a tremor in the international landscape; by having more respect for the problems confronting the oldest and most worldly member of the executive branch; and if it felt that someone should be called to account for the ripples that spread across the policy pond from time to time, it could see to the appointment of a permanent official, at the undersecretary level, who could devote a reasonable amount of his time to answering questions on the Hill. It would help even more if congressmen from states where there is comparatively little interest in or understanding of foreign affairs could take more time out from their preoccupations to study world problems and thereby develop a strong sense of leadership on this subject among their constituents.

In exchange, the Department might try to soft-pedal some of the cynicism it inevitably acquires in the course of its duties, to devote more time to cultivating personal relations between the two branches of government. Since both work for the same boss —the American people—it is all the more unfortunate that in many cases they seem to be at loggerheads, that they do not mingle more often in formal or informal Washington gatherings; that there are not more opportunities for off-the-record discussion and exchange of views. Better understanding and greater tolerance might result.

"There ought to be a law" forbidding the appointment of ambassadors to pay off political debts. With the possible exception of 5 or 10 per cent of the total, all diplomatic posts should be filled by qualified career men—the exceptional outsider to be selected solely for his ability to contribute to the interests of the nation, not to the pocketbooks of the politicians. This bedrock rule in diplomacy was laid down in 1718 by François de Callières, father of French diplomatists:

A wise prince will not fall into the fault common to many princes, namely, that of regarding wealth as the first and most necessary quality in an ambassador. Indeed he will serve his own interests much better by choosing an able negotiator of mediocre fortune than one endowed with all the wealth of the Indies but possessing a small intelligence, for it is obvious that the rich man may not know the true use of riches, whereas the able man will assuredly know how to employ his own ability. And the prince should further remember that it is within his power to equip the able man with all the necessary means, but that it is not in his power to endow with intelligence one who does not possess it.

De Callières further observed: "Since peace and war and the welfare of nations depend upon it, the best minds, the most sagacious and instructed of public servants should be appointed to the principal foreign posts." His recommendation—so carefully heeded by the French and British and others who know something about the diplomatic art—is as applicable to the American Foreign Service as if it had been penned especially for it. "The veriest fool," de Callières also wrote,

would not entrust the command of an army to a man whose sole badge of merit was his successful eloquence in a court of law. . . . All are agreed that military command must be learned by long service in the army. In the same manner it should be regarded as folly to entrust the conduct of negotiations to an untrained amateur unless he has conspicuously shown in some other walk of life the qualities and knowledge necessary for the practice of diplomacy.

If diplomatic novices conspicuously showed such qualifications, and brought gain or honor by their reputation to the United States, no career officer would object to an occasional invasion of his precincts by a distinguished outsider. Myron T. Herrick made an everlasting impression in France; Thomas Nelson Page, the author, was appropriately cast as ambassador to Italy; and Brand Whitlock, mayor of Toledo, rose to dramatic heights during World War I in Belgium. At the same time, it must be remembered that those were the days when it did not matter so much if an ambassador lacked all the qualifications of a professional.

In recent times, Ellsworth Bunker has served with distinction in Buenos Aires, Rome, and India, and David K. E. Bruce, ambassador in London—who once did time as a vice consul—has displayed the talents of the best professional in a series of important posts.

Those who look to ambassadorships for their political reward might be taken care of in another way. They could be made Honorary Knights of the Conference Table, or Grand Potentates of a colorful order such as the Mystic Shrine; or members of a club that entitled them to wear a rosette in the buttonhole, like the Legion of Honor. Creating a new class of citizens would be no more undemocratic than appointing an ambassador for services to a political party.

As Aristotle phrased it over two thousand years ago, "The road to every public office should be open to all; and the offices themselves should be closed except to those who have traveled the road and arrive fully prepared."

Reforms in policy making, like charity, should begin at home; the Department should relax the restrictions that tend to hold its chiefs of mission in telegraphic or written bondage. If an able man is chosen for a post, and is backed by a capable staff, he should be given the discretion to act more in accordance with the dictates of his judgment. The man on the scene occupies a vantage point; he knows the local personalities, the nuances of local politics, the psychological moment to approach the foreign office. His instincts should be more relied upon, even if he should occasionally make a mistake; his initiative should be encouraged, so that he can move with events instead of waiting for instructions from Washington. At home, much more must be done: decisions must be sharpened by cutting away the underbrush; responsible decision makers must take the responsibility of making decisions. The committee system should be drastically overhauled. Conflicts with competing agencies should be resolved by authority of the Secretary of State, the senior member of the Cabinet; and indecisiveness in the policy councils should not be countenanced while special emissaries fly forth to investigate what the ambassador on the spot might rightfully be expected to cover in his reports.

It might even help the Department in its attempt to formulate policies and discharge its prescribed duties if it were let alone for a change by those who are tempted to tinker with the machinery. Alternate reorganizations, reductions in force, augmentations and retrenchments, as have taken place regularly over the years, do not make for either efficiency or good morale. What sense was there, in one of the periodic "economy" waves that occurred during the early 1950's, to drop overboard fifty career Foreign Service professionals—most of whom, incidentally, found ready and lucrative employment in the business world? A second secretary of embassy in my office at Oslo, for example, is today vice president of a leading bank instead of spending his energies in the thankless employ of Uncle Sam. If State's leadership in foreign affairs could be recognized, its financial needs treated adequately, if not generously, and its internal structure left intact for a while, it might function to the much greater satisfaction of its employees and the taxpayer alike.

3. One of the administrative experts brought in from the business world for a look at the grotesqueries of government bureaucracy used to say that if business were run like government, it would perpetually be in the red.

It may be a forlorn hope that the growth of any bureaucratic tree can be arrested, or that the thick foliage on branches of the civil service can be trimmed, even though President Johnson has preached thrift, economy, and a cutback in the number of federal jobs. If it were possible to wield the ax in a manner that would increase rather than impair efficiency, however, certain specific strokes might add to the Department's operational competence— such as abandoning use of the multiplication tables in thinking of the organization, and emphasizing instead a judicious employment of the pruning shears. This means, among other things, that pressure should be applied on all federal agencies, either by the President or Congress, to reduce the platoons of job holders overseas, thus reducing the demands on State for logistic support, liaison, or co-ordination. It might also mean putting an end to the proliferation of office space, as well as of personnel. Parkinson's law might be amended to read, "Work expands to fill the space available"; if space were unavailable, it is barely possible that units would not expand, that the vicious circle would be at least temporarily broken.

But the immediate need of the Department and the Foreign

Service is for money where it will do the most good. No more scandalous situation can be imagined than that of a great world power caught short of funds to conduct its international business. Yet this happens every year: the travel freeze, the anemic budget for representation, the lack of wherewithal to meet emergencies, the consequent setback to morale, all form a recurrent pattern. It is conceivable that the available funds might be used to better purpose, and trips of assistant secretaries curbed to places where ambassadors are already on the ground, but there is no doubt that a proper injection of money would do wonders for the Department's self-confidence.

Two facts of life on the international front bespeak the necessity for strong support of the Foreign Service: First, the inevitable crises of a world in ferment, the costs of which cannot be estimated in advance; and second, the leadership expected of the executive agent of the President in carrying out United States foreign policy. The former entails all sorts of emergency expenditures —deploying our forces when and where needed, holding conferences, a spate of cables. The latter requires bold assertion of the State Department's role over the activities of other government agencies in their relation to foreign countries, so as to produce an efficient national instrument speaking for the cause of freedom. On a shoestring appropriation, orderly planning is not possible; and the most orderly plan can be quickly disrupted by events that are not foreseeable.

The place to begin, perhaps, is in the Bureau of the Budget, that tough-jawed watchdog of the Treasury which allows no departmental request without minute inspection. Small yearly increases have never solved the problem of budgetary deficiencies. If the Foreign Service is to discharge its duty to the public efficiently, realistic provision should once and for all be made, not only for salaries and expenses and representation but for the unspecified contingencies which are as certain as sunrise. A small slice of the amount spent annually on aid to other nations, to aid the attainment of our own national objectives, would provide the answer. If approved by the Bureau of the Budget, it would be more difficult for Congressman Rooney's committee on appropriations to turn down.

In summary, to bring about improvement, and help clear the air in Foggy Bottom, a number of reforms are indicated, though without public interest, Congressional approval, and Presidential support, the possibility of realizing any of them is slim indeed. A six-point program might run as follows:

First, a determined effort must be made to arrest the bureaucratic growth. It would be desirable, as we learn how to handle our foreign problems with greater economy of personnel, to trim down the whole "foreign affairs complex" by a quarter to a third. We might aim to eliminate rather than accumulate papers, and learn whether two persons can be trained to do what three do at present. One must recognize, however, the built-in difficulties of curtailing projects already in full bloom, as well as the attendant pangs of reductions-in-force which any entrenched bureaucrat would be sure to resist. The sole practical solution seems to be by attrition—calling a halt to the expansion of all bureaus and letting new "job opportunities" wither away with the passage of time.

Second, the Foreign Service and its entire State Department backstop should be a purely professional career. Political appointments, whether through influence, friendship, connections, or campaign contributions, should—with the rare exception of a most distinguished American—be completely eliminated in favor of recruitment, training, and promotion from the bottom. Admission standards should be tougher instead of easier. Nobody, in other words, should become a general without rising from the ranks as a soldier. Ambassadors should be confirmed by the Senate Foreign Relations Committee only after critical questioning of their fitness to serve as chief of mission; experienced career officers could generally stand on their record, but if there must be some who enter by the side door, at or near the top, they should be given intensive courses of indoctrination, lasting at least three months, before appearing for examination by the committee. Ambassadorial assignments should extend over three or four years at a post, regardless of a new President in the White House.

Third, to attract the best talent, salaries and allowances in the Foreign Service should be as liberal as those in private industry, with mandatory increases at stated intervals to meet increased costs of living. This would include a sliding scale of retirement annuities, so that retired officers or their widows would not have to contemplate the shrinking purchasing power of a fixed income, which, if they live long enough, might bring them perilously close to destitution. Appropriations for the State Department should be raised so as to cover crises, emergencies, conferences, household maintenance and operating expenses for all our embassies; in short, all expenses in line of duty should be borne without question by the government. Above all, substantial funds should be provided for representation—the everyday business of diplomacy —so that even at the most expensive posts there would be no need of appointing an ambassador on the basis of his wealth.

Fourth, the stultifying system of committee clearances should be ruthlessly overhauled. Authority to make decisions should go hand in hand with responsibility. Less emphasis should be placed on managing and administering household problems and more on speeding up and streamlining the policy-making process. Excessive reporting should be stopped, to help reduce paper work.

Fifth, to raise morale in what is essentially a most honorable lifework, a massive effort should be made to get in touch with the American people, to acquaint them with what the Foreign Service does and what it does not do, what the State Department can and cannot do, and what the career can offer to those who are qualified. To begin with the foundation, the Department and the Service should lay stress on the human element in foreign relations and should, accordingly, humanize their establishment instead of giving to many the impression of a cold and soulless corporation.

Sixth, the President of the United States, whoever he may be, should give the Secretary of State the power to run the show in foreign affairs without interference—to deploy the skills and resources of his department to the best advantage without obstruction by others. He should rely on the experts and give them authority commensurate with their professional qualifications. If he has confidence in his Secretary of State—and if he does not, he should have one in whom he does, as demonstrated by Truman's switch from Byrnes to Marshall—he should back him to the hilt in the conduct of international relations, and make this clear to any and all other government departments concerned. Troubleshooters from outside the career sometimes create more trouble than they shoot.

❦❦❦❦❦❦ THIRTEEN ❦❦❦❦❦❦

Hope Springs Eternal

In a salute to the Service on the forty years that have elapsed since the Rogers Act made possible the present career, President Johnson reminded all whom it might concern that "these have been years when the Foreign Service has contributed enormously to this country's security." The President also recalled that "the Foreign Service is the front line of our effort in the field of foreign affairs. And while the very nature of the work done by the front line often denies it the public recognition it deserves, the assistance given to a young and struggling nation, the rift repaired here, the smoldering fire damped down there—all contribute importantly to world peace." To this tribute, he added one more thought: "Our future does rest with the diplomatic corps—and I am happy to say that the shoulders of our corps are broad and strong."

Indeed, broad and strong shoulders are needed if in the future the corps is to carry the combined load of responsibility, leadership, public criticism, bureaucratic oversize, and deficit financing which now weigh heavily upon it. Forty years have seen the United States emerge from the cocoon of isolationism and try its wings as the champion of freedom and democratic institutions everywhere. Never before have the eyes of other nations been turned toward us so expectantly in peacetime; never before have we been faced with such uncompromising duty to ourselves as well as to others; never before have we had to conduct our international relations in the awful knowledge that a misstep or a misstatement can lead to nuclear holocaust.

235

❀ ❀

To forecast developments over the next forty years would tax the art of divination, but their general outline five or ten years from now should be clear enough. Still more new and nonviable states—such as the sliver of independence in West Africa known as Gambia—will strain the structure of the United Nations, crowd the agenda of countless conferences, and beset the policy makers with added difficulties. We need no crystal ball to see that a rising generation of Africans, gradually replacing those trained in the colonial tradition, will have stupendous problems of statehood to contend with. We know that the monolithic nature of Soviet communism is changing and that the satellite block is developing its own lines of policy in the economic sphere. Peking, as a would-be center of power, is certain to make its presence on the globe increasingly felt—and the shadow of its atom bomb will not be any less. The population explosion in Latin America, its equivalent in Asia, and the economic headaches in both regions are likely to be matched only by the interlocking problems of France, European unity, and the Atlantic alliance. As defender of the cause of freedom in a dangerous world, the sun never sets on our foreign problems, and the watch we must keep on them can never be relaxed.

If the needs and commitments of the nation were so great a decade ago, it is staggering to think how much greater they will be in the future. Multilateral diplomacy is the mode. In the gamut of international organizations, summit conferences, specialized agencies of the United Nations and regional groupings of nations for economic or political purposes, the United States must be either a participant or an attentive spectator. As the speed of transportation and communication has accelerated, distant peoples have been brought into close relationships, the world's economy has become more and more interdependent; and political events must be accurately analyzed as soon as they have happened. All of this has put a greater premium than ever on the vision, capability, and resourcefulness of the men and women who compose the Foreign Service.

So complex have our foreign problems become that, at best, one

can only hope to have some of them understood by the people all
of the time, or perhaps all of them understood some of the time;
but never to have all of them understood all of the time. Probably
decades will be required before Americans accustom themselves to
the world role which has been thrust upon them, and realize that
the subtleties of most foreign issues are so difficult to grasp that
only those who live and work with the questions full time are
qualified to decide what should be the answers. But it is certainly
unbecoming for those who are neither versed in the problems nor
aware of what goes on backstage, to downgrade in spoken or written word the Foreign Service as a calling. In no other country
would the diplomatic profession be regarded with the suspicion in
which it is held in the United States. To overcome this handicap, a
conscious effort must be made to get the Service across—to persuade Americans to rally round the flag held aloft in their name
by our officers in the far corners of the world.

The crux of the problem probably lies in creating in Congress,
and in the public, that awareness of which the *New York Times*
spoke—an awareness of the danger in weakening the Service because of meager appropriations, an awareness of what it stands for
and what it does, an awareness of the type of American who is
needed to serve his country abroad, and who is deserving of a loyal
constituency at home to back him up. In American folklore there
is a line that implies it is better not to shoot the piano player if a
good performance is to be expected. It is conceivable that if the
sniping stopped, morale might rise, appreciation might follow,
and applause might even come from the most unlikely segment of
the audience. The American Legion, for instance, ever on the alert
for risks to our security, responded to an invitation from the Secretary of State to make a firsthand survey of the Departmental
scene. It named a responsible committee of five which, after exhaustive investigation, found that the Department "is made up by
and large of capable and dedicated public servants in whom the
Nation can place much confidence. . . . The personal attitude of
these Department leaders is tough and realistic." Considering the
source, such a verdict is truly laden with praise.

At least the Foreign Service Officer may be allowed to hope. He may hope that his income will be progressively boosted to keep up with the cost of living, and that in time his pecuniary reward will be commensurate, especially in the upper brackets, with what private industry is willing to offer; for as President Johnson has noted, the power and prestige associated with a government job lose their appeal when their concomitant is debt. He may hope that, in due course, the taxpayer will be convinced that his investment is well placed, that the Foreign Service Officer and his family in their distant outposts render at the very least what the President has called "a dollar's worth of value for every dollar's worth of pay"—if not more for good measure. He may hope that his countrymen will gradually come to have confidence in him and in his integrity; that as comprehension dawns about the vital nature of his work, an informed electorate will demand of Congress better treatment for those in the front line; that efforts by the State Department to reach the public will be greatly expanded, for constituents and friends do not just grow like Topsy—they must be cultivated. He may hope also that his ranks will be swelled, not by the hordes of administration and management, but by recruits of high caliber who possess what Secretary of the Navy Paul Nitze has publicly asked for in his admirals: flexibility of mind, analytical thought processes, creativity and imagination; for only those with such attributes can expertly focus on all points in a policy decision and successfully relate them one to the other.

Reason for hope exists in certain small beginnings that have been made in the field of public relations. Foreign Service Officers on leave in their home towns are encouraged to talk in public at luncheons or civic functions; speakers are furnished by the Department to address student groups, clubs, chambers of commerce, and business or labor organizations; a program of "community meetings on foreign policy" has been launched in selected grass-roots areas of the nation. Now and then a diplomatic drama goes on the airwaves, which gives its audience an inkling about the Foreign Service and its mission. But this is modesty of a high order. The bridge between government and public is not easily built; to construct it well, many times the available funds are needed, much more speaking and writing are required.

It is invariably astonishing to the five "public" members of the annual Selection Boards to read the case histories of Foreign Service Officers. Often with preconceived notions about cooky pushers, these widely respected and representative Americans, chosen from private life to lend objectivity to the findings, meet with the other panel members to review the performance of every officer, to promote the praiseworthy, and to comb out the less deserving. To these outsiders, the stark record is usually a revelation; if every citizen had the same opportunity to examine it, he would join the public members of a recent board who wrote to the Secretary of State: "We can be proud of the men and women who represent us to the rest of the world." For the sake of the nation, this must continue to be so.

What is not on the record are the reasons why these men and women devote their lives to work from which they can anticipate little public thanks or recognition. Intellectual curiosity about the world, a sense of adventure and the satisfaction of representing the nation in the conduct of its foreign business may explain why they embark upon this career. What holds them at their task is that indefinable spirit of public service, so difficult to put in so many words, so unfathomable in its attraction. When Dean Acheson was Secretary of State, he compared this spirit to that "which animates great military outfits, groups of men who have lived together and fought together and have pride in their organization."

"Every time I go home," he told a group at an honor awards ceremony in the State Department, "I find that there are scores of other people who are staying later than I have stayed. I see lights all over the building. Sometimes when I get home and want to talk to one of my colleagues and telephone him at his home I find he isn't there at all, he is still at the Department. I find that my colleagues and all of you give up your holidays, give up your evenings, give up your weekends to stay and work on projects which have fired your imagination. Sometimes I have to order my colleagues to get out of that building, to go away and stay away for a few days, and I find, as many Secretaries of State have found before me, that no one pays the slightest bit of attention to these orders."

The hard core Foreign Service Officer would like nothing better than to see the quality of the service he performs for his fellow Americans improved by adequate funds, by the elimination of politics, by a high standard of entrance requirements, and by a top-notch organization in which the human equation in his profession is not sacrificed to the Moloch of bureaucracy. He does not look for thanks, but his morale would be infinitely improved if more faith were placed in his talents and his sincerity of purpose.

When career officer G. Frederick Reinhardt was appointed ambassador to Italy, he was asked by Senator Bourke B. Hickenlooper of the Foreign Relations Committee how he proposed to make ends meet at the costly Rome post. Reinhardt replied that he hoped Congress would be generous enough to grant him extra funds. "Hope," said the senator drily, "springs eternal."

So it is with the rest of the Service. If hope did not spring eternal, the going would be a good deal rougher than it is.

Index

Foreign Service (*cont.*)
  size of, 27–33, 55, 58, 62
  solutions to problems of, 219,
    221–229, 231–233, 240
  unification of, 39, 57
  See also Foreign Service Officers;
    State, Department of
Foreign Service Act, 54, 68
Foreign Service Association, 173
Foreign Service Institute, 224–225
Foreign Service Journal, 162–163
  quoted, 162, 169–170
Foreign Service League, 161–162
Foreign Service List, 28
Foreign Service Officers
  allowances for, 107, 114–115,
    122, 124, 139, 163, 233
  ambassadorial appointment of,
    chances for, 199–200
  assignment and promotion of,
    57
  "auxiliary," 67
  average age of, upon entry, 148
  capabilities, increasing of, 224–
    225
  career, 11, 15, 89, 182–183
  civil service status of, 53
  classification of, 129–130
  commissions of, 130
  compared to British and French,
    56
  deaths of, heroic and tragic, 42–
    43, 142–144
  disagreement of, with policy, 90
  educational backgrounds of,
    145–150, 157
  effects of bureaucracy on, 6
  effects of false economies on,
    123–125
  effects of McCarthyism on, 167–
    173
  entertainment of Congressmen
    by, 113–114

Foreign Service Officers (*cont.*)
  examination and selection of,
    145, 156–157, 221–222
  expenses of, 104–106, 112–113,
    222
  female, 148, 152
  fringe benefits of, 135–136
  of future, 220
  "generalists," 33–35
  home leave for, 57
  home states of, 147–149
  housing of, 53–54, 118, 122
  images of, 2, 4–11, 15, 71, 136
  languages, proficiency in, 154–
    155, 225–226
  living conditions of, 127–128,
    131–132, 134, 139–140
  merit system applied to, 53
  and party politics, 85–86, 165
  patriotism of, 4
  political appointees, 11, 15, 82–
    85
  as presidential advisers, 77
  professional life of, 6–11, 130–
    145
  quality of, 152–157, 221, 223,
    238–240
  recruitment of, 150–154, 232
  remuneration of, 42, 49–50, 56–
    57, 129–130, 135, 163, 222,
    223, 238
  requisites of, 129
  Reserve, 130, 152, 209
  resignation of, 90, 152
  responsibilities of, 4, 130, 132–
    134
  retirement of, 122, 201–202
  sabbaticals for, 224
  social obligations of, 113–114
  "specialists," 33–34, 220
  training of, 129–130, 154, 223–
    224, 232
  transfer of, 90, 138